New Mythologies in Design and Culture

New Mythologies in Design and Culture

Reading Signs and Symbols in the Visual Landscape

REBECCA HOUZE

Bloomsbury Academic
An imprint of Bloomsbury Publishing Plc

BLOOMSBURY
LONDON • OXFORD • NEW YORK • NEW DELHI • SYDNEY

Bloomsbury Academic

An imprint of Bloomsbury Publishing Plc

50 Bedford Square	1385 Broadway
London	New York
WC1B 3DP	NY 10018
UK	USA

www.bloomsbury.com

BLOOMSBURY and the Diana logo are trademarks of Bloomsbury Publishing Plc

First published 2016

© Rebecca Houze, 2016

British Library Cataloguing in Publication Data
A catalogue record for this book is available from the British Library.

ISBN: HB: 978-0-8578-5521-3
PB: 978-0-8578-5762-0
ePDF: 978-1-4742-7771-6
ePub: 978-1-4725-1849-1

Library of Congress Cataloging-in-Publication Data
A catalogue record for this book is available from the Library of Congress.

Typeset by Fakenham Prepress Solutions, Fakenham, Norfolk NR21 8NN
Printed and bound in India

For Gabriel and Lucian

CONTENTS

LIST OF ILLUSTRATIONS

Plates

Figures

ACKNOWLEDGMENTS

There are many individuals who deserve special thanks for their encouragement and contribution to this project. First and foremost, I am grateful to my students and colleagues at Northern Illinois University, who have given me the opportunity to examine the visual landscape from diverse points of view, especially Janie Wilson-Cook, Brooke Stover, Tara Quell, Jamie Jacobs, Stuart Henn, Chrysoula Gardiakos, and the many graduates of NIU's program in Visual Communication. Their insights into design have challenged me to think more critically and imaginatively about fascinating topics—from IKEA to video games. I am also indebted to the community of scholars active in the Design History Society, Design Studies Forum, and the Gender Studies Program at the University of Notre Dame, especially Pamela Robertson Wojcik and Barbara Green, who have invited me to present these ideas over the years. Some of the essays included here I first read as papers at: the 2013 Design History Society conference on sport; the conferences on food and childhood, hosted by the Gender Studies Program at the University of Notre Dame in 2012 and 2014; and the 2015 annual meeting of The Space Between: Literature and Culture, 1914–45. I am also grateful to Professor Yu Zhongwen, and his colleagues at Wuhan University of Technology, who invited me to present a series of lectures on these topics to their design students in China.

I thank the editorial staff of Bloomsbury, as well as the former Berg Publishers, who so enthusiastically encouraged this project, and who have worked with me patiently to refine and clarify the ideas in these chapters, especially Tristan Palmer, Simon Cowell, Simon Longman, Rebecca Barden, and Abbie Sharman. I owe the opportunity to work on this book to Grace Lees-Maffei, who invited me years ago to co-edit with her *The Design History Reader*, a project through which I was first introduced to these dynamic publishers. My outside readers provided valuable suggestions and insights that likewise have helped me to shape my arguments.

I am grateful to the many individuals and institutions who generously granted permission to use the images included, especially Gabriel O'Leary, Lucian O'Leary, and Margaret O'Leary, who created some of them. Yolanda B. Houze deserves special thanks for her editorial assistance, as does Janie Wilson-Cook for her technical expertise in helping to prepare the images for publication. Many thanks are due as well to Northern Illinois University's Division of Research and Innovation Partnerships, College of

Visual and Performing Arts, and School of Art and Design, each of which provided financial support for this project. The interpretations of signs and symbols that follow are exclusively my own and are in no way endorsed by the companies represented, including those who have given permission to use images of their brands and products.

The boyhood interests of Gabriel and Lucian O'Leary, to whom this book is dedicated, inspired this project. Their many hours playing with Lego, Minecraft, and the Nintendo DS, their fervent interest in sports attire, as well as the many bedtime stories we've read together over the years, are at the heart of my endeavor to better understand and interpret these popular myths of the everyday. Most importantly I thank my creative and intellectual partner, collaborator, and frequent co-author, Peter O'Leary, for sharing with me his keen understanding of myth. Peter deserves special credit for his insights into the ominous nature of television, the menacing cloud, Freud's uncanny, Michael Jordan, and William Faulkner.

Introduction

What are signs and symbols in the visual landscape? And how do we read them? A sign seen from the interstate highway communicates quickly. Its simplified iconic form tells us that we may replenish our hungry bodies and thirsty cars at the next exit. A gateway—a pair of golden arches—beckons to us from the distance. Not far beyond we recognize a large bull's-eye—concentric circles in red and white. The unmistakable symbol tells us that if we continue moving in that direction we will surely hit the target; that is, we will find everything we need to buy. These signs shout to us loudly from a distance. Others we can hold in our hands, and near our eyes and ears, where they flicker with images and whisper suggestively. The smooth, cool, glass touch screen is alive with tantalizing sounds and sights that enable us to interact both with others and with the endless stream of information which it provides. These signs and symbols are not only practical tools, designed to provide us with new knowledge or to satisfy our physical needs, but are also seductive invitations to play. They are central to our imaginative lives and to the construction of our identities.

As we move through the day we continuously navigate the built environment. In doing so, we encounter many images and objects, which are both strange and familiar. They are part of a shared language, a visual vocabulary of the collective imagination. Our clothing, the spaces we inhabit, the tools we use for work and for leisure, our vehicles of transportation, and even the food we eat, are all designed, but the individual experience of this visual landscape is idiosyncratic and often accidental. Though clothing, cars, or kitchens may have been designed with particular uses in mind, their meanings shift from one context to another.

The experience of the visual landscape as something fragmented and diverse may be peculiar to modernity, first having emerged in Europe during the early modern period. It gathered steam with the industrialization of the nineteenth century, when novel forms of architecture and furnishings, fashions, printed journals, newspapers, advertisements, and other ephemera, increasingly began to define it. Poet and cultural critic Charles Baudelaire described the visual landscape of Paris in the 1860s as the domain of the *flâneur*, the stylish observer of everyday life in the city.[1] By the turn of the twenty-first century, however, this experience was increasingly and less optimistically understood as a symptom of the postmodern condition.[2] But our experience of the postmodern visual landscape today is not necessarily one of chaos and confusion. By contrast, we combine and piece together disparate elements of that landscape into a comprehensible language of forms. The signs we encounter resonate through culture, history, politics, and social change.

This book was inspired, as its title suggests, by the work of literary critic and semiotician Roland Barthes, whose memorable observations of French popular culture in the 1950s were first published in the French literary magazine, *Les Lettres Nouvelles*. In 1957, Barthes collected his short essays in the volume *Mythologies*, for which he wrote the theoretical concluding chapter, "Myth Today." In this, he examined the way in which socially constructed notions become naturalized through a linguistic process he described as "myth." Barthes wrote: "Myth is a type of speech."[3] More specifically, it is "depoliticized speech," of which the ideological underpinnings are obscured. In his well-known analysis of a photograph on the cover of *Paris Match*, depicting a young black boy in uniform, saluting, Barthes demonstrated that the image on one level signified the soldier's patriotism, but on another reassured its white bourgeois audience of the validity of French colonialism in Africa, at a time of increasing political unrest.

Barthes's essays, in general, dwell on seeming trivia, such as the meaning of wine and milk, laundry detergents, travel guides, professional wrestling, and striptease, but "Myth Today" is more pointedly political. The essays in *New Mythologies in Design and Culture*, likewise, seek to demonstrate the political and ideological underpinnings of popular myths of daily life at the beginning of the twenty-first century, and they emerge, like Barthes's impressions, from "a feeling of impatience with the 'naturalness' which common sense, the press, and the arts continually invoke to dress up a reality which, though the one we live in, is nonetheless quite historical."[4]

It may seem anachronistic to use Barthes's essays as the inspiration for the collection of ideas in this book, particularly when Barthes himself, in the preface to the 1970 edition of *Mythologies*, wrote that he could no longer have performed his ideological critique of culture and semiotic dismantling of language in quite the same way. Following the May 1968 uprisings, he explained, semiological analysis became more differentiated and complex.

In the decades that followed Barthes's initial publication of *Mythologies*, and in tandem with more complex, post-1960s modes of inquiry, a new field, design history, emerged. This relatively young academic discipline has its roots in the products of industrialization, and in the paradigm shift that took place during the nineteenth century, when factory goods began to be produced using not only organized systems of divisions of labor, which had existed since antiquity, but more significantly, new forms of energy and new types of machines with which goods could be made more rapidly. This shift gave rise to the urban centers of Europe and North America, with their visionary new architecture and institutions, as well as their shifts in social class, gender roles, and attitudes toward race. By the beginning of the twentieth century mechanized production had become increasingly automated in both Europe and North America. In addition, new systems of education, collection, and attention to objects of all sorts, from carpets and pianos to firearms, prompted new types of analysis by cultural critics, educators, anthropologists, and art historians, who examined objects in relationship to culture and to history.

In the second half of the twentieth century, however, as scholars inter-rogated the ways in which such products, objects, and images had been produced, consumed, mediated, and circulated, using a variety of Marxist, feminist, and poststructuralist approaches, Barthes's *Mythologies* likely seemed rather simplistic. This book, however, while recognizing the limita-tions of semiotic readings of images, also challenges that presumption. Rather, it argues that we continue to be influenced by the world of signs in which we live today, often in ways that may be invisible on the surface. In fact, there has lately been a resurgence of new interest in Barthes, which is reflected in the new translation of his complete *Mythologies* into English, as well as by the publication of academic readers, including the book of essays on contemporary culture edited by Peter Bennett and Julian McDougal.[5]

It is important, indeed urgent, that we continue to peel away the layers of signification, locating myth in historical context. Unless we do so, we cannot understand what motivates us to long for that perfect pair of athletic shoes, what compels us to buy one electronic device rather than another, or what causes us to insist that our children play with wooden blocks instead of video games.

This is not a book of literary criticism, however, in the tradition of those that have been devoted to deeply understanding the work of Roland Barthes over the years, collected, for example, in the four volumes of Barthes studies edited by Neil Badmington.[6] Nor is it simply a polemical examination of brands in the globalized economy. It is rather a study of how we read the images that surround us such that we rarely notice them, and that when we do, we do not give them much thought. These images, and the ideas they signify, are located in graphic signage, in corporate identity systems, and, sometimes, in objects, too. To be sure, this book is critical, but it also hopes to present a reflective and thought-provoking call for change in our consumption habits, legislation, and worldview. The nine chapters that follow are offered here merely as examples of the infinite ways in which one might meditate on the visual aspects of designed images and objects. The subjects are arbitrary and personal, chosen according to my own interests and experiences as a teacher, scholar, and parent, experiences that are as challenging today as they were for those of Barthes's generation. The individual analyses are grounded in design history as an interdisciplinary approach, which draws from linguistics, psychoanalysis, sociology, anthropology, business and economic history, as well as from other theories of material cultural.

By calling our reading of such signs and symbols "new mythologies," I invoke not only Barthes's linguistic definition of myth, but also myth as a story with cultural meaning that transforms over time. Sigmund Freud, for example, reinterpreted the ancient Greek myth of Oedipus as a prism for reading the psychosexual dimensions of contemporary Viennese society at the turn of the twentieth century.[7] Claude Lévi-Strauss similarly analyzed the structural relationship of societal kinship patterns through the retelling of folk tales and the production of ceremonial, talismanic masks in the Pacific Northwest.[8] Our contemporary myths at the beginning of the twenty-first century are surely even more nuanced, globalized, and diffused. They migrate across space and time and infiltrate our imaginations in meaningful ways. What does the Nike Swoosh mean in China? Why do new Apple products continue to generate excitement?

Grant McCracken describes our relationship to these kinds of things as "displaced desire." Consumer goods, he believes, are "bridges to hopes and ideals."[9] Applying his ideas, we might agree that to purchase a product branded "green" is less about that product's functional potential to reduce our exposure to environmental toxins, or to prove that it was produced without exploiting the workers who made it, than it is about the way it makes us feel as consumers. Particularly potent objects and images, often deemed "iconic," similarly constellate around themselves myriad attitudes and emotions that may be as connected to feelings of identity as to the ways in which they have shaped new modes of living.[10] Television, a rather eccentric new technology when it was first introduced in the 1920s, quickly led the way to new modes of communication. But by the 1960s, the television, as object and institution, was also promoted as a symbol of democracy and capitalism, taking the place of the hearth as social center of the home, and ushering in a new era of telecommunication, the future implications of which cannot yet be fully comprehended.

In order to uncover the multiple layers of signification, which Barthes described so vividly as "a sort of constantly moving turnstile," it is necessary to conduct some research into unfamiliar territory.[11] The essays that follow, therefore, combine semiotic or linguistic analysis with historical and sociological methods of interpretation. As a historian of Central European art and culture at the turn of the twentieth century, I have been particularly influenced by Adolf Loos, an early twentieth-century Viennese architect, whose infamously acerbic essays on aspects of popular Austrian design, from toilets to ladies' fashion, were first published in Vienna's newspapers.[12] Readers may also find connections to other works of cultural criticism that comment on the way in which we interact with our designed world, such as Marshall McLuhan's enigmatic 1951 study, *The Mechanical Bride: Folklore of Industrial Man*, and Vance Packard's best-selling critique of advertising, *The Hidden Persuaders*, which, like *Mythologies*, was first published in 1957.

Iconic symbols, such as McDonald's "Golden Arches," are so ubiquitous in our visual landscape and popular imagination as to be virtually invisible. We are barely aware of them as we speed along the expressway, or walk along a busy street. Once we begin to think about them with more attention, however, we find ourselves asking, what is the meaning of gold? What is the purpose of an arch? How have our interpretations of these things changed over time, from one historical period to another, and from one cultural context to the next?

Initially I expected this project to reveal themes of the struggle for sustainability and social responsibility against the desire for corporate profit. In writing the essays, however, I began to discover recurrent threads that I could never have predicted: Thomas Jefferson makes frequent appearances in these chapters, as does Walt Disney. And the reader will encounter more than once themes of violence, childhood, and the quest for gold, and will dwell at length on the meaning of color and dreams.

One must approach an investigation of this sort with a sense of humor, disturbing though its implications may be. I admit that, like Barthes, I claim "to live to the full the contradiction of my time, which can make sarcasm the condition of truth." As we wander through the visual landscape in the following chapters, with sense of humor intact, we will encounter many contradictions, surprises, a little sarcasm, and possibly some truth, too, along the way.

Notes

1   Charles Baudelaire, "The Painter of Modern Life" (1863), in *The Painter of Modern Life and Other Essays*, trans. and ed. Jonathan Mayne (London: Phaidon, 1995), 1–41.

2   Jean-François Lyotard found evidence of the postmodern condition in the eclectic patchwork of contemporary popular culture, the experience of which can be schizophrenic. For Frederic Jameson, this condition emerges from its economic context that he described as "late capitalism," a mode that emerged after the Second World War. See Jean-François Lyotard, *Postmodernism Explained: Correspondence 1982–1985* (1988; reprint, Sydney: Power Publications, 1993); Frederic Jameson, *Postmodernism; or, the Cultural Logic of Late Capitalism* (1991; reprint, Durham, NC: Duke University Press, 1994).

3   Roland Barthes, "Myth Today," in *Mythologies*, trans. R. Howard and A. Lavers (1972; reprint, New York: Hill and Wang, 2012), 217–74. The

original volume of *Mythologies* was published in French by Éditions du Seuil in 1957.

4 Barthes, *Mythologies*, xi.

5 The 2012 English language edition of *Mythologies* includes several essays that did not appear in the 1972 selected edition of the text, translated by Annette Lavers. See also Peter Bennett and Julian McDougal (eds), *Barthes' "Mythologies" Today: Readings of Contemporary Culture* (London: Routledge, 2013).

6 Neil Badmington (ed.), *Roland Barthes: Critical Evaluations in Cultural Theory*, 4 vols (London: Routledge, 2010).

7 Sigmund Freud, "The Interpretation of Dreams" (First Part) (1900), in *The Standard Edition of the Complete Psychological Works of Sigmund Freud*, translated by James Strachey, 24 vols (London: Hogarth Press, 1953–74, 1995), vol. 4, 261–4.

8 Claude Lévi-Strauss, "The Structural Study of Myth" (1955), in Claude Lévi-Strauss, *Structural Anthropology*, translated by Claire Jacobson and Brooke Grundfest Schoepf (New York: Basic Books, 1961), 207–31; Claude Lévi-Strauss, *The Way of the Masks*, translated by S. Modelski (Seattle: University of Washington Press, 1975).

9 Grant McCracken, *Culture and Consumption: New Approaches to the Symbolic Character of Consumer Goods and Activities* (Bloomington, Indiana: Indiana University Press, 1990), 104–17. Adrian Forty likewise investigates the emotional and psychological aspects of design in *Objects of Desire: Design and Society From Wedgwood to IBM* (London: Thames and Hudson, 1986).

10 Grace Lees-Maffei (ed.), *Iconic Designs: 50 Stories About 50 Things* (London: Bloomsbury, 2014), 6–23.

11 Barthes, *Mythologies*, 233.

12 Adolf Loos, *Ins Leere Gesprochen: Gesammelte Schriften 1897–1900* (1921; reprint, Vienna: Georg Prachner Verlag, 1981, 1997); Adolf Loos, *Trotzdem, 1900–1930* (1931; reprint, Vienna: Georg Prachner Verlag, 1982, 1997).

CHAPTER ONE

Green

Thoughts on Sustainability

The color green has many associations. It describes bright new plants that burst forth from the frozen ground in springtime, as well as the fresh foods we like to eat. In Islam, green is the color of Paradise, symbolized as a lush and verdant garden. Exotic emerald and other deep mineral greens often suggest riches and luxury, a signification that echoes in the color of the United States one-dollar bill. But green has also been recognized in history and folklore as the color of sickness, envy, and poison. The term "green," which increasingly is used today to market products deemed environmentally friendly, also suggests progressive politics and sustainability. This first chapter takes as its point of departure one such symbol, a new logo designed for the multinational company BP (British Petroleum). As we meditate on the historical and symbolic meaning of green in BP's signage, we begin a journey that takes us from the discovery of Pennsylvania's green-tinted oil fields in the 1870s to the emergence of green political parties a century later. By the second half of the twentieth century, as the world became ever more dependent on oil, environmentalists responded to the oil industry's destructive practices by advocating for new legislation to protect planet Earth. As we examine the more recent symbols of the Iranian Green Movement, and related events of the Arab Spring, we are reminded of the bright green lozenge of BP's first house flag. The green flag, emblazoned with a red cross and golden lion, represented the dual national origins of the Anglo-Persian oil company, origins that likely continue to resonate today beneath the surface of the company's new emblem.

In 2002, BP redesigned its company logo as a green and yellow "Helios," named after the sun god of the ancient Greeks. The friendly symbol, part sunshine and part flower, evokes the life-giving forces of the natural world. It radiates four concentric rings of eighteen petals, or rays, in deepening colors from white, to yellow, to lighter and darker shades of green.[1] The new logo, designed by the San Francisco-based global consulting firm

Landor Associates, incorporated the identities of three recently purchased petroleum companies, Amoco, Arco, and Burmah Castrol, within a new BP that aspired to environmental leadership and progressive use of new energy sources, including an exploration of alternative fuels "beyond petroleum," which Landor Associates promoted on its corporate website.[2]

Many objected, however, to the use of this symbol by the oil industry, calling it a disingenuous "greenwashing" campaign designed to obscure BP's environmentally dangerous policies and record.[3] In 2010, following the fatal explosion on BP's oil rig, *Deepwater Horizon*, which killed eleven oil workers and spilled an estimated 4.9 million barrels (205.8 million gallons) of oil into the Gulf of Mexico, Greenpeace UK organized a campaign to redesign the BP Helios logo, which elicited nearly 2,000 clever, cynical, moving, and powerful variations, from oil-dripping sunflowers and smothered seabirds, to skulls and crossbones, in which "BP" stood for "brazen polluter," "bloody poison," and "bent on profit" (see Plate 1).[4]

From the garden city designs of the late nineteenth century to the Arab Spring at the beginning of the twenty-first, the color green frequently has signaled political, social, or environmental change. The word green in English derives from the verb "to grow," an origin that is shared by Germanic and Slavic languages, as well as by Latin and ancient Greek.[5] The color green, as a description of new vegetation, is, likewise, found in Sanskrit, Turkic, and some Asian languages. In 2009, following the reelection of conservative Iranian President Mahmoud Ahmadinejad, protests ensued with supporters of opposition leader Mir-Hossein Mousavi demanding that the results of the vote be annulled. Mousavi's reformist coalition, the Green Path of Hope, adopted the color green, the traditional color of Islam, in protest signs and banners, calling for a "Green Revolution," which would be "defined by peace and democracy."[6]

In 2010, a wave of revolutionary demonstrations swept across North Africa, the Arabian peninsula and the Middle East, resulting in the overthrow of the governments of Tunisia, Egypt, Libya, and Yemen. Collectively these events, which may have been instigated, in part, by the Iranian elections the previous year, came to be described as the "Arab Spring," recalling not only a seasonal period of fresh new growth and change, but also other world historical struggles for democracy. The 1848 revolutions in Europe, which were called "the springtime of the people," the 1968 Prague Spring, and the 2005 protests in Egypt and Lebanon, which were likewise referred to as an "Arab Spring," were each important precedents.[7]

Today, the word and color "green," in addition to signifying springtime and Islam, also connote environmentally friendly policies for sustainable production, and use of clean and renewable energy sources, such as solar and wind power, as well as the political ideologies of their advocates. Many corporations seeking to shape their image in this light have adopted both the color and word as a marketing strategy.[8]

The term "Green Revolution," however, was first coined in the 1960s in reference to new agricultural technologies—the use of pesticides and fertilizers chemically engineered to increase food production in developing parts of the word, especially India.[9] This campaign, while promising to alleviate global hunger, also introduced a host of environmental dangers. American writer and biologist Rachel Carson criticized the use of the chemical pesticide DDT in her influential 1962 book, *Silent Spring*, which drew attention to the fragile planet, and argued for protections for it that are still being debated today.

Trademark as Shield

While BP's adoption of the sunflower motif in 2000 was new, its use of the color green was not. Rather fortuitously BP's logo before the redesign had already featured the company's initials in yellow letters on a green shield. The original green and yellow colors were, thus, reincorporated into the Helios logo with a newly attributed environmental meaning.

The origins of the British Petroleum company date to the late nineteenth century when the Burmah Oil company was founded in Scotland by entrepreneur William Knox D'Arcy, who began oil exploration in Southeast Asia. In 1901, D'Arcy signed a concession agreement with Mozaffar ad-Din Shah Qajar of Persia (modern-day Iran) to search for oil. By the 1920s, the Anglo–Persian Oil Company (APOC), which was formed in 1909, had established a monopoly over Persian oil in the region. The company changed its name first in the 1930s to the Anglo–Iranian Oil Company (AIOC), and then again in the 1950s to British Petroleum (BP).[10] But the brand name BP was used as early as 1917 to market a line of motor fuel called BP Motor Spirit (the general term then used in the UK to refer to motor fuel).[11]

During the First World War (1914–18), a Petroleum Pool Board controlled the UK's distribution of fuel products; individual trademarks were prohibited and packaging was produced in "war colors" (dull tan or khaki-colored metal canisters).[12] At the end of the war, the BP letters were reintroduced, and in 1920, A. R. Saunders, an employee in BP's marketing department, won a competition to design the first logo, which he produced with the angular serif initials "B.P." in quotation marks in black on a red shield.[13] Throughout the 1920s, both the shield logo and the two-gallon cans of BP Motor Spirit were packaged and advertised in a variety of colors, including blue, green, yellow, and red. One printed advertisement from 1923 featured the BP Motor Spirit brand name emblazoned over a British flag, and promoted British Petroleum as the distributer for APOC, with an illustration of the company's new refinery at Llandarcy, Wales, a town named for D'Arcy. A caption under the flag proclaimed: "The Sign that means the 'Best Possible'."[14]

The origin of the heraldic shield as an identifying signifier can be traced to ancient Rome, where it was used to designate military units on the battle-field. It was also used in Europe in the twelfth and thirteenth centuries, where heraldic insignia were worn as badges, flown as flags, and used as seals for both protection and identification. A "coat" of arms, a real jacket worn by knights to protect their armor, was also marked with the identi-fying symbols that figured prominently on their battle shields. Valentin Groebner writes that:

> These heraldic images were not just visual insignia meant to represent political institutions and leaders, that is, to stand in for them or to announce their presence in their absence. They were also material objects, embodied signs.[15]

With the rise of the merchant class during the early modern period, heraldic insignia was used not only by the court, but also by guilds and other organi-zations with legal permission to "bear arms," and some have argued that medieval and Renaissance heraldic symbols may be seen as predecessors to the modern corporate logo.[16] Thus, the shield not only identifies and represents the company, communicating its identity to an audience, but also implicitly protects it. But from what?

Though the color of BP's Motor Spirit packaging varied through the 1920s, it seems that the green and yellow cans, which were registered as an international trademark by BP's French subsidiary in 1928, had become the most popular color pairing three years later, when the company's marketing department decided to standardize the look of the brand. According to BP's own corporate history, the green and yellow color scheme was envisioned in the spring of 1923, while two senior executives, J. E. J. Taylor and Edmond le Paix, enjoyed together a "very agreeable" lunch at a restaurant outside Paris.[17] In addition to attributing the French executives' color choice to their pleasant mood while enjoying a meal in the spring weather, BP recounts that the company's bright red petrol pumps and delivery trucks (the color of London's now iconic double-decker buses and telephone booths) were not popular at that time with residents in the British countryside, where they were felt to clash with the picturesque, natural green scenery.

More significantly around this same time BP began to fly a new house flag that symbolized the dual nationality expressed by the name "Anglo–Persian." It utilized the colors of the Persian flag—red, white, and green—and featured the red cross of St. George on a white background, upon which floated a green lozenge with an image of a golden lion, the national symbol of both England and Persia. The Middle Eastern legend of St. George's slaying of a dragon in the sea near Beirut was brought back to Europe during the Crusades, the medieval European Christian military campaigns to secure access to the Holy Lands. In Syria and Palestine the identity of St. George sometimes overlapped with that of Khidr, described in the Quran as companion to Moses, a servant of God and possessor of great wisdom, whose name in Arabic means "evergreen."[18]

In 1931, BP attempted to standardize the Persian green-and-gold color scheme in an updated shield logo, and in the 1940s, BP's international subsidiaries were again persuaded to adopt the yellow-and-green color scheme, though its use by individual franchises varied in shade. What is the relationship, then, between Britain and Persia as embodied within this sign? What is the relationship between access to the holy land by Christian crusaders in the twelfth and thirteenth centuries and access to the region's oil by multinational companies in the twentieth? Who wears this shield? Who does it identify or protect?

Arguably the most successful of the American industrial designers of the early to mid-twentieth century was the French–American émigré Raymond Loewy, who was responsible for the Chrysler corporation's exhibit building at the 1939 World's Fair, and who appeared, in 1949, on the cover of *Time* magazine, surrounded by his many famous designs. Loewy worked on a wide range of products in the 1940s and 1950s for companies as diverse as Studebaker, Greyhound, Coldspot, and Lucky Strike. In 1957, Loewy's French firm, Compagnie d'Esthétique Industrielle (CEI), was hired to redesign BP's corporate identity with an updated logo and comprehensive architectural scheme for its filling stations worldwide (see Plate 2).[19]

Loewy recalls that, because BP was committed to retaining the green-and-yellow color scheme (which he found "drab"), he tried to find a better, brighter shade of green for the shield, working with a psychologist at Dartmouth College to discover which colors could most easily be perceived in all possible weather conditions.[20]

In order to understand Loewy's work for BP within the larger context of oil company design at mid-century it is important to consider the designs of Tom Geismar and Eliot Noyes of Chermayeff & Geismar Associates, who were, likewise, influenced by the early twentieth-century approaches to modern corporate identity pioneered in Germany, Austria, and Switzerland, as well as by American innovations in corporate advertising.[21]

In 1964, Chermayeff & Geismar Associates revised the trademark for Mobil Oil, replacing with a bold letter "O" the company's traditional red-winged horse or Pegasus symbol, which had been used since 1911.[22] The red O stands out brightly between the blue letters of the word "Mobil," on a white rectangular signboard, calling attention to the round shape that resembles the circular wheel of an automobile, and signifies mobility. The classical, geometric circle further evokes perfection, a sense of calm, and feeling of timelessness. Geismar and Noyes mirrored the roundness of the letter O in their design of the cylindrical gasoline pumps in smooth stainless steel, beginning in 1968, which rebranded the Mobil filling station as a clean and modern, even clinical space, and dispelled any previous associations with the greasy, dirty, disorganized automotive shop.

Exxon, Amoco, and Chevron, each like Mobil, descended from John D. Rockefeller's American company, Standard Oil, which was founded in 1870. The later companies were formed after 1911, when the U.S. Supreme Court broke up Standard Oil's monopoly, finding that it had violated the 1890 Sherman Anti-Trust Act, which protected consumers from corporate monopolies.[23] The simple, iconic trademarks in red, white, and blue of the later companies visually recall their predecessor's first emblem, a blue torch with red flame, and ensure that the powerful family of former Standard Oil brands stays intact in the viewer's imagination.

The Standard Oil torch may also signify light, since petroleum was first used in the form of kerosene for lamps, or it may allude to the strange encounters with oil by early European settlers in the Pennsylvanian region, who witnessed springs and rivers on fire, burning the oil that had risen to and settled on their surfaces. Children's author L. Frank Baum, best known for the "Oz" stories, was born in upstate New York, near the Pennsylvania oil fields. His father made a good profit skimming the dark green oil off the river before Rockefeller and others began drilling in the region.[24]

But let's get back to the color green.

Green Means "Go"

Is there also something urgent about the color green itself that makes it particularly well suited to advertising? American psychologist Harlow Gale conducted clinical studies of attention to color in the late nineteenth century at the University of Minnesota in one of the first laboratories for consumer research in the United States.[25] Gale was interested in new developments in color printing and in the colorful signage and printed posters that had begun to saturate the visual landscape in the 1890s. He discovered that men and women responded differently to variously colored lettering schemes, and further, that their attention was related to their feelings of like and dislike for particular colors.[26] Gale's data was compiled and analyzed in the early twentieth century by American psychologist Daniel Starch, pioneer of marketing and consumer research, whose books on advertising were influential in the field for decades.[27] Psychologists, including A. P. Guilford and Louis Cheskin, carried out many studies of the use of color in advertising in the 1930s and 1940s. In 1945 Cheskin founded the Color Research Institute in Chicago. He published influential books on color during his career, including the 1951 *Color For Profit*.[28] By the mid-twentieth century the advertising industry relied heavily upon such psychological studies of consumer behavior, which coincided with the popularity in the United States of Freudian psychoanalytic therapy in the medical realm and of psychoanalytic methods of criticism in academia. Journalist Vance Packard's best-selling 1957 book, *The Hidden Persuaders*, billed by its publisher as "the classic examination of how the Media manipulate what you think, what you feel and what you spend," attacked the subliminal methods used by advertisers to entice consumers to buy products that they did not even know they wanted.[29]

The colors green and red began to be used for railroad traffic lights in the late nineteenth century, and were subsequently adopted by the automobile industry where green ubiquitously came to signify "go" and red "stop." The reasoning behind the color choice, presumably, is that it is more urgent to stop in a traffic situation; thus the stronger and more alarming red, associated with danger, is used for that purpose. The United States Department of Transportation later also adopted the color green for its interstate highway signage.[30] Though this color scheme is not international it does contribute in the United States to the unconscious association of the color green with mobility. Green is eye-catching. By the later twentieth century, as the built landscape of commerce became more homogenous in the U.S., the color green could stand out sharply as a familiar beacon, for example, in the bright green signage of ATMs (automatic teller or banking machines) or in the ubiquitous green logo and store awnings of Starbucks coffee shops. In both cases the color green compels customers not only to go, but also to spend.

Sunflower

In addition to the powerful signification of its green color we must also consider the floral shape of BP's Helios logo. In 1864–5 William Morris, the artist, writer, and social theorist at the forefront of the British Arts and Crafts movement, depicted himself as King Arthur of medieval legend in a splendid robe of large golden sunflowers. He included his self-portrait in a set of stained glass windows that he designed for All Saints church, in Middleton Cheney, Northamptonshire.[31]

The sunflower motif was prevalent in designs of the Arts and Crafts, Aesthetic, and later Art Nouveau movements, dating to the last quarter of the nineteenth century, in which contexts it signified both a rejection of industry and the embrace of modernity. In the nineteenth century, Morris and other critics connected to the Arts and Crafts movement, including most notably John Ruskin, criticized the modern factory system on both moral and aesthetic grounds.[32] The products of modern industry, Ruskin and Morris believed, lacked integrity, and the means of their production were exploitative and unethical. Modern factory workers labored long hours in inhuman conditions, were poorly compensated, and led impoverished lives.[33] At the same time, in the British Empire's colonies abroad, raw materials—the necessary ingredients for industry—were extracted from the land. If indigenous plants, animals, or human inhabitants of colonized regions were not readily useful for industry they were invisible, and those that were useful were consumed.

The deleterious effects of industrialization in England set into place some of the world's first environmental protections, including: the 1863 British Alkali Acts, which regulated air pollution in the production of soda ash; the 1865 establishment of the Commons Preservation Society; the 1869 Sea Birds Preservation Act; the 1875 Public Health Act to regulate the production of coal smoke; and the 1893 National Trust for Places of Historic Interest or Natural Beauty. In his 1898 treatise, *To-Morrow: A Peaceful Path to Real Reform*, reissued in 1902 as *Garden Cities of Tomorrow*, planner and social critic Ebenezer Howard envisioned a new type of suburban dwelling that promised to better integrate nature and human living. His first experiments were the towns of Letchworth and Welwyn Garden City, founded in Hertfordshire in 1903 and 1920 respectively.[34]

In the United States, conservationist John Muir, landscape architect Frederick Law Olmsted, and architect and city planner Daniel Burnham, among others, drew attention to the landscape of North America, calling for its preservation, while also designing parks and city spaces like Chicago's lakefront and New York's Central Park that enhanced its natural features.[35] Muir, concerned that California's beautiful Yosemite Valley would be destroyed by the timber and mining industries, succeeded in establishing the area as a National Park in 1892 with the help of his newly founded Sierra Club.[36] His ideas, like those of Olmsted and Burnham, were inspired not only by a critique of industry, but also by a philosophy of the redemptive aspects of the natural world, and a sense of the sublime that was articulated in the transcendentalist philosophy of American writers Ralph Waldo Emerson and Henry David Thoreau, both of whom were themselves influenced by French Enlightenment philosopher Jean-Jacques Rousseau.[37]

In Art Nouveau, the fashionable urban style that emerged in parts of Europe and North America as an outgrowth of the Aesthetic Movement in England in the years before the First World War, plants and flowers, especially those in early stages of growth, signified youth. Art Nouveau architecture referenced the organic forms of nature as well as the new possibilities of industry, as seen for example in the architectural ornament of Louis Sullivan's multi-storied office buildings in Chicago, or the train stations designed by Austrian architect Otto Wagner for Vienna's new city rail system in the 1890s (see Plate 3).

Associated most directly with Paris at the time of the 1900 Exposition universelle, Art Nouveau, "the new art," was visible in the evocative, vine-like forms of Hector Guimard's decorative, iron subway station entrances, as well as in tantalizing commercial advertisements illustrated by Alphonse Mucha.

To the chagrin of environmentalists, the new Helios (or sunflower) logo designed for BP in 2002 by Landor Associates is similar to that which is currently used by the Green Party of Canada. It is also generally reminiscent of leaf and flower logos used by a number of different local, national, and international green party organizations.

The first green party to adopt the sunflower motif was West Germany's Die Grünen, founded in March 1979, which used it for a political poster promoting the party in the elections of that year. The poster depicted a childlike drawing of trees, flowers, and a smiling sunshine. Punctuated by a green and yellow sunflower, it announced: "We have merely borrowed the earth from our children (*Wir haben die Erde nur von unseren Kindern geborgt*)" (see Plate 4).

The Preamble to the 1980 Federal Program of the Green Party of West Germany (*Die Grünen Bundesprogramm*) outlined a platform of social and ecological interests "in which the wanton destruction of natural resources and raw materials goes hand in hand with the destructive interference with the laws of nature and natural cycles." The party members wrote, "We are convinced that we have to halt the exploitation of nature and of human beings, in order to control the acute and serious threats to life itself."[38]

In Europe, as in North America, the organization of green political parties in the 1980s was the culmination of the cultural shift toward environmental awareness that began to percolate more politically in the 1960s, but which had been consistent among social critics, progressive thinkers, and reformers since the time of William Morris.[39] The Green Party of the United States, founded in 1984, follows "four pillars" of ecological wisdom, social and economic justice, grassroots democracy, and nonviolence.[40] No members of the Green Party of the United States currently hold office in the United States federal government, although journalist and consumer advocate Ralph Nader was the Green Party of the United States' candidate during both the 1996 and 2000 presidential elections. Nader rose to prominence in 1965 with the publication of his book, *Unsafe at Any Speed: The Designed-In Dangers of the American Automobile*, a scathing critique of the automobile industry and, in particular, of the American manufacturer, Chevrolet. Due to its unstable axle the Chevrolet Corvair, a popular, sporty car produced from 1961–3, had the tendency to roll over, which had caused a number of fatalities.[41]

Following the Second World War, the conservation activities of nineteenth-century environmentalists took on greater urgency as the world faced new challenges of air and water pollution, nuclear proliferation, and overpopulation. In the United States, coinciding with the turbulent era of agitation for the civil rights of African Americans and women's rights to equal pay and reproductive choice, as well as protest against the Vietnam War, a host of environmental protections was legislated, including the National Environmental Policy Act (1969), the establishment of the Environmental Protection Agency (1970), the Clean Air Act (1970), the Clean Water Act (1972), and the Endangered Species Act (1973). Among the most important catalysts for these changes was biologist and writer

Rachel Carson's gripping 1962 book, *Silent Spring*, an account of the dangers of the chemical pesticide DDT, in which she wrote:

> Over increasingly large areas of the United States, spring now comes unheralded by the return of the birds, and the early mornings are strangely silent where once they were filled with the beauty of bird song. This sudden silencing of the song of birds, this obliteration of the color and beauty and interest they lend to our world have come about swiftly, insidiously, and unnoticed by those whose communities are as yet unaffected.[42]

DDT (dichlorodiphenyltrichloroethane) was first synthesized in 1874 by Austrian chemist Othmar Zeidler. Swiss scientist Paul Hermann Müller discovered the properties of DDT as an insecticide in 1939, when it was hailed as a means of eradicating insect-borne disease in the agricultural industry. Müller was awarded the Nobel Prize in Physiology and Medicine for his discovery in 1948, before the hazards of the substance to human and environmental health were discerned.[43] Carson warned:

> Along with the possibility of the extinction of mankind by nuclear war, the central problem of our age has therefore become the contamination of man's total environment with such substances of incredible potential for harm—substances that accumulate in the tissues of plants and animals and even penetrate the germ cells to shatter or alter the very materials of heredity upon which the shape of the future depends.[44]

Carson's polemic, which predicted the extinction of many species, including the American bald eagle—the national symbol of the United States—generated widespread bipartisan support for the banning of DDT, with certain exceptions for use by the World Health Organization (WHO) in countries with endemic malaria, and for public health emergencies at home. Some in the chemical industry who stood to lose financially from the new legislation, however, objected to her arguments and sought to refute her scientific claims. Carson, who passed away only two years after the publication of her book, has also been the target of more recent attacks by foes, who attempt to undermine scientific discovery that threatens the financial interests of powerful industries, the profits of which have depended traditionally on harm to human health and the environment.[45]

In tandem with the revelation that certain chemicals could be used to control pests that threatened agricultural production, a "Green Revolution" to alleviate global hunger was initiated. The idea that certain newly engineered hardy grains could be grown, with the help of synthetic fertilizers and pesticides, in parts of the developing world that had been devastated by famine, emerged, at least in part, from a place of social concern. The negative side effects of artificially controlling the natural growing cycle, however, quickly became apparent. The initiative in the early 1960s to introduce a new, high-yielding variety of rice to India's Punjab was organized by agricultural developer Norman Borlaug, whose research was supported by the Rockefeller and Ford foundations. The term "Green Revolution" was used in 1968 by William Gaud, former director of the USAID (United States Agency for International Development), who said: "These and other developments in the field of agriculture contain the makings of a new revolution. It is not a violent Red Revolution like that of the Soviets, nor is it a White Revolution like that of the Shah of Iran. I call it the Green Revolution."[46]

Similarly influential on the global environmental movement were the photographs of Earth taken from outer space by NASA's ATS–3 satellite between 1967 and 1969. The first of these photos was featured on the cover of the *Whole Earth Catalogue*, a collaboratively authored manual of tools and information for sustainable living, edited by American writer and social activist Stewart Brand. The first photograph taken from space by the crew of NASA's Apollo 17 mission on December 7, 1972 was even more potent. The stunning image, popularly called "The Blue Marble," clearly depicts the coastline of Africa, Madagascar, and the Arabian Peninsula. It signified a call to action for environmentalists in the 1970s, and intersected with feminist metaphors of earth as a life-giving goddess, as well as with the Gaia hypothesis, the scientific theory that planet Earth, like Gaia, the ancient Greek personification of Mother Earth, is a self-regulating ecosystem that maintains conditions for life.[47]

In 1964, British graphic designer Ken Garland published the "First Things First Manifesto" in the *Guardian* newspaper. The document, an ethical call to action for graphic designers, was signed by twenty-one others who joined Garland in objecting to using their talents to sell commercial products, from cat food to cigarettes, which "contribute little or nothing to our national prosperity," instead of producing useful things like street signs and educational aids, and of promoting trade, education, culture and a "greater awareness of the world." The signatories wrote:

> we have reached a saturation point at which the high pitched scream of selling is no more than sheer noise ... we are proposing a reversal of priorities in favour of the more useful and more lasting forms of communication. We hope that our society will tire of gimmick merchants, status salesmen and hidden persuaders, and that the prior call on our skills will be for worthwhile purposes.[48]

Garland's use of the term "hidden persuaders" was most certainly a reference to Packard's groundbreaking 1957 book of the same title.

In his widely read polemic, *Design for the Real World: Human Ecology and Social Change*, first published in 1971, Austrian–American industrial designer Victor Papanek similarly urged his colleagues to forgo wasting their talents on streamlining "toasters for the rich," and to devote their energies instead to design for social good.[49] Among his innovative projects of the 1970s were contraceptive packaging for women unable to read, leaning stools for restless school children, and irrigation systems made from recycled tires for use in the developing world. Papanek was a follower of visionary American architect and engineer R. Buckminster Fuller, best known for his geodesic dome, an alternative, self-sustaining structure composed of lightweight poles that hold together through the principle of "tensegrity," tensile integrity and strength. Fuller's experimental concept of "Dymaxion" structures, a neologism combining the words "dynamic," "maximum," and "ion," which he explored in the 1920s in the form of houses and cars, and later in world maps, combined his interest in technology, international peace, and the ecological systems of the planet. In the midst of the space exploration of the 1960s, Fuller described the planet as "spaceship Earth," a technological wonder that must be carefully maintained in order to transport its passengers (humanity) into the future.[50] Instructions for building a version of Fuller's geodesic dome were published in the *Whole Earth Catalogue*.[51]

The rich period of socially conscious design in the 1960s and 1970s was greatly influenced by the alternative economics of Ernst Friedrich Schumacher, who in his 1973 book, *Small is Beautiful: Economics as if People Mattered*, rejected the notion that prosperity for some eventually benefits the whole of society. Rather, Schumacher noted with urgency, such an approach will hasten the extinction of the human species. "The modern economy is propelled by a frenzy of greed and indulges in an orgy of envy, and these are not accidental features but the very causes of its expansionist success." The lust for fossil fuels in particular, he believed, and the treatment of them as income, rather than capital to be saved and preserved for the future, would result only in economic and environmental disaster.[52]

Today environmental concerns have reached a critical point. The fact of global warming, caused by increased carbon emissions in the atmosphere, which result from the burning of fossil fuels, has surpassed the threats of famine, chemical toxicity, or nuclear annihilation that preoccupied the last quarter of the twentieth century. In his 1992 *Hannover Principles*, written on the occasion of the first United Nations Earth Summit, in Rio de Janeiro, Brazil, architect William McDonough asserted that humanity and nature must coexist and that responsible design must respect the earth's ecology and rely upon sustainable and renewable sources of energy, above all, the sun.[53] In his 2002 manifesto written with German chemist Michael Braungart, *Cradle to Cradle: Remaking the Way We Make Things*, McDonough proposed a system of design that relies upon solar energy and produces only things that can naturally biodegrade, returning to the earth, or can be perpetually recycled and reused.[54] The rhetoric of environmentally conscious ideology, coded "green," has now entered the vernacular such that one may speak of green energy, green building, green technology, green living, and even green-collar jobs. But one often questions the marketing of green products, which began with Gary Anderson's 1970 design of a new recycling symbol for the Container Corporation of America. The symbol, a simplified circle of arrows signifying an endless cycle of use and reuse, was criticized by designer Karrie Jacobs as confusing the slick corporate style branding of the mid-twentieth century with antithetical environmental concerns.[55]

Paradise

Though BP's oil spill at the Macondo well in the Gulf of Mexico was the worst accidental spill in history, it pales in comparison to the estimated eight million barrels of oil released into the Persian Gulf by Iraqi forces retreating from Kuwait during the United States Gulf War in 1991. Now on the cusp of a post-industrial world, the West continues to struggle with its addiction to oil and with its relationship to the Orient, which Edward Said described as "the place of Europe's greatest and richest colonies, the source of its civilizations and languages, its cultural contestant, and one of its deepest and most recurring images of the Other."[56] The histories of the environmental movement, the global oil industry, and the recent democratic movements in the Middle East are closely and complexly intertwined. Said wrote a new preface to his classic 1979 text, *Orientalism*, in the aftermath of the attacks by terrorists on the twin towers of the World Trade Center in New York on September 11, 2001. The tragic event led directly to the U.S. invasions of Iraq and Afghanistan in 2003, and of the ensuing wars there, which have lasted for more than a decade. Said wrote:

> Even with all its terrible failing and its appalling dictator, were Iraq to have been the world's largest exporter of bananas or oranges, surely there would have been no war, no transporting of an enormous army, navy, and air force 7,000 miles away to destroy a country scarcely known even to the educated American, all in the name of "freedom."[57]

The attacks of September 11 were later determined to have been carried out by affiliates of the radical, militant Sunni Muslim organization, al-Qaeda, based in Afghanistan and led by Osama bin Laden, a member of the wealthy Saudi Arabian bin Laden family, with its own ties to the global oil industry. The mourning and fury of Americans in the days and months that followed the attacks gave way to the U.S. Congress's decision, under the administration of President George W. Bush and his team of powerful advisors, to invade Iraq and Afghanistan, an act that has been criticized by the international community. While Afghanistan was governed at the time and is still largely controlled by a conservative fundamentalist Muslim movement known as the Taliban, Iraq was led by a ruthless and oppressive dictator, Saddam Hussein, who, the U.S. intelligence organizations claimed, was harboring "weapons of mass destruction," a claim that fueled a hysterical fear of the "Arab Other," and which garnered from the U.S. Congress and the American public a tacit support for war. The Bush administration argued urgently that this was the moment for Americans and Western European nations to step in and restructure the governments of Iraq and Afghanistan, preparing the way for Western-style freedom and democracy in the Middle East—an unfinished project that had begun in the first U.S. Gulf War of 1990–1, which was led by President Bush's father, the former President George H. W. Bush. Iraq's strategic location as an oil-exporting nation in the Persian Gulf, insisted President Bush's Secretary of Defense, Donald Rumsfeld, had "nothing ... literally nothing" to do with it.[58]

In retrospect, the U.S. twenty-first century wars in Afghanistan and Iraq have been costly, not only in human lives, but also for the American economy.[59] Bush's successor, President Barack Obama, was elected in 2008, in part because of his early and vociferous opposition to that war. After reporting on the war for several years, journalist Peter Maass asked: "Had Americans marched on Baghdad for the sake of oil rather than democracy or weapons of mass destruction?"[60] Describing a conversation with "Alain," the French senior executive of a "West European oil company," Maass writes:

> For Alain, geology was nearly as sexy as sex itself. He excitedly talked up the physical wonders of Iraq, which has some of the largest [oil] reservoirs in the world, with high-quality oil close to the surface and easy to move to seaports. His awe was of the sort Frenchmen usually reserve for discussions about the beauty of the mistresses they possess or desire.[61]

Maass's description of the erotic and covetous desire for Iraq's oil fields recalls Said's critique of French novelist Gustave Flaubert's tantalizing encounter with the Egyptian courtesan, Kuchuk Hanem, which Said read as a metaphor for the larger discourse of Western power and domination in the Orient.[62] It is hard to see the twenty-first-century wars in Iraq and Afghanistan now as anything other than imperialism and strategic positioning for global energy resources, specifically oil, with erotic, orientalist overtones, but this kind of covetous and violent posturing was certainly nothing new.

When oil was first discovered by European settlers in the Allegheny region of what is now Pennsylvania in the first half of the nineteenth century, it was considered something of a nuisance that interfered with obtaining saltwater from wells and springs, which could be distilled to produce salt. A few enterprising individuals, however, following the lead of native North American peoples in the region, decided that the gooey, slick substance floating on the surface of springs and rivers might be bottled and sold as a therapeutic remedy for a variety of ailments, from cholera to consumption.[63] A few years later the oil's useful properties as a lubricant for machinery, and as a lamp fuel, helped to spur interest in its production, not only from water surfaces, but also from underground wells, from which it could be pumped. By the 1860s, prospectors, many of whom had failed to find gold in the west, began to arrive in the region by the thousands to try their luck at leasing land and drilling for oil. Alongside the rush of prospectors grew an extensive transportation system of oil pipelines and railroads, as well as shipping and horse-drawn carriage transport routes. The most significant use of refined oil was gasoline fuel for powering automobiles; they were first produced in the U.S. in large quantities by the Ford Motor Company in the early twentieth century.

A half century later, after witnessing the German Autobahn system during the Second World War, President Dwight D. Eisenhower became committed to building a similar network of interstate highways in the United States. With the passage of the Federal Aid Highway Act of 1956, he developed a national system of roads.[64] Standard Oil of Indiana (Amoco) constructed five highway rest stops along the interstate toll roads in Illinois, the Tollway Oases. These respites featured Amoco filling stations and restaurants run by Fred Harvey, a concession company that originally built hotels and restaurants along railroad lines in the early days of rail travel. An oasis is an isolated area of vegetation in a desert, usually surrounding a water source, such as a spring. The Tollway "oases" were envisioned as peaceful, rejuvenating pauses in the desert of traffic, where one could refresh both self and automobile. A 1959 television advertisement featured a soothing woman's voice singing, "Take it easy, take the tollway."[65] In 2010, the Illinois Tollway Oases were rebuilt and today feature Mobil filling stations, as well as a host of fast food franchises and snack shops.

In 1954, BP, Exxon, Royal Dutch Shell, and others formed a consortium for oil production in Iran, the goal of which was to protect Western (especially British and American) oil interests against possible Soviet expansion in the area, and which had the effect of bolstering the regime of Iran's new king Mohammad Reza Shah Pahlavi.[66] Oil was wielded as a political weapon most notably during the 1973 embargo on oil exports to Western nations by the members of OPEC (the Organization of Petroleum Exporting Countries), whose founding members in 1960 included Venezuela, Iran, Iraq, Saudi Arabia, and Kuwait. The embargo, which was enacted in response to the United States and its Western allies' support of Israel during the 1973 Yom Kippur War, caused a global shortage of gasoline. Prices quadrupled and rations were instituted, leading the drivers of thirsty American cars into a desert of long lines at the gas station, and leading the American economy into a recession.[67]

After nearly a century of development, the oil industry began to experience major environmental disasters with greater and greater frequency. In 1967, the oil supertanker SS *Torrey Canyon* was wrecked off the coast of Cornwall in southwest England, spilling an estimated 32 million gallons of crude oil into the sea. The experimental clean-up, which relied upon solvent emulsifiers to break up the oil, proved disturbingly to be as toxic and detrimental to sea life as the oil itself. While the accident was attributed to a mistake in the design of the ship's steering control, it is noteworthy that the ship itself was owned by a subsidiary of the Union Oil Company of California, and was chartered for the voyage by BP, which used it to transport crude oil from the Kuwait National Petroleum Company refinery at Mina al-Ahmadi.

Just two years later, Union Oil spilled 4.2 million gallons of oil off the coast of Santa Barbara, California, when its drilling platform in the Dos Cuadras Offshore Oil Field exploded. The public outcry in response to the ecological destruction, which killed thousands of sea birds and mammals, spurred to action further environmental legislation, expanding upon that which had been initiated following the publication of *Silent Spring*. The environmental catastrophe of the Santa Barbara oil spill, which was widely publicized on television, and in a June 13, 1969 article in *Life* magazine, led directly to the establishment of Earth Day in the next spring.[68] At the 1969 UNESCO Conference in San Francisco, U.S. peace activist John McConnell proposed that such an event be held each year on the first day of spring. Modifying the vocabulary of civil rights sit-ins, Senator Gaylord Nelson, from the state of Wisconsin, concurrently proposed an Earth Day to be held on April 22, 1970, as a "teach-in," a national day of education and awareness about the environment, which is still observed in many American schools today.

Since the 1960s, large oil spills have occurred all over the globe, including: in Nova Scotia, Canada; South Africa; France; Italy; Angola; Oman; Russia; Iran; and Trinidad and Tobago. Two of the largest, including BP's 2010 *Deepwater Horizon* accident, happened in the Gulf of Mexico. The first of these took place in 1979 in the Bay of Campeche, when the Mexican state-owned Pemex (Petrólos Mexicano) drilling rig stationed at the exploratory well *Ixtoc I* had a blowout that gushed 140 million gallons of oil into the ocean, before it could be stopped. Similarly, although ranked only in 36th place for its trifling 11 million gallons of spilled oil, the 1989 crash of the tanker *Exxon Valdez* in Alaska's Prince William Sound is widely considered to have been the most environmentally damaging of the spills. It was particularly difficult to clean up the spilled oil in the remote location, a problem that was exacerbated by Exxon's slow response to the accident, which devastated marine life in the beautiful, pristine habitat. The Exxon Shipping Company was transporting oil from the Prudhoe Bay oil fields of Alaska to Long Beach, California, when the intoxicated captain and fatigued crew ran into the Sound's dangerous Bligh Reef. Subsequent investigations revealed that in addition proper inspections of the ship had not taken place, nor had equipment for monitoring icebergs been installed.

In the aftermath of BP's 2010 oil spill in the Gulf of Mexico, which resulted from the company's safety negligence, as well as that of the American multinational oil field service company, Halliburton, and the Swiss-based offshore drilling company, Transocean Ltd., BP's chairman Carl-Henric Svanberg outraged many when he referred insensitively to Louisiana's inhabitants as the "small people" of the Gulf coast.[69] Perhaps he felt some sympathy, albeit in a paternalistic manner, for those who make their living by fishing in the Gulf waters and providing hotels and restaurants for tourists to the region, many of whom needed to be compensated by BP in order to get back on their feet. In 2012, two years after the oil spill, BP made $25 billion in annual profits, a fact that made it likely difficult for the company's executives to relate to those whose livelihoods depend on a modest income of at best about $40,000 per year, according to the Bureau of Labor Statistics. Their living is based not on the fluctuation of oil futures and stock market investments, but rather on day-to-day events, like the number of fish they can catch or the number of visitors who travel through the area to view the pretty scenery.

Louisiana is one of America's great ecological and cultural treasures. Some of the country's greatest music was born there, especially early jazz. Louisiana, and the city of New Orleans in particular, is known for its exotic foods, hybrid languages, and unfamiliar customs. It is a place of decadent escape, mystery, and magic, as well as one of intense poverty. Its multi-ethnic roots include the traditions of African American slaves as well as the intermarriages of French settlers and Caribbean natives. But Louisiana was also the name given to the swathe of cheap land sold to the United States by Napoleon Bonaparte in the early nineteenth century under the "Louisiana Purchase." Napoleon chose not to settle what at that time may have been perceived as an insect-infested and disease-ridden swampland, but which today is essential to American trade.

Located at the mouth of the Mississippi River, Louisiana's wetlands stretch into the sea, facilitating the endless flow of goods in and out of its waters.[70] Beautiful, primitive, and exotic Louisiana, populated largely by black people, is in many ways "America's Other." This fact became uncomfortably clear when the United States government was shockingly slow to respond to the victims of the 2005 hurricane Katrina, one of the deadliest in history, in which at least 1,833 people perished. The hurricane devastated the Gulf region, destroying entire neighborhoods in New Orleans, and leaving many homeless, stranded, and desperate. Today, many climate scientists have suggested that such violent storms will only become more prevalent with global warming and the continued unchecked burning of fossil fuels.

Animal, Vegetable, Mineral

Despite its many associations with health and life, in the animal world green can, by contrast, signify poison. The green coloring of reptiles and insects is sometimes a shield used for protection. It is a signal to birds and other animals that they should stay away, sending the deceptive message that they will taste bad or make their predators sick, though the seductive green feathers of some species of birds can also attract mates. Green is the color of certain types of fungi that grow on food, signaling that it has spoiled. The color green can signify sickness, too, particularly seasickness or nausea, which may cause a greenish pallor. Green may signify youth, inexperience, or naïveté, though not necessarily in a negative way, as in "she's still green." Green is the color of money. Green can also evoke outdoor recreation and military survival, notable for example in the dull green color of military fatigues, including those uniforms worn by the U.S. Army Special Forces, the Green Berets, as well as in the dark green color of canvas tents, camp stoves, and other outdoor equipment. In folklore, green is often associated with nature, as in the Green Knight of Arthurian legend. But green is also the color of envy, the notorious green-eyed monster, and one of the seven deadly sins.

In the mineral world, green frequently signifies wealth, rarity, and luxury, most notably in the deep green color of emerald gemstones, but also in other mineral materials, such as jade, malachite, celadon, turquoise, and jewels and glazes tinted by chromium. Frank L. Baum's glittering Emerald City of Oz, memorably evoked in *The Wizard of Oz*, the 1939 film version of his story with a Technicolor art deco cityscape of green, crystalline towers, is an illusory place of dreams. But Dorothy, Baum's young protagonist, magically displaced from her dour, sepia-toned, dust bowl Kansas home, learns the Potemkin truth of Oz, once the curtains are drawn back, and she discovers that the Great and Terrible Wizard of Oz is just a man. In fact, he is the dream incarnation of the friendly traveling salesman from Omaha, Nebraska, whom she encountered earlier at home. He is not exactly a snake oil salesman, but rather a self-described "humbug."[71] How did Oz, the itinerant merchant peddling his bottles of oil, grow so inexplicably powerful? Is the green of BP's Helios symbol a sign of rejuvenating new life for the planet and an assurance of its sustainable future? Or is the promise of such a future, like Oz, merely an illusion, cynically used to mask the destructive practices of an exploitative industry? Can we reconcile our desire for the riches of oil with the needs of a healthy environment? Or is BP's green rather the green of envy, sickness, and capital that has already poisoned us for generations to come?

Notes

1   "Brief History of the Brand & Logo," BP Corporate Archive, n.d., received by personal communication, May 15, 2014.

2   "BP Moving beyond on a global scale," Landor Associates [website], copyright 2010, available online: http://landor.com/#!/work/case-studies/bp/ (accessed May 14, 2014). See also "BP parts with shield logo and 'Amoco' name," *National Petroleum News* 92/5 (May 2000): 46; Gregory Solman,

"BP: Coloring Public Opinion?" *Adweek* (January 14, 2008), available online: http://www.adweek.com/news/advertising/bp-coloring-public-opinion-91662 (accessed May 14, 2014).

3 James Ridgeway, "BP's Slick Greenwashing," *Mother Jones* (May 4, 2010), available online: http://www.motherjones.com/mojo/2010/05/bp-coated-sludge-after-years-greenwashing (accessed May 14, 2010); Joe Nocera, "Green Logo, but BP is Old Oil," *New York Times* (August 12, 2006), available online: http://www.nytimes.com/2006/08/12/business/worldbusiness/12nocera. html?pagewanted=all&_r=0 (accessed May 14, 2014).

4 "Behind the Logo competition winners," Greenpeace UK [website], available online: http://www.greenpeace.org.uk/files/bp/rebranded/index.html?utm_source=ebulletin20100802 (accessed May 13, 2014).

5 "green, adj. and n.1," *Oxford English Dictionary Online* (March 2014), copyright Oxford University Press, available online: http://www.oed.com/view/Entry/81167?rskey=MYFwxF&result=2 (accessed March 2014).

6 Mohsen Makhmalbaf, "I speak for Mousavi. And Iran," The *Guardian* (June 19, 2009), available online: http://www.theguardian.com/commentisfree/2009/jun/19/iran-election-mousavi-ahmadinejad (accessed May 18, 2014).

7 Dieter Langewiesche, "The Role of the Military in the European Revolutions of 1848," in Dieter Dowe et al. (eds), *Europe in 1848: Revolution and Reform* (New York: Berghahn Books, 2001), 694–707; Vladimir Kusin, *The Intellectual Origins of the Prague Spring: the Development of Reformist Ideas in Czechoslovakia 1956–1967* (Cambridge: Cambridge University Press, 2002); Marc Lynch, *The Arab Uprising: The Unfinished Revolutions of the New Middle East* (New York: Public Affairs, 2012).

8 Pauline Madge, "Design, Ecology, Technology: A Historiographical Review," *Journal of Design History* 6/3 (1993): 149–66; Pauline Madge, "Ecological Design: A New Critique," in Richard Buchanan, Dennis Doordan, and Victor Margolin (eds), *The Designed World: Images, Objects, Environments* (Oxford: Berg, 2010), 328–38, originally published in *Design Issues* 13/2 (Summer 1997): 44–54.

9 Richard Manning, *Against the Grain: How Agriculture Has Hijacked Civilization* (New York: North Point Press, 2005).

10 R. W. Ferrier, *The History of the British Petroleum Company*, vol. 1, *The Developing Years 1901–1932* (Cambridge: Cambridge University Press, 1982).

11 Ibid.

12 Donald F. Dixon, "Inter-War Changes in Gasoline Distribution: A US–UK Comparison," *Business and Economic History* 26/2 (Winter 1997): 632–48.

13 "Brief History of the Brand & Logo."

14 Phil Easdown, "The British Petroleum Co. Ltd.," Vintage Garage [website], available online: http://www.vintagegarage.co.uk/histories/british%20 petroleum%20co%20ltd.htm (accessed May 14, 2014).

15 Valentin Groebner, *Defaced: The Visual Culture of Violence in the Late Middle Ages*, trans. Pamela Selwyn (New York: Zone Books, 2008), 52–3;

Michel Pastoureau, *Traité d'héraldique* (3rd edn, Paris: Picard, 1997), first published in 1979.

16 Paul Rand, "Logos, Flags, and Escutcheons," in Michael Bierut, William Drenttel, Steven Heller, and D. K. Holland (eds), *Looking Closer: Critical Writings on Graphic Design* (New York: Allworth Press, 1994), 88–90. Originally published in the *AIGA Journal of Graphic Design* 9/3 (1991).

17 "History of the use of the colours green and yellow," BP Corporate Archive, n.d., received by personal communication, May 15, 2014.

18 Oya Pancaroğlu, "The Itinerant Dragon-Slayer: Forging Paths of Image and Identity in Medieval Anatolia," *Gesta* 43/2 (2004): 151–64.

19 Evert Endt, "The French Connection: The Compagnie de l'Esthéthique Industrielle," in Angela Schönberger (ed.), *Raymond Loewy: Pioneer of American Industrial Design* (exh. cat., Berlin: International Design Center; Munich: Prestel Verlag, 1990), 173–81.

20 Raymond Loewy, *Industrial Design* (Woodstock, NY: Overlook Press, 1979). See also Harry A. Burdick, Edward J. Green, and Joseph W. Lovelace, "Predicting Trademark Effectiveness," *Journal of Applied Psychology* 43/5 (October 1959): 285–6.

21 Jay Doblin, "Trademark Design," in Michael Bierut, Jessica Helfand, Steven Heller, and Rick Poynor (eds), *Looking Closer 3: Classic Writings on Graphic Design* (New York: Allworth Press, 1999), 180–6. Originally published in *Dot Zero*, 2 (1967). The approach of Doblin's generation was described in Wally Olins, *The Corporate Personality* (London: Design Council, 1978), an influential study of corporate identity written by one of the leaders in the field at the British consulting agency Wolff Olins. For a critical interpretation see Steve Baker, "Re-Reading 'The Corporate Personality'," *Journal of Design History* 2/4 (1989): 275–92. See also Richard Hollis, *Swiss Graphic Design: The Origin and Growth of an International Style, 1920–1965* (New Haven: Yale University Press, 2006).

22 "Mobil's High-Flying Trademark," American Oil and Gas Historical Society [website] (April 20, 2014), available online: http://aoghs.org/popular-oil-history-articles/high-flying-trademark/print/#comments_controls (accessed May 27, 2014).

23 The lawsuit was brought in the wake of journalist Ida Tarbell's two-volume exposé, *The History of the Standard Oil Company*, which was published in nineteen installments in *McClure's* magazine between 1902 and 1904. Tarbell documented Standard Oil's practice of colluding with other industries, including the railroad, to undersell products and drive out competitors, and to raise its prices artificially. Ida Tarbell, *The History of the Standard Oil Company*, 2 vols (New York: McClure, Phillips and Company, 1905). See also United States Public Law 94–435, Title 3, Sec. 305(a), 90, Stat 1383.

24 William Leach, *Land of Desire: Merchants, Power, and the Rise of a New American Culture* (New York: Pantheon, 1993), 56.

25 John Eighmey and Sela Sar, "Harlow Gale and the Origins of the Psychology of Advertising," *Journal of Advertising* 36/4 (Winter 2007): 147–58. For a

more general history of color in design see also Regina Lee Blaszczyk, *The Color Revolution* (Cambridge, MA: MIT Press, 2012).

26 Eighmey and Sar, 153.

27 Daniel Starch, *Advertising: Its Principles, Practice, and Technique* (New York: Scott, Foresman, 1914); Daniel Starch, *Principles of Advertising* (New York: McGraw Hill, 1923).

28 J. P. Guilford, "Affective Value of Color as a Function of Hue, Tint, and Chroma," *Journal of Experimental Psychology* 17 (1934): 342–71; Louis Cheskin, *Color for Profit* (New York: Liveright, 1951). See also Louis Cheskin, *How to Predict What People Will Buy* (New York: Liveright, 1957).

29 Vance Packard, *The Hidden Persuaders* (1957; reprint, New York: Simon and Schuster, 1980).

30 National Joint Committee on Uniform Traffic Control Devices, *Revisions to the Manual on Uniform Traffic Control Devices For Streets and Highways* (Washington, DC: Department of Commerce, Bureau of Public Roads, 1954).

31 Fiona MacCarthy, *William Morris: A Life for Our Time* (New York: Knopf, 1995), color plate IX.

32 William Morris, "Useful Work Versus Useless Toil" (1884), in *The Collected Works of William Morris*, 24 vols (London: Longmans, Green, and Company, 1910–15), vol. 23, 98–120; John Ruskin, *Unto This Last, and Other Essays on Art and the Political Economy* (London: J. M. Dent, 1907), first serialized in 1860 in *Cornhill Magazine*.

33 Charles Dickens, *Hard Times: For These Times* (London: Bradbury and Evans, 1854), first serialized in 1854 in *Household Words*.

34 Ebenezer Howard, *Garden Cities of To-Morrow*, ed. F. J. Osborn (1902; new edn, Cambridge, MA: MIT Press, 1965).

35 Frederick Law Olmsted, "The Misfortunes of New York" (1877), and "Chicago: Taming the Waterfront" (1871), in Frederick Law Olmsted, *Civilizing American Cities: Writings on City Landscapes*, ed. S. B. Suton (1971; reprint, New York: De Capo Press, 1997), 43–51, 156–96; Daniel H. Burnham and Edward H. Bennett, *Plan of Chicago* (Chicago: The Commercial Club, 1909); Carl Smith, *Plan of Chicago: Daniel Burnham and the Remaking of the American City* (Chicago: University of Chicago Press, 2006).

36 John Muir, "Features of the Proposed Yosemite National Park," in John Muir, *Nature Writings*, ed. William Cronon (New York: Library of America, 1997), 687–700, originally published in *Century Magazine* (September 1890).

37 Henry David Thoreau, *Walden, or, Life in the Woods* (Boston: Ticknor and Fields, 1854); Ralph Waldo Emerson, *Nature* (Boston: James Munroe and Company, 1836). See also Gilbert F. La Freniere, "Rousseau and the European Roots of Environmentalism," *Environmental History Review* 14/4 (Winter 1990): 41–72.

38 "Federal Programme 1980: Preamble," in Eva Kolinsky (ed.), *The Greens in West Germany: Organisation and Policy Making* (Oxford: Berg, 1989), 239–43.

39 Madge, "Design, Ecology, Technology," 150.

40 The Green Party of the United States, organized as a federation of state green parties that focuses on electoral politics, is not to be confused with the Greens/Green Party USA, a grassroots advocacy organization founded in 1984 to draw attention to environmental issues.

41 Ralph Nader, *Unsafe at Any Speed: The Designed-In Dangers of the American Automobile* (New York: Grossman, 1965).

42 Rachel Carson, *Silent Spring* (1962; new edn, Boston: Mariner Book, 2000), 103.

43 Malcolm Gladwell, "The Mosquito Killer," *The New Yorker* (2 July 2001): 42–51.

44 Carson, *Silent Spring*, 8.

45 Naomi Oreskes and Erik M. Conway, *Merchants of Doubt: How a Handful of Scientists Obscured the Truth on Issues from Tobacco Smoke to Global Warming* (New York: Bloomsbury, 2010), 216–39.

46 Gordon Conway, *The Doubly Green Revolution: Food For All in the Twenty-First Century* (Ithaca: Comstock Publishers, 1998). See also H. K. Jain, *The Green Revolution: History, Impact and Future* (Houston: Studium Press, 2010); Vandana Shiva, *The Violence of the Green Revolution: Ecological Degradation and Political Conflict in Punjab* (Dehra Dun: Research Foundation for Science and Ecology, 1989); Vaclav Smil, *Enriching the Earth: Fritz Haber, Carl Bosch, and the Transformation of World Food Production* (Cambridge, MA: MIT Press, 2004).

47 The Gaia hypothesis was formulated by English environmental scientist James Lovelock, born in 1919 in Ebenezer Howard's experimental Letchworth Garden City, and American microbiologist Lynn Margulis. J. E. Lovelock, "Gaia as seen through the atmosphere," *Atmospheric Environment* 6/8 (August 1972): 579–80; James E. Lovelock and Lynn Margulis, "Atmospheric homeostasis by and for the biosphere: the Gaia hypothesis," *Tellus* 26/1–2 (1974): 2–10.

48 Ken Garland, "First Things First" (1964), in Michael Bierut, Jessica Helfand, Steven Heller, and Rick Poynor (eds), *Looking Closer 3: Classic Writings on Graphic Design* (New York: Allworth Press, 1999), 154–5.

49 Victor Papanek, *Design for the Real World: Human Ecology and Social Change* (New York: Pantheon Books, 1971); Victor Papanek, *Design for Human Scale* (New York: Van Nostrand Reinhold, 1983); Victor Papanek, *The Green Imperative: Natural Design for the Real World* (New York: Thames and Hudson, 1995); See also Madge, "Design, Ecology, Technology," 153–4.

50 R. Buckminster Fuller, *Operating Manual for Spaceship Earth* (New York: Simon and Schuster, 1969); R. Buckminster Fuller, *Utopia or Oblivion: The Prospects for Humanity* (New York: Bantam Books, 1969).

51 Access to Tools: Publications from the Whole Earth Catalogue, 1968–1974 [website], exhibition at the Museum of Modern Art, New York, April 11 to December 10, 2011, available online: http://www.moma.org/interactives/exhibitions/2011/AccesstoTools/ (accessed June 5, 2014).

52 E. F. Schumacher, *Small is Beautiful: Economics as if People Mattered* (New York: Harper and Row, 1973), 28–9. Schumacher's treatise contradicts the macroeconomic view presented in John Maynard Keynes, *The General Theory of Employment, Interest, and Income* (London: Macmillan, 1936). Schumacher was equally critical of the use of nuclear energy, due to the dangers of transporting it and storing its waste, as well as its potential use for war. Other influential books by environmentalists during this period included Charles Reich, *The Greening of America: How the Youth Revolution is Trying to Make America Livable* (New York: Random House, 1970); Paul R. Erlich, *The Population Bomb* (New York: Ballantine Books, 1971); Barry Commoner, *The Closing Circle: Man, Nature, and Technology* (New York: Knopf, 1971); and Timothy O'Riordan, *Environmentalism* (London: Pion, 1976).

53 W. McDonough and M. Braungart, *The Hannover Principles: Design for Sustainability, for the City of Hannover, Germany, EXPO 2000, the World's Fair* (Charlottesville, VA: William McDonough Architects, 1992). See also William McDonough, "Design, Ecology, Ethics, and the Making of Things," *Colonnade* 10/3 (Fall 1994): 9–14, reproduced in Kate Nesbitt (ed.), *Theorizing a New Agenda For Architecture: An Anthology of Architectural Theory 1965–1996* (New York: Princeton Architectural Press, 1996), 400–7.

54 William McDonough and Michael Braungart, *Cradle to Cradle: Remaking the Way We Make Things* (New York: North Point Press, 2002). The book is dedicated "To our families, and to all of the children of all species for all time."

55 Karrie Jacobs, "Disposability, Graphic Design, Style, and Waste," in Michael Bierut, William Drenttel, Steven Heller, and D. K. Holland (eds), *Looking Closer: Critical Writings on Graphic Design* (New York: Allworth Press, 1994), 183–90, originally published in the *AIGA Journal of Graphic Design* 7/4 (1990).

56 Edward Said, *Orientalism* (1979; new edn, New York: Vintage Books, 1994, 2003), 1.

57 Said, *Orientalism*, xx.

58 Donald Rumsfeld, quoted in Peter Maass, *Crude World: The Violent Twilight of Oil* (New York: Vintage Books, 2009), 4.

59 Daniel Trotta, "Iraq war costs U.S. more than $2 trillion: study," *Reuters*, available online: http://www.reuters.com/article/2013/03/14/us-iraq-war-anniversary-idUSBRE92D0PG20130314 (accessed June 5, 2014); Mark Thompson, "March was First Month Without U.S. Fatalities in Iraq or Afghanistan in 11 Years," *Time* (April 1, 2014), available online: http://time.com/45160/zero-us-fatalities-iraq-afghanistan–11-years/ (accessed June 5, 2014).

60 Maass, *Crude World*, 4.

61 Maass, *Crude World*, 104.

62 Said, *Orientalism*, 6.

63 Tarbell, *The History of The Standard Oil Company*, vol. 1, 5.

64 United States Public Roads Administration, *Toll Roads and Free Roads: Message from the President of the United States Transmitting a Letter From*

the Secretary of Agriculture, Concurred in by the Secretary of War, Enclosing a Report of the Bureau of Public Roads, United States Department of Agreiculture, on the Feasibility of a System of Transcontinental Toll Roads and a Master Plan for Free Highway Development (Washington, DC: U.S. Government Printing Office, 1939); United States National Interregional Highway Committee, *Interregional Highways: Message From the President of the United States, Transmitting a Report of the National Interregional Highway Committee, Outlining and Recommending a National System of Interregional Highways* (Washington, DC: U.S. Government Printing Office, 1944); Owen D. Gutfreund, *Twentieth-Century Sprawl: Highways and the Reshaping of the American Landscape* (Oxford: Oxford University Press, 2004).

65 Illinois Tollway television advertisement featuring "Mary MacToll," 1959, available online: http://www.youtube.com/watch?v=hedT-mNvHJg (accessed May 23, 2013).

66 Mary Ann Heiss, "The United States, Great Britain, and the Creation of the Iranian Oil Consortium, 1953–1954," *International History Review* 16/3 (August 1994): 511–35.

67 James Bamberg, *British Petroleum and Global Oil, 1950–1975: The Challenge of Nationalism* (Cambridge: Cambridge University Press, 2000).

68 David Snell, "Iridescent Gift of Death," *Life* 66/23 (13 June 1969): 22–7. See also John Wills, *U.S. Environmental History: Inviting Doomsday* (Edinburgh: Edinburgh University Press, 2013), 126; Stephanie LeMenager, *Living Oil: Petroleum Culture in the American Century* (Oxford: Oxford University Press, 2014), 20–65.

69 Garance Franke-Ruta, "BP chairman says firm cares about 'the small people,'" *The Washington Post* (June 16, 2010), available online: http://voices.washingtonpost.com/44/2010/06/bp-chairman-says-firm-cares-ab.html (accessed May 22, 2014); Campbell Robertson and Clifford Krauss, "BP May Be Fined Up to $18 Billion for Spill in Gulf," *The New York Times* (September 4, 2014), available online: http://www.nytimes.com/2014/09/05/business/bp-negligent-in–2010-oil-spill-us-judge-rules.html?_r=0 (accessed May 13, 2015).

70 "Port Industry Statistics," AAPA (American Association of Port Authorities) [website], available online: http://www.aapa-ports.org/Industry/content.cfm?ItemNumber=900 (accessed June 9, 2014).

71 L. Frank Baum, *The Wonderful Wizard of Oz* (1900; reprint, New York: Harper Trophy, 1987), 216.

CHAPTER TWO

Gateway

Travel, Triumph, and Striking Gold

One of the most familiar and ubiquitous signs in the United States, if not around the globe, is that of McDonald's, the burger restaurant that first opened in San Bernardino, California, in 1940. McDonald's distinctive bright yellow logo formed of two parabolic arches was designed later, in 1962, by Jim Schindler, who drew upon the owner Dick McDonald's original idea to incorporate two large arches into the building design of a 1953 McDonald's restaurant in Phoenix, Arizona. When seen from an angle the arches look like a letter "M" (see Fig. 2.1).

Stanley Clark Meston, architect of the Phoenix restaurant, initially rejected the idea of including the arch feature in his building, so the task was delegated to sign maker George Dexter, who produced them in sheet metal trimmed with yellow neon. Meston designed the same style of building with incorporated arches, however, for a subsequent 1955 McDonald's restaurant in Des Plaines, Illinois, which is considered to be the first of the present-day chain businesses. The restaurant's owner, Ray Kroc, a Czech–American entrepreneur from Oak Park, Illinois, was so impressed by the original California restaurant that he decided to build a franchise, which made use of standardization to ensure the quality and consistency of products in every business location.[1]

What is the meaning of this sign, nicknamed the "Golden Arches"? Its message is thickly layered. On a primary level, the sign signifies the food itself. Its color scheme is evocative of red ketchup and yellow mustard; the looping letter M signifies not only "McDonald's," but is also reminiscent of the famous, thin-cut, slightly droopy fries that customers receive with each meal.[2] The particular shape of the arching letter M also suggests a relationship to the swooping optimism of mid-century modern design, seen, for example, in Finnish–American architect Eero Saarinen's 1947 design of the Jefferson National Expansion Memorial, otherwise known as the St. Louis Gateway Arch. The McDonald's golden arches are thus an entrance, or gateway, to another place.

Fig. 2.1 McDonald's restaurant, Downy, California, designed by Stanley Meston, 1958. Photo by Bryan Hong, 2007. Creative Commons.

Gold

Beneath the surface of the Golden Arches is a complex web of references. The golden yellow letter M stands not only for the name of the restaurant, but also for McDonald's as fulfillment of the American dream of westward expansion, immigration, technological innovation, prosperity, and economic and political power. Many of the first European explorers to the New World, and later adventurers who traversed the continent, came in search of gold. Spanish explorers were awestruck by golden mountainsides carpeted with native California poppies (*Eschscholzia californica*), which, according to local legend, filled the soil with gold. Meanwhile, the development of profitable timber, mining, and railroad industries in the nineteenth century resulted from this westward expansion. Wealth was generated, in the end, not from the elusive gold, but rather from the apparatus that developed around the search, which included merchants of all sorts, such as the German–American denim manufacturer, Levi Strauss, who established his blue jean business, Levi Strauss & Co., in San Francisco, California, in 1853.

The California Gold Rush began in 1848, with the discovery of gold at Sutter's Mill, a sawmill in Coloma, California, owned by John (Johann) Sutter and operated by James W. Marshall, an American carpenter of English descent from New Jersey.[3] Sutter himself was a Swiss pioneer who had traveled extensively with a group of German immigrants from the St. Louis region to both the New Mexico and the Oregon Territories, and beyond that to Honolulu, and Sitka, Alaska, finally settling in 1838 in what is now San Francisco. It was there that he established the fort that he called "New Helvetia," or "New Switzerland."[4] A subsequent wave of immigration began the following year with thousands of hopeful prospectors dubbed the "forty-niners." Many of California's new arrivals from Europe had fled the political revolutions of 1848–9, energized by students and intellectuals, including Karl Marx and Friedrich Engels who published "The Communist Manifesto" in 1848.[5] Many others crossed the Pacific from China to pursue work in America. The Treaty of Guadalupe–Hidalgo, at the end of the Mexican–American War (1846–9), ceded California to the United States. When it became a new state that same year the exclamation "Eureka!" ("I have found it!") was incorporated into the state's official seal, designed by U.S. Army Major Robert S. Garnett, who explained that it could refer both to California's admission to the union, and to the discovery of gold.[6] The etymology of the word "Eureka" may be traced to its use by the ancient Greek mathematician, Archimedes, who discovered the physical principle of mass displacement while determining that a local goldsmith had cheated King Heiros of Syracuse by fabricating for him a less-than-pure gold crown.[7]

In 1846, just two years before the discovery of gold at Sutter's Mill, American explorer John C. Frémont described the strait connecting the San Francisco Bay to the Pacific Ocean as the "Golden Gate," comparing it to the harbor of Istanbul, at the juncture of the Bosphorus Strait and the Sea of Marmara. He named it: "Chrysopylae, or Golden Gate; for the same reasons that the harbor of Byzantium (Constantinople afterwards) was called Chrysoceras, or Golden Horn."[8]

For Frémont, San Francisco's Golden Gate resembled the harbor of Byzantium, not just topographically but also in its potential for facilitating commerce with Asia. In its reference to gold, therefore, McDonald's invokes a long history of political and ethnic conflict, expansion, settlement, and of trying and finding one's luck, as both an individual and a nation.

The California dream of instantaneous wealth and a happy life in an ideal climate and bountiful land is signified not only by the individual success of the McDonald's family business, but also, more broadly, by the glamor and luxury of the Hollywood film industry in Los Angeles, and, today, by the high-tech industries of Silicon Valley in the Bay Area to the north. The warm, lush, and lazy California dream is a special version of the American dream, which is more typically premised on hard work, rather than luck, as a means to prosperity.

The term "American Dream" was coined by American writer and historian James Truslow Adams, in his 1931 book, *Epic of America*, in which he described the phenomenon as "that dream of a land in which life should be better and richer and fuller for everyone, with opportunity for each according to ability or achievement," although the basic idea had already been expressed by many thinkers from statesman Benjamin Franklin to writer Mark Twain.[9] The American Dream also became an important theme for many twentieth-century American writers, including John Steinbeck and Toni Morrison, who were ambivalent toward or critical of its illusory nature.[10]

The idea of the American dream as a sign of social and political transformation and progress became central to the mid-twentieth-century Civil Rights Movement, as invoked by one of its leaders Dr. Martin Luther King, Jr., in his 1963 "Letter from a Birmingham Jail." King's vision, expressed even more profoundly in his memorable speech, "I Have a Dream," delivered at the Lincoln Memorial, Washington, D.C., on August 28, 1963, has continued on into contemporary American politics, most notably in President Barack Obama's 2006 reinterpretation, *The Audacity of Hope: Thoughts on Reclaiming the American Dream.*[11]

Fast

In 1948, The Irish–American McDonald brothers introduced a new method for standardized production, which they called the "Speedee Service System." Identical items from the simplified menu of burgers, fries, and milkshakes were produced continuously so that a customer could receive his or her food instantaneously; dishes and eating utensils were eliminated, and all meals were served in paper bags. While McDonald's was not the first burger restaurant in the United States to make use of such standardization and disposability in food preparation and service, what it did was build on a method that had been tried and tested successfully by others, including the White Castle hamburger restaurant, established in 1921 in Wichita, Kansas.[12]

White Castle's founders, Walter A. Anderson and Edgar Waldo "Billy" Ingram, were influenced by the efficiency of assembly line production demonstrated by Henry Ford's manufacture of automobiles in the early twentieth century. Many designers of kitchens and electrical appliances in the 1920s, including Christine Frederick in the United States, and Margarete Schütte-Lihotsky in Germany, also used scientific principles of production and engineering based on the theories of Frederick Taylor and Henry Ford.[13] These innovators were concerned with using the least amount of energy to produce the greatest quantity of product, thus maximizing profit. Sanitation was also a concern for kitchen designers in the 1920s. White Castle, for example, utilized stainless steel kitchens and clad their buildings in white porcelain enamel, while McDonald's allowed customers to see into the kitchen, providing complete transparency in the process of food preparation.

The hamburger has multiple stories of origin. Its American incarnation seems to have originated in the nineteenth century in New York City's seaport district, among German street vendors who sold low-grade shredded beef, mixed with spices. German sailors had an appetite for this food reminiscent of their native Hamburg. Similar food sold as "Hamburg steak," sometimes blended with onions, could be found across the country through the turn of the twentieth century, from Athens, Texas, to New Haven, Connecticut, to St. Louis, Missouri, where it was served at the Tyrolean Alps restaurant at the 1904 Louisiana Purchase Exposition. In each case, the key features of the food were its inexpensive, informal, urban, fast, and slightly foreign nature, often served in a context of recreation and entertainment.

Beef has long conjured romantic images of cattle grazing on the open range and of cowboy herdsmen in the American West. At the same time, however, the beef industry in the early twentieth century was also associated with the deplorably unsanitary, immoral, politically corrupt, and financially exploitative conditions of human and animal misery portrayed in Upton Sinclair's 1906 novel, *The Jungle*. Recounting a tour through a slaughter-house, Sinclair describes the visitors' reactions to the appalling scene:

> the car was assailed by a most terrifying shriek; the visitors started in alarm, the women turned pale and shrank back [...] There were high squeals and low squeals, grunts, and wails of agony; there would come a momentary lull, and then a fresh outburst, louder than ever, surging up to a deafening climax [...] The party descended to the next floor, where the various waste materials were treated. Here came the entrails, to be scraped and washed clean for sausage casings; men and women worked here in the midst of a sickening stench, which caused the visitors to hasten by, gasping.[14]

Sinclair's shocking portrait of the abusive Chicago meatpacking district, in which were processed both hogs and cattle, and the struggle of its Lithuanian–American immigrant workers, launched a government investigation which led to the passage of the Pure Food and Drug Act that same year. The fast food hamburger restaurant, thus, contains all of these overlapping, if not contradictory, ideas of America—a place of open spaces, of agricultural bounty, of technological innovation, as well as a bustling home for immigrants, and the embodiment of their dreams of industry, creativity, and prosperity. Sinclair's frightening image of the horrors of industrial agriculture and settlement in the urban metropolis was smoothed away in the postwar fast food restaurant by its reassurance of cleanliness and efficiency, and its cheerful celebration of middle-class suburban life, comfort, and financial security.

Further, the romantic ideal of cattle grazing on the open range is translated by the fast food restaurant into the romance of the automobile and its illusion of freedom. Just as the Western cowboy roams freely on horseback, driving his herd of beef across the land, the driver of the automobile is master of the country he traverses. Sinclair, in his later 1927 novel, *Oil!*, a story of the early twentieth-century oil industry in California, described the thrill of driving on the open road, a sensation that, with its speed and danger, felt more like flight. As the motoring protagonist and his son meet a car driving in the opposite direction on a narrow two-lane road, Sinclair writes, "'Whoosh!' went the other projectile, hurtling past; a loud swift 'Whoosh!' with no tapering off at the end." As the pair continues driving, Sinclair describes their feeling of euphoria:

> [T]hey were free, and the car leaped forward into a view—oh, wonderful! Hill below hill dropping away, and a landscape spread out, as far as forever; you wanted wings, so as to dive down there, to sail out over the hilltops and the flat plains. What was the use of speed limits, and curves, and restraining gears and breaks?[15]

McDonald's was established in tandem with modern transportation. The McDonald family first opened its original Airdrome restaurant, a hot dog stand, near the airport on Huntington Drive, also known as U.S. Route 66, in Monrovia, California, a northeastern suburb of Los Angeles, in 1937. Three years later, the family closed the hot dog stand, and moved forty miles east to San Bernardino, California, where it opened a drive-in barbeque restaurant, which they named McDonald's. Patrick McDonald, proprietor of the first restaurant, had emigrated in 1877 from Ireland to the United States, where he met his wife, Margaret, who had come to the U.S. in 1884. Their two sons, Richard James "Dick" McDonald, and Maurice James "Mac" McDonald, carried on the business into the 1950s, from which point it developed into the global franchise we know today.

To begin with, the McDonald's restaurants were drive-ins: that is, customers would drive their cars into the parking lot of the restaurant, where attractive female servers would wait on them.[16] Customers could eat in their cars, with meals conveniently delivered on trays that could be attached to the driver's window. Once the Speedee Service System was introduced, carhops were eliminated, and customers were obliged to park their cars and walk up to the service counter to place an order. Today, the drive-in element remains an important feature of many McDonald's restaurants in the United States, which are typically designed to accommodate both walk-in customers, and drivers who may circle around to the back of the building and place an order directly from their car by way of a speaker. They then continue circling to pick up the order from a second window. Thus, it is unnecessary for customers to leave their cars at all; food can be eaten in the car while driving, or taken to another location.

Such drive-in restaurants proliferated in the United States with the construction of highways in the mid-twentieth century. Along Route 66, one of the first such interstate highways, extending from Chicago to Los Angeles, buildings were designed to cater to the driver—service stations, fast food restaurants, and motels. Such businesses required signage that could be easily seen from a distance, beckoning to their rapidly moving potential customers as they sped through the landscape.

Large, colorful signs, brightly lit with neon and incandescent bulbs in quirky and amusing shapes, were the most visible part of these new businesses, whether free standing, close to the side of the road, or cleverly incorporated into the architecture. Dynamic, angular, or soaring shapes, clear plate glass, and shiny aluminum, embodied the quality that writer Thomas Hine described as "Populuxe," and suggested a futuristic optimism in the possibilities of modern transportation, fast and efficient, as well as the pleasures of middle-class life, obtainable with disposable income in a booming economy at the end of the Second World War. "The essence of Populuxe is not merely having things," Hine wrote. "It is having things in a way that they'd never been had before, and it is an expression of outright, thoroughly vulgar joy in being able to live so well."[17]

Architects Robert Venturi, Denise Scott Brown, and Steven Izenour identified two types of roadside structures from this period: the "duck," a sculpture building-as-sign (as in the case of the 1931 Long Island Duck restaurant), and the "decorated shed," a mere box whose signage was applied to its surface. The new McDonald's restaurant, with golden arches incorporated into the building, blended these two attention-catching types in an appealing and memorable design.[18]

By the 1960s, the new culture of wealth designed around the automobile was most apparent in Las Vegas, Nevada, where the sensual pleasures of driving, dining, and spending money culminated in the grand casinos, themselves symbols of pleasure, riches, luck, style, and good fortune, but also, on the darker side, of greed, desperation, corruption, exploitation, addiction, and organized crime. Architect Venturi was not discouraged, however, by the less salubrious side of Las Vegas. Rather, in his postmodern celebration of popular culture and its lively signage, he urged his architects to embrace the complexities and contradictions embodied by Las Vegas, and to understand the structure and flow of the automotive and commercial strip as the life-blood of contemporary culture.[19]

While the completion of the transcontinental railroad, in 1869, opened North America to further settlement and economic development in the nineteenth century, and created vast urban centers, the decision to invest in an infrastructure of new highways after the Second World War gave rise to new suburban development and a new way of living that depended upon the automobile. Modernist architects and urban planners from Le Corbusier to Frank Lloyd Wright had imagined new and better designed cities with middle-class neighborhoods that revolved around the personal vehicle, where one could have easy access to all sorts of services from schools and parks to grocery stores and museums.

The suburban supermarket and shopping mall began to replace the small urban corner store, changing patterns of consumption and daily life. Among the earliest examples were those designed, in the 1950s, on the outskirts of big cities such as Detroit and Minneapolis by Austrian–American architect Victor Gruen.[20] At the supermarket, a family could purchase everything it needed for the week in a single trip to the store, packing it all into the car, and then preserving it at home in a refrigerator. Or better yet, Mom or Dad could simply stop at a drive-in restaurant and pick up dinner ready-made, served in throwaway wrappers. Convenient, efficient, fast.

Triumph

The visual similarity between the distinctive Golden Arches and the contemporaneous Gateway Arch, the Jefferson National Expansion Memorial in St. Louis, Missouri, has long been a source of speculation.[21] The Gateway Arch, designed in 1947 by architects Eero Saarinen and Hannskarl Bandel, is an inverted steel catenary arch, 630 feet tall and 630 feet wide (see Fig. 2.2).

Each leg is 54 feet (16.45 m) wide at the base, gradually narrowing to just 17 feet (5.18 m) wide at the highest point of the arch. Inside the arch is a tram that carries visitors to windows in an observation deck at the top of the structure. One of the earliest uses of the term "catenary" is attributed to U.S. President Thomas Jefferson, who in 1788 described a bridge design with an arch of "perfect equilibrium," or, in other words, the shape that a hanging chain assumes under its own weight, when supported only at its ends.[22]

Although research indicates that the designer of the Golden Arches was not influenced specifically by Saarinen, with whose work McDonald's architect Stanley Meston and sign maker George Dexter may not have been at all familiar, it is nevertheless clear that both structures emerge from a similar cultural context of mid-century modernism that departs from the rectangular forms of the International Style to celebrate organic and ergonomic forms suggestive of speed, flight, and the contours of the human body. Similar architectural forms, derived in part from the Scandinavian modern movement, evoking the shapes of bird wings as much as those of airplanes, may be seen in the undulating poured concrete of Saarinen's unprecedented 1956 TWA terminal for New York's John F. Kennedy airport, and in the curvaceous, ergonomic molded plywood and fiberglass chairs designed by Charles and Ray Eames during that same period.

The Gateway Arch commemorates the beginning of the 1804 westbound journey of explorers Meriwether Lewis and William Clark. Lewis and Clark were commissioned by President Thomas Jefferson to travel upstream from St. Louis along the Missouri River to its source, traverse the continental divide in the Rocky Mountains, and to locate the western terminus of the same waterway in the Pacific Ocean.[23] Their expedition was organized in

Fig. 2.2 Jefferson National Expansion Memorial, St. Louis, Missouri, designed by Eero Saarinen and Hannskarl Bandel, 1947. Photo by Sue Ford/NPS. Courtesy National Park Service, Jefferson National Expansion Memorial.

part to better understand the new lands that would be acquired shortly thereafter as part of the Louisiana Purchase, the transfer from France to the United States of a vast territory of 828,000 square miles, encompassing land from the Rocky Mountains to the Mississippi River, and from present-day Canada to the Gulf of Mexico. The sale of what now comprises the middle third of the United States was negotiated between the governments of Thomas Jefferson and the French Emperor Napoleon Bonaparte for approximately $15 million or about 3 cents per acre.[24]

The monumental triumphal arch was used historically to celebrate imperial power and conquest, most notably in ancient Rome. The first-century Roman Arch of Titus inspired Emperor Napoleon's neoclassical Arc de Triomphe, constructed in Paris between 1806 and 1836 to commemorate those who fought and died in the French Revolutionary and Napoleonic wars (1792–1802, and 1803–15).

Before Saarinen envisioned his monument for St. Louis, architect Pier Luigi Nervi, under the directorship of Marcello Piacentini, chief architect for Italian fascist dictator Benito Mussolini, had already designed a sleek, parabolic arch to be used as a monumental gateway at the 1942 Esposizione Universale of Rome. The event had been first planned in 1935, but was never held due to the outbreak of the Second World War. Nervi's arch made reference to the Roman imperial tradition within the context of Italian fascist Neoclassicism, but was also swooping and futuristic.[25] The Jefferson National Expansion Memorial, like the transcontinental railroad before it, is a powerful symbol that celebrates the triumph of manifest destiny, the controversial and contested notion of westward expansion, and the conquest of the North American continent.[26]

Author Thomas Friedman, in his 1999 book *The Lexus and the Olive Tree*, posited the "Golden Arches Theory of Conflict Prevention," which states that no two countries with a McDonald's restaurant will ever declare war on each other. This concept, which is central to the classically liberal philosophy that free-market capitalism fosters political and economic stability, peace, and prosperity, suggests that the "soft power" of cultural imperialism—the introduction of American products and brands to a global market—is every bit as powerful as the "hard power" of military control.[27] Are the Golden Arches, then, a triumphal monument? A symbol of peace through economic domination? A sign of manifest destiny? A gateway to the era of global capitalism?

But arches signify more than triumph, conquest, or even peace. More significantly, they are passageways and ports of entry from one world into another. The St. Louis Gateway Arch remembers the westward journey of Lewis and Clark into unknown territories, a voyage through geographical and imaginative space. Monumental arches are similar to other kinds of structures and transportation routes, like railways, roads, and bridges, which lead us through the landscape. Arches were often used as gateways to the festive temporary grounds of world's fairs in the nineteenth century, where viewers could glimpse exotic places and future possibilities promised by industry and empire. Monumental bridges, with their massive arched spans, also serve as civic monuments, signaling technological achievement, and humankind's dominion over the natural world, as well as the more intangible cultural and aesthetic relationships of civilization to nature.

Rainbows are the most elusive and ephemeral arched gateways found in nature. And it is not surprising, perhaps, that legend describes a pot of gold at the base of the intangible and unreachable spectrum of color. In American mythology the rainbow is a gateway to an imaginary better place. Oz, as we discussed in the first chapter, was a magical, colorful paradise vividly imagined by L. Frank Baum in his 1900 children's book, *The Wonderful Wizard of Oz*. The tale's protagonist, Dorothy, played by actress Judy Garland in the 1939 film version, famously evoked its wonder in her wistful performance of the song, "Over the Rainbow."[28] The enchantment of Oz, that land "over the rainbow," is intensified in the film by the cinematic transition from Dorothy's grim, black-and-white life in depression-era Kansas at the beginning of the story to her waking in the Technicolor world of dreams beyond.

The wide-eyed Judy Garland, with all of her Hollywood glamor and tragedy, became an icon for America's gay (today LGBTQ) community, which, in 1978, also adopted a rainbow-colored flag to symbolize gay pride. San Francisco artist and civil rights activist Gilbert Baker designed the flag. For the 1978 San Francisco Pride parade Baker, who, like Dorothy, was born in Kansas, produced a hand-dyed version, similar to the flags symbolizing world peace that were popular on college campuses throughout the 1960s.

By the 1960s San Francisco became identified as a kind of Oz, a land of promise, home to the gay community, and a bastion of free-thinking idealism. California has often been historically at the cutting edge of controversial, progressive policy and legislation in the United States, from its efforts in the 1970s to set in place stricter state regulations than required by the federal government for polluting vehicle emissions and fuel efficiency, to its 2008 Supreme Court case ruling affirming that all citizens, including same-sex couples, have a fundamental right to marriage.[29] In 2011, California adopted a version of the DREAM Act (Development, Relief, and Education for Alien Minors), a bipartisan bill proposed by Senator Richard Durbin of Illinois and Senator Orin Hatch of Utah, which would provide permanent U.S. residency for certain undocumented young people enrolled in college or enlisted in military service.[30]

The San Francisco Golden Gate Bridge, designed by Joseph Strauss, Irving Morrow, and Charles Ellis, was built in the midst of the Great Depression, between 1933 and 1937. With its bright orange paint and celebratory art deco forms, not dissimilar to the colorful art deco Emerald Cityscape of Oz, the bridge was an optimistic feat of modern engineering. Spanning Frémont's "Golden Gate," the bridge is a triumphal arch of sorts, a monument to the American dream, and to California as land of promise. But the American dream is dialectical; its promise on the one end necessitates the possibility of failure on the other.

Therefore, is the promise of the American dream, as portrayed by Theodore Dreiser in his 1925 novel, *An American Tragedy*, too much to bear?[31] What are we to make of the fact that so many suicides are attempted on the Golden Gate Bridge?

Slow

I recently had a moment of despair while driving to a store at which I wanted to purchase camping equipment, so that I could spend a few days in nature. To do this, I had to drive my car on the Illinois Tollway to a suburb outside Chicago, where such a store was located among hundreds of others that need lots of space in order to contain the vast quantities of goods they keep in stock. After exiting the Tollway, I could see my destination ahead, only a quarter of a mile away from me; however, this particular exit was situated at a major intersection of numerous highways, each some lanes wide, such that I was obliged to wait at a traffic light with dozens of other idling cars, exhaust spewing, for several minutes before driving into the parking lot. Even if I had wanted to, I could not have reached the store by any other means of transportation, as it is not accessible by train or bus. In fact, there are no sidewalks, crosswalks, under- or over-passages along most major suburban thoroughfares in the United States, where it would be considered unsafe to walk or even to ride a bicycle.

Today, the utopian optimism of futuristic modernist designers, architects, and urban planners has given way to the dystopia of suburban sprawl, with its wasteful use of space, environmental damage, traffic jams, and the physical atrophy of the body that sits for long hours, trapped in a car. The alarming rates of obesity and increase in number of patients suffering from diabetes and heart disease are certainly not improved by the habit of eating fatty, sugary, processed food while sitting in the car. The personal vehicle, for many, is no longer a freedom, but rather a prison.[32] The contemporary suburb with its vast expanse of strip malls replacing farmland, and before that prairie, forest, desert, or wetland, is Frank Lloyd Wright and Le Corbusier's dream of modernist urban planning turned to nightmare. And just as the modern fast-food restaurant emerged within the context of mid-century transportation and urban planning, its criticism coincided with the environmental backlash against such development.[33]

Within the past few decades, a new food movement, with its origins in the environmentalism of the 1960s and 1970s, has constellated around anti-industrial concepts of locally grown and pesticide-free meats and produce, small farmers, and fair trade policies.[34] In 1986, the Slow Food movement, organized by Carlo Petrini, emerged in response to the opening of a McDonald's restaurant in Rome.[35] Petrini's outrage stemmed not only from his indignation at fast food's encroachment on the soil from which emerged one of the world's oldest and most delicious culinary traditions, but more significantly, of course, from Italy's acquiescence to global corporate interests, and to the American imperialism signified by McDonald's. (A similar affront was felt by Europe in 2001 when the Seattle-based Starbucks coffee company opened a shop in Vienna, the first coffee capital in the West. The Central European city's influential coffee culture developed after invading Ottoman soldiers left behind coffee beans in 1683.[36])

Among the most vocal proponents of food reform in the United States are journalists Michael Pollan and Eric Schlosser, and chef Alice Waters. Pollan's work dwells on the ethics of eating and of the complex social relationship between human beings and the natural environment.[37] Waters's renowned Chez Panisse restaurant in Berkeley, California, established in 1971, celebrates meals prepared with simple, fresh, and locally grown market foods, a tradition that she absorbed while living in France in the 1960s. All three have been active participants in Petrini's Slow Food International, of which Waters served as Vice President since 2002. Waters organized the San Francisco event, Slow Food Nation, in 2008.

It is popular today to speak of addiction, not only to life-threatening narcotics, pharmaceuticals, or other illicit drugs that dangerously alter the body's chemistry, or to nicotine, caffeine, and alcohol, but also to love, chocolate, shopping, sugar, corn, beef, salt, fast-food, cheap goods, even cheaper labor, energy, and oil. The term "gateway drug" is a colloquialism used to describe, on the one level, a seemingly benign or mildly addictive substance that can lead to the use and abuse of a more significant or deadly one, such as the use of marijuana leading to the use of heroin or cocaine. If McDonald's is a "gateway," to what does it lead? Can our addiction to cheap burgers and fries be extricated from the way in which such food is produced, from our dependence on United States government subsidies for corn producers to our addiction to oil?[38]

When the U.S. went to war in Iraq in 2003, following the terrorist attacks on September 11, 2001, it suffered a great deal of criticism from the international community, which opposed America's unilateral retaliatory aggression. In an absurd and somewhat irrational show of support for the American invasion in defiance of its international detractors, especially France, two American Congressmen called for a rejection of the term "French fries" on the U.S. House of Representatives cafeteria menu, calling for its replacement with the ostensibly more patriotic "Freedom fries," predictably eliciting yet more ridicule from abroad.[39] American food has always had a fraught relationship to French cuisine, which is just one manifestation of the complex connection of American culture to French culture, and beyond that to Enlightenment ideas of freedom and government dating to the American Revolutionary War (1775–1783) and French Revolution (1789–1799). The term "French fries," like the word "catenary," is attributed to Thomas Jefferson, who once referred to "potatoes fried in the French manner," describing the way in which French-cut potatoes were narrowly sliced before being cooked in oil.[40]

Despite the effort by fast food restaurants to assure customers of their sanitary production through transparency and use of industrial materials, traces of Sinclair's *The Jungle* linger, particularly in the periodic outbreaks of food poisoning by the *E. coli* (*Escherichia coli 0157:H7*) bacterium, a potentially deadly organism that lives normally in the intestines and feces of cattle, and which can contaminate meat that is improperly butchered, or in some cases, produce grown in the vicinity of cattle farms, which is improperly cleaned. Thorough heating can eliminate many pathogenic organisms, including *E. coli*, but if a contaminated burger escapes proper preparation, it can induce severe vomiting, diarrhea, and in some tragic instances organ failure or even death. It is particularly dangerous to children. In 1993, four children died from eating burgers contaminated with *E. coli* at a Jack-in-the-Box fast food restaurant in Washington State.[41]

Fear over the dangers of beef consumption had already exacerbated in 1986, however, when cattle infected with BSE (*bovine spongiform encephalopathy*), also known as "mad cow disease," were discovered in the UK. This especially gruesome disease developed and spread because cattle, typically herbivores, had been given feed consisting of the ground-up bones of other cattle that had been infected with the virus. The human variant of mad cow disease, Creutzfeldt–Jakob disease, which can be contracted from eating contaminated beef, causes severe neurological degeneration resulting in dementia, seizures, and death. Beyond responding to the problem of food poisoning from contaminated beef, food activists and environmentalists reject the unsustainable methods of industrial agriculture upon which the fast food industry relies. Among their many concerns are the monoculture and genetic engineering of crops, inhumane treatment of livestock necessitating the blanket use of antibiotics, wasteful usage of land by livestock, and greenhouse gasses emitted as a result, wasteful packaging, transport, and storage of food products, and their deleterious effects on basic human health, leading to obesity, diabetes, high cholesterol, and heart disease.

In 2004, American filmmaker Morgan Spurlock released his award-winning documentary, *Super Size Me*, which traced the results of his experimental thirty-day McDonald's diet. In February 2003, Spurlock set about eating three meals a day, chosen from the McDonald's menu. He prohibited himself from consuming any products outside the menu, and agreed to the restaurant's suggestion to "Super Size Me," every time the offer was extended to him. The Super Size marketing campaign, promoted by McDonald's, ostensibly gave customers a better value by increasing the quantity of their meal without increasing its price. During one month, in which he consumed 5,000 calories per day, Spurlock monitored his health with three physicians, who by the end of the month urged him to stop the experiment, finding that his rapid weight gain of over twenty-four pounds, and dangerous increase in both body mass and cholesterol levels, had put his organ function at risk.

The "all you can eat" concept is an important promotional strategy in American food culture, which can likely be traced to what cultural historian

Jackson Lears has called an "iconography of abundance," in the late nineteenth and early twentieth century advertisements for food products.[42] I once encountered a sign for an all-you-can-eat breakfast buffet at a hotel restaurant in a resort town in Hungary, which advertised without irony, when translated into English, "unlimited American-style consumption." I have also noticed that the Illinois Tollway Oases snack shops carry today only "king-sized" items, so that one is obliged to purchase (and will very likely eat) a giant bag of chips, candy bar, or soda. In 2013, Michael Bloomberg, Mayor of New York City, attempted to institute a city-wide ban on sugary soda drinks larger than 16 ounces sold in restaurants and entertainment venues. For many this seemed to be a sensible idea in the midst of a national crisis of obesity, but others were outraged that their personal freedom might be infringed upon by such a regulation. The soda ban did not go into effect.[43]

Spurlock's work is related to that of Eric Schlosser, who investigated multiple aspects of the industry in his 2002 book, *Fast Food Nation*, which was later also released as a film. Journalist Naomi Klein questioned not just McDonald's ethics in its mass-production of food, but also the ethics of a global system in which exploitative multinational corporations have so much financial and political power over the individual.[44] Postmodern theorist Jean-François Lyotard associated McDonald's with the inauthenticity, fragmentation, and disjointedness of youth culture in the 1980s, writing, "you eat McDonald's at mid-day and local cuisine at night; you wear Paris perfume in Tokyo and dress retro in Hong Kong; knowledge is the stuff of TV game shows."[45] When the first McDonald's restaurant opened in Moscow in 1990, following the fall of the iron curtain, one critic playfully described it as the "world's largest chain of free bathrooms."[46]

By the late twentieth-century, the "Mc" in McDonald's had become a cliché pejorative prefix suggestive of standardization, inauthenticity, commercialization, or globalization. A "McMansion," for example, is a grandiose, yet characterless, suburban home; a "McJob" is a low-paying job in which workers are interchangeable, require few skills, and have little possibility for advancement. The company's "i'm lovin' it" campaign, launched in 2003, seemed, therefore, trite. Who, after all, would "love" McDonald's? With its absence of capital letters, colloquial slur, and graphic smile logo, which also recalled the form of the Golden Arches, as well as the smiling shape of the traditional red French fry box, the tagline "i'm lovin' it" was casual, unsophisticated, and lighthearted, extending to its adult customers the infantilizing concept of the "Happy Meal," marketed for children, and a central feature of the franchise since 1979. McDonald's has also appealed to children over the years with its cast of entertaining, costumed characters, including Grimace, the Hamburglar, and the original clown, Ronald McDonald, dressed in red and yellow. Many McDonald's restaurants also feature play equipment so that restless children need not sit with their families while eating.[47] The bright red-and-yellow plastic booths of the earliest venues, it might be argued, extended the playful atmosphere of the nursery school to the parents as well.

McDonald's is both fast and slow, a distraction that lulls us into complacency; the convenience of a pre-made and disposable world, the ease and quantity of consumption of which renders our bodies sluggish and immobile. As Dorothy and her friends make their journey to Oz, they encounter many obstacles. Among them is an enchanted field of poppies, the narcotic effect of which lures the travelers into irresistible sleep. The field of poppies in the film is dazzling, colorful, and enticing, just as presumably the golden hillsides of California appeared to the Spanish who believed its soil to be filled with the precious mineral. The poppies' opiate pleasures however, like those evoked by the Golden Arches, are deceptive and dangerous, even deadly.

Notes

1 Alan Hess, "The Origins of McDonald's Golden Arches," *Journal of the Society of Architectural Historians* 45/1 (March 1986): 60–7. See also D. J. Huppatz, "McDonald's Golden Arches Logo, USA," in Grace Lees-Maffei (ed.), *Iconic Designs: 50 Stories About 50 Things* (London: Bloomsbury, 2014), 47–9.

2 Observation of McDonald's French fries by Jay Lees-Maffei. Grace Lees-Maffei, personal communication, December 2011.

3 H. W. Brands, *The Age of Gold: The California Gold Rush and the New American Dream* (New York: Doubleday, 2002).

4 Albert L. Hurtado, *John Sutter: A Life on the North American Frontier* (Norman: University of Oklahoma Press, 2006).

5 Karl Marx and Friedrich Engels, *Manifesto of the Communist Party*, trans. Samuel Moore (London: William Reeves, 1888), originally published as *Manifest der Kommunistischen Partei Veröffentlicht im Februar 1848* (London: Office of the Bildungs-Gesellschaft für Arbeiter, 1848).

6 "The Great Seal of California," *The Illustrated London News* (January 12, 1850): 21; Louis A. Garnett, "The True Story of the Origin of the Great Seal of the State of California," *San Francisco Chronicle* (10 December 1899): 10.

7 "Archimedes," in David Sacks and Lisa R. Brody, *Encyclopedia of the Ancient Greek World* (revised edition, New York: Facts on File, Inc., 2005), 40.

8 John Charles Frémont and Jessie Benton Frémont, *Memoirs of My Life* (Chicago: Belford, Clark and Co., 1887), 512.

9 James Truslow Adams, *Epic of America* (Boston: Little, Brown & Co., 1931); Benjamin Franklin, *The Autobiography of Benjamin Franklin* (1771–90), ed. Leonard Woods Labaree (New Haven: Yale University Press, 1964); Mark Twain, *The Adventures of Huckleberry Finn* (New York: Charles L. Webster and Co., 1885).

10 John Steinbeck, *The Grapes of Wrath* (New York: Viking Press, 1939); Toni Morrison, *Song of Solomon* (New York: Knopf, 1977).

11 Martin Luther King, Jr., "Letter from a Birmingham Jail" (April 16, 1963), reproduced in Martin Luther King, Jr., *Why We Can't Wait* (New York: Signet Classic, 2000), 64–84; Dr. King's speech, "I Have a Dream," August 28, 1963, Washington, DC, available online: http://www.archives.gov/press/exhibits/dream-speech.pdf (accessed August 29, 2014); Barack Obama, *The Audacity of Hope: Thoughts on Reclaiming the American dream* (New York: Crown Publishers, 2006).

12 David Gerard Hogan, *White Castle and the Creation of an American Food: Selling 'em by the Sack* (New York: New York University Press, 1997).

13 Christine Frederick, *Household Engineering: Scientific Management in the Home* (Chicago: American School of Home Economics, 1920), 19–98; Frederick Winslow Taylor, *The Principles of Scientific Management* (New York: Harper & Brothers, 1911). The American labor-saving kitchen was upheld as a symbol of national identity at the 1959 American National Exhibition in Moscow, where it was touted by then Vice-President Richard Nixon as evidence of the supremacy of Western capitalism. See Susan E. Reid, "The Khrushchev Kitchen: Domesticating the Scientific Technological Revolution," *Journal of Contemporary History* 40/2 (2005): 289–316; "Nixon and Khrushchev Argue in Public as U.S. Exhibit Opens: Accuse Each Other of Threats," *The New York Times* (July 25, 1959): 1–3, reproduced as Richard Nixon and Nikita Khrushchev, "The Kitchen Debate," in Carma Gorman (ed.), *The Industrial Design Reader* (New York: Allworth Press, 2003), 172–4.

14 Upton Sinclair, *The Jungle* (1906; reprint, New York: Bantam Books, 1981), 34–7.

15 Upton Sinclair, *Oil!* (1926; New York: Penguin, 2007), 2–8.

16 Eric Schlosser, *Fast Food Nation: The Dark Side of the All-American Meal* (Boston: Houghton Mifflin, 2002).

17 Thomas Hine, *Populuxe* (1986, reprint; New York: Knopf, 1987), 4.

18 Robert Venturi, Denise Scott-Brown, and Steven Izenour, *Learning From Las Vegas: The Forgotten Symbolism of Architectural Form* (Cambridge, MA: MIT Press, 1972).

19 Robert Venturi, *Complexity and Contradiction in Architecture* (New York: Museum of Modern Art, 1966).

20 M. Jeffrey Hardwick, *Mall Maker: Victor Gruen, Architect of an American Dream* (Philadelphia: University of Pennsylvania Press, 2003); Malcolm Gladwell, "The Terrazzo Jungle," *The New Yorker* (15 March 2004): 120–7. See also Le Corbusier, *The City of Tomorrow and Its Planning*, trans. Frederick Etchells (1929; reprint, New York: Dover Publications, Inc., 1987); Frank Lloyd Wright, *The Disappearing City* (New York: W. F. Payson, 1932), and its later iterations, Frank Lloyd Wright, *When Democracy Builds* (Chicago: University of Chicago Press, 1945); Frank Lloyd Wright, *The Living City* (New York: Horizon Press, 1958).

21 Hess, "The Origins of McDonald's Golden Arches," 66.

22 "catenary, *n.* and *adj.*," *Oxford English Dictionary Online* (September 2012), copyright Oxford University Press, available online: http://www.ulib.niu.edu:2846/view/Entry/28884?redirectedFrom=catenary#eid (accessed November 13, 2012).

23 Meriwether Lewis and William Clark, *The Journals of Lewis and Clark*, ed. John Bakeless (1964, reprint; New York: Signet Classics, 2011).

24 "Treaty Between the United States of American and the French Republic, April 20, 1803," in Richard Peters, Esq (ed.), *The Public Statutes at Large of the United States of America, from the Organization of the Government in 1789, to March 3, 1845* (Boston: Little, Brown and Company, 1867), 201–6.

25 Silvia Barisione, *The Birth of Rome: Five Visions for the Eternal City* (exh. cat., Miami Beach, The Wolfsonian and Florida International University, 2013).

26 The origin of the term "manifest destiny" is attributed to journalist John O'Sullivan who, in 1845, described what some believed to be America's providential mission to expand settlement across the North American continent, in part through the annexation of Texas. John O'Sullivan, "Annexation," *The United States Democratic Review* 17/5 (July–August 1845): 5. See also Anders Stephanson, *Manifest Destiny: American Expansionism and the Empire of Right* (New York: Hill and Wang, 1995).

27 Matthew Fraser, "Peace Through McDomination," *National Post* (September 20, 2003): A19. Excerpt from Matthew Fraser, *Weapons of Mass Distraction: Soft Power and American Empire* (Toronto: Key Porter, 2003). See also Thomas Friedman, *The Lexus and the Olive Tree: Understanding Globalization* (New York: Farrar, Straus & Giroux, 1999). Friedman's theory precedes the moment during which the United States and its NATO allies began to bomb Belgrade, which had no shortage of McDonald's restaurants.

28 Also commonly referred to as "Somewhere Over the Rainbow," the ballad, composed for the film by Harold Arlen, with lyrics by E. Y. Harburg, won the Academy Award for Best Song in a 1939 film.

29 Mark B. Brown, Weert Canzler, Frank Fischer, and Andreas Knie, "Technological Innovation Through Environmental Policy: California's Zero-Emission Vehicle Regulation," *Public Productivity and Management Review* 19/1 (September 1995): 77–93; Joe Garofoli, John Wildermuth, and Demian Bulwa, "Judge Strikes Down Same-Sex Marriage Ban," *San Francisco Chronicle* (August 5, 2010), available online: http://www.sfgate.com/news/article/Prop-8-judge-strikes-down-same-sex-marriage-ban-3179346.php (accessed August 29, 2014). It is important to note, however, that California's progressive urban centers are often balanced by its more conservative suburban communities, which have led the state over the years to elect conservative governors, including Ronald Reagan and Arnold Schwarzenegger.

30 Nanette Asimov and Wyatt Buchanan, "[California Governor] Jerry Brown Signs Dream Act for Illegal Immigrants," *San Francisco Chronicle* (October 8, 2011), available online: http://www.sfgate.com/news/article/Jerry-Brown-signs-Dream-Act-for-illegal-immigrants-2327890.php (accessed August 29, 2014).

31 Protagonist Clyde Griffiths rises from his modest background as the son of traveling evangelists to fashionable society, but in order to maintain his

place in the social order he is driven to increasingly dark and deceptive actions, resulting in murder, conviction, and execution. Theodore Dreiser, *An American Tragedy* (1925, reprint; New York: Penguin, 2010).

32 Dolores Hayden, *Building Suburbia: Green Fields and Urban Growth, 1820–2000* (New York: Pantheon Books, 2003); Robert Bruegmann, *Sprawl: A Compact History* (Chicago: University of Chicago Press, 2005).

33 Andres Duany, Elizabeth Plater-Zyberk, and Jeff Speck, *Suburban Nation: The Rise of Sprawl and the Decline of the American Dream* (New York: North Point Press, 2000).

34 Michael Pollan, "The Food Movement, Rising," *New York Review of Books* 57/10 (June 10, 2010): 31–3, available online: http://www.nybooks.com/articles/archives/2010/jun/10/food-movement-rising/ (accessed August 29, 2014).

35 Carlo Petrini, *Terra Madre: Forging a New Global Network of Sustainable Food Communities* (White River Junction, VT: Chelsea Green, 2010).

36 Harold B. Segel, ed., *The Vienna Coffeehouse Wits, 1890–1938* (West Lafayette, IN: Purdue University Press, 1993), 1–40.

37 Michael Pollan, *The Omnivore's Dilemma: A Natural History of Four Meals* (New York: Penguin Press, 2006); Michael Pollan, *In Defense of Food: An Eater's Manifesto* (New York: Penguin Press, 2008).

38 Pollan, *In Defense of Food*, 121–2.

39 The United States representatives who introduced the measure were Robert W. Ney of Ohio and Walter B. Jones, Jr., of North Carolina, both Republicans. Sheryl Gay Stolberg, "An Order of Fries, Please, But Do Hold the French," *New York Times* (March 12, 2003): A51; Stephen Dinan, "A lost appetite for 'French' food; House renames fries, toast," *The Washington Times* (March 12, 2003): A1; Christina Bellantoni, "Hill Fries Free to be French Again; GOP in House Mum About It," *The Washington Times* (August 2, 2006): A01.

40 Marshall Fishwick, "The Savant as Gourmet," *The Journal of Popular Culture* 32/1 (Summer 1998): 51–8.

41 "Company News: Jack in the Box's Worst Nightmare," *The New York Times* (February 6, 1993), available online: http://www.nytimes.com/1993/02/06/business/company-news-jack-in-the-box-s-worst-nightmare.html (accessed August 29, 2014).

42 Jackson Lears, *Fables of Abundance: A Cultural History of Advertising in America* (New York: Basic Books, 1994), 104.

43 Eugene Voloh, "New York's Highest Court Strikes Down New York City Big Soda Ban," *The Washington Post* (June 27, 2014), available online: http://www.washingtonpost.com/news/volokh-conspiracy/wp/2014/06/27/new-yorks-highest-court-strikes-down-new-york-city-big-soda-ban/ (accessed August 29, 2014).

44 Naomi Klein, *No Logo* (New York: Picador, 2000), 387–91.

45 Jean-François Lyotard, *Postmodernism Explained: Correspondence 1982–1985* (1993; reprint, Sydney: Power Publications, 1998), 8.

46 Finn Sivert Nielsen, "Eye of the Whirlwind: Russian Identity and Soviet Nation-Building. Quests for Meaning in a Soviet Metropolis," (MA Thesis, University of Oslo, 1987, 2004).

47 Amy Ogata, "McDonald's," in Juliet Kinchin and Aidan O'Connor (eds), *Century of the Child: Growing By Design 1900–2000* (exh. cat., New York: Museum of Modern Art, 2012), 204–5.

CHAPTER THREE

Bull's-eye!

A Meditation on Targets

Have you ever wondered why little boys (and some girls, too) love to play with guns? Cap guns, squirt guns, guns made of cardboard paper rolls and duct tape, guns made of Lego bricks, toast bitten into the shape of guns. Boys like to shoot projectiles of all sorts—slingshots, rubber bands, rocks, baseballs, paper airplanes—but guns are really fun, especially when dramatized with the percussive sound of gunfire. Some parents today, ideologically opposed to the use of firearms, may try to restrict this urge, but boys find ways to play with guns. American vernacular English is saturated with firearm metaphors and figures of speech drawn from gun culture: *bite the bullet, dodge the bullet, silver bullet, shoot from the hip, stick to your guns, it's worth a shot, he's gun-shy, she's trigger-happy.*[1]

This chapter explores the mythology of the archetypal bull's-eye symbol. Simple, iconic, and rich in meaning, the bull's-eye or target, composed of concentric circles, has been used successfully for more than a century to establish numerous corporate identities, including those of the London Underground and Transport system, Lucky Strike cigarettes, and Target retail stores. The form may have originated from the practice of using ringed cross-sections of trees as shooting targets for archery and, later, games of darts.[2] Though it is an old symbol that predates the use of firepower, the relationship of the bull's-eye target to the shooting of guns pervades its symbolic meaning in the modern context. The industrialization of firearm production and the use of firepower in modern warfare have profoundly influenced design, as much as they have affected social, economic, and political history from the late eighteenth century to the present. What do rail travel, smoking, or shopping have to do with shooting? At first glance these activities seem unrelated. Upon closer examination, however, it is apparent that, like the oil, automobile, and fast food industries, they shape important aspects of a collective imagination that continues to evolve today. In the following discussion of these three symbols we discover that a target is effective not only because it directs and focuses our attention on a particular object, venue, or activity, but also, implicitly, because it signifies war.

Faster than a Speeding Bullet

When London Transport first adopted its circular red and white emblem in 1908 it was officially called the Underground "Bullseye" (see Fig. 3.1).

The design, which was later revised by Frank Pick, managing director of the Underground Electric Railways Company of London, and the typographer Edward Johnston, evolved quickly into the familiar red-and-white roundel with rectangular blue bar, and by the 1930s was incorporated in clever ways into signage, posters, and even the architecture of the stations themselves.[3] Pick reported that the maritime Plimsoll Load Line, designed by Samuel Plimsoll, inspired his idea for the trademark. (The circle bisected horizontally by a bar indicates the water surface level at which a ship may safely maintain buoyancy.) Art historian and London resident Ernst Gombrich remarked that the circle had always signified, for him, the city of London, and the horizontal bar, the train crossing it.[4]

The effectiveness and longevity of the London Transport roundel, as it is called today, is likely due in part to its legibility when seen from a train

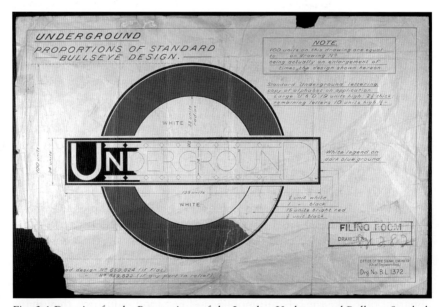

Fig. 3.1 Drawing for the Proportions of the London Underground Bullseye Symbol, designed by Edward Johnston, c. 1925. ©TfL from the London Transport Museum Collection.

moving rapidly through a station. Johnston's railway typeface, designed in 1916 for use with the bull's-eye symbol, further contributed to the rider's ability to recognize the signage. Johnston, an Arts and Crafts calligrapher, created an elegant sans-serif alphabet, inspired by the proportions of classical letterforms, that would influence his student, Eric Gill, to design his famous Gill Sans typeface a decade later. By the 1920s, many type designers experimented with letterforms evocative of the machine age, without decoration, which they believed had universal application, and could be read with great speed.[5]

The term "bull's-eye," like the Plimsoll line, has its origins in nautical terminology. The word was used in the very late eighteenth and early nineteenth centuries to refer to round windows in ships, as well as ocular openings through which to pass a rope. The term also describes a round protuberance of blown glass, which can resemble the round, protruding eye of a bull or ox. It was first used to describe a shooting target, however, in the 1833 *Regulations for the Instruction, Formations, and Movements of the Calvary*, published by the London War Office. It appeared just a few years later as a figure of speech in Charles Dickens's 1841 novel, *The Old Curiosity Shop*.[6]

By 1908, London's underground rail system was complex, having developed in multiple stages since the 1860s. Swiss modernist architect Le Corbusier illustrated its confusing twists and turns as a bewildering tangle of intersecting tubular passageways beneath Piccadilly station.[7] For Le Corbusier, writing in the 1920s, rail traffic was a relic of the past, which he contrasted with his radical vision of future cities, in which individual cars would drive on efficiently organized highways. But the bright, cheerful Underground Bullseye, and soothing typeface, as well as the new color-coded diagrammatic map of the various subway lines, designed in 1931 by Harry Beck, assured riders that they need not fear entering the dark and dangerous underworld. The company's modern signage and avant-garde posters promised instead a clean, comfortable, stylish, and convenient traveling experience and guided the train's users clearly and confidently through the city. Beck's map became the template for every such public transportation visual communication system that followed.

Nearly thirty years after the introduction of the London Underground Bullseye, a new sort of train, the Chicago, Burlington, and Quincy Railroad's Pioneer Zephyr, named after Zephyrus, Greek god of the west wind, made its sensational debut at the 1934 Century of Progress exhibition in Chicago. Made of shiny, shot-welded stainless steel, with a clean diesel engine, the Zephyr travelled 1,015 miles from Salt Lake City, Utah, to arrive at the fair in just thirteen hours and five minutes at an average speed of seventy-seven miles per hour.[8] The shape of the train captured the essence of speed imaginatively in its engine's smooth, aerodynamic form. Featured in the third issue of *Superman* comics, published in winter 1940, just as the U.S. entered the Second World War, a streaking Zephyr-like train mirrored the superhuman speed of Superman himself, as he set out, heroically, to fight for truth and justice, stronger than steel and faster than a speeding bullet.[9]

After the Second World War, while the United States enthusiastically paved over miles of rails to develop its interstate highway system, Europe and Japan explored more aggressively the possibility of high-speed train travel.[10] Japan's Shinkansen was the first such system to be developed, with a high-speed rail service between Osaka and Tokyo completed in 1964, opening on the eve of the Tokyo Olympics. The train, which sped from city to city at 120 miles per hour, was sleek, with a rounded, almost anthropomorphic engine that resembled the aerodynamic forms of airplanes in the 1940s and 1950s. Because of its bullet, or missile-like, shape, which also recalled the forms of bombs and bomber planes, it was nicknamed the "bullet train." Tadanao Miki, one of the train's designers, was well known for his design of the Ginga WWII Navy divebomber airplane. Greg Votolato notes that the shape of the Shinkansen engine resembled that of the Douglas DC3 airliner, the most popular model of airplane worldwide between 1935 and 1950.[11]

Echoes of the London Underground Bullseye may be seen in the circular red, white, and blue emblem of the British Royal Air Force, used in the First World War, as well as in Marvel Comics' hero Captain America's patriotic "vibranium" steel shield, which first appeared in 1941, and in the 1964 symbol for the British rock band, The Who, designed by painter Brian Pike. The bull's-eye symbol in various combinations of red, white, and blue, thus signifies broadly the patriotic nationalism of the first half of the twentieth century, in both the U.K. and the U.S. Mods appropriated the British Royal Air Force roundel in the 1960s, attaching it to their U.S. Army surplus parkas, with the Union Jack and other coded cultural symbols. The stylish, well-dressed youth wore the embellished jackets while riding their Italian motor scooters. The enduring popularity of the London Underground roundel is evident, even today, in its merchandise that depicts the subway's signage, with instructions such as "Mind the Gap," or "Way Out," which recall 1960s counterculture expressions like "groovy" or "far out," as much as they direct its passengers to an exit. Why, we might ask ourselves, does the fashionable war emblem continue to resonate? Is the archetype of the chic and patriotic London Transport Bullseye "target" also present in the stylish and easy-to-see-from-a-distance British Royal Air Force roundel? Is the symbol's meaning implicit in the bullet-like forms of the Zephyr and Shinkansen? Is speed or swiftness as a sign of modernity intrinsically related to shooting, the mechanism of industrialized military victory?

Lucky Strike Green Has Gone to War!

In what other ways is the target associated with war through its use in product design? Around the time that the Zephyr-like train appeared on the cover of *Superman* comics, Raymond Loewy redesigned the Lucky Strike cigarette package for the American Tobacco Company, updating the lettering and changing the background color of the cigarette package from green to white (see Fig. 3.2).[12]

The new Lucky Strike logo, a red bull's-eye encircled by a green band, which was printed on both the front and back of the package, increased the brand's visibility, and began to be popularly described as a "target." By relocating the label's text to the side of the package, Loewy opened up space on the back of the box for a second image of the target, which could then be seen no matter how it was placed, and which resulted in additional advertising. Widely considered by graphic artists today to be a masterful stroke of genius itself, Loewy's redesign was pragmatic. The American Tobacco Company could no longer use the ink color green during wartime production, since its chromium-based dye relied upon copper, which had been rationed. Furthermore, Loewy points out, the dark green dye was expensive, and "had a slight smell." By contrast, the updated package, "owing to its impeccable whiteness," Loewy wrote, "looks, and is, clean. It automatically connotes freshness of content and immaculate manufacturing."[13] The distinctive new look of Loewy's white package and its iconic target—sharp, modern, and eye-catching—was also popularized by the "Lucky Strike Green Has Gone to War!" advertising campaign, which appealed to the patriotic sentiments of smokers.

Lucky Strike brand cigarettes make a memorable appearance in "Smoke Gets in Your Eyes," the first episode of the American television network AMC's stylish hit dramatic series, *Mad Men*, which aired in 2007. In the opening scene, set in the year 1960, the show's protagonist, Don Draper, a handsome, enigmatic advertising executive, strikes up a conversation with his waiter in a smoky, dimly lit restaurant. Distractedly jotting his flashes of inspiration on a cocktail napkin, Draper notes that his black waiter smokes Old Gold cigarettes, whereas he himself smokes Lucky Strikes. Asking why, he learns that his waiter had become attached to the brand during the Second World War, when the U.S. military sent free cartons each week to servicemen abroad. Draper, probing further asks, "Could I persuade you to try another brand, say, my Luckies?" The waiter reluctantly agrees that, if necessary, he could switch brands, since he loves smoking, though his wife would rather that he quit. She had read in *Reader's Digest*, the waiter reports, that cigarettes can kill you. "Ladies love their magazines," the waiter sighs. Draper, writing "I LOVE SMOKING," while smiling knowingly, responds, "Yes they do."

The brand names of both Old Gold and Lucky Strike cigarettes recalled the association of tobacco with gold, which had been legendary since

Fig. 3.2 Lucky Strike package designed by Raymond Loewy, 1942. Used with approval of Loewy Design, LLC. (www.RaymondLoewy.com)

Virginia colonist John Rolfe (the husband of Pocahontas) first cultivated a domestic tobacco crop from Spanish seeds.[14] He called his special variety of the plant Orinoco, after the adventures of Sir Walter Raleigh, who traveled the South American Orinoco River in search of El Dorado, a mythical city of gold. The golden leaves of the tobacco plant were even used in Jamestown, Virginia, as a form of currency.[15] The name "Lucky Strike" is believed to be a reference to the 1849 Gold Rush during which time (like the expression "Eureka!") it described the good fortune of striking gold. The name of the Lucky Strike brand dates to 1871, when it was registered by the Virginia-based company, R. A. Patterson, as a brand of chewing tobacco, sold in green tins decorated with a red medallion, encircled by gold lettering. The first Lucky Strike cigarette package maintained the older Patterson package design, reinterpreted as a deep green paper box with a circular red medallion and arc of gold lettering.

When Lucky Strike cigarettes were first introduced in 1916, the brand was owned by what had been the most powerful tobacco producing entity by the turn of the twentieth century, the American Tobacco Company. In 1911, the U.S. Supreme Court dissolved ATC's monopolistic holding of numerous private tobacco companies, which, like Standard Oil, had violated the Sherman Anti-Trust Act.[16] The original companies comprising ATC, however, like the many descendants of Standard Oil, continued to enjoy great economic success over the years.

James Buchanan "Buck" Duke, of Durham, North Carolina, together with his brother, inherited in 1890 the family tobacco business that had been started by their father. Buck Duke revolutionized the industry by licensing the use of a new rolling machine, invented in 1880 by James Albert Bonsack, and by engaging in aggressive advertising campaigns, as well as by purchasing the companies of his competitors. Duke's packages of cigarettes were stiffened with trading cards featuring sports themes and images of scantily clad actresses that appealed to young customers, especially boys, who were as interested in collecting the cards as they were in the cigarettes themselves. Historian Allen Brandt writes: "Duke had discovered important incentives for smoking in the cultural rituals of youth."[17]

From its very beginnings physicians, social reformers, temperance advocates, and others who attacked the cigarette industry claimed that smoking, like drinking alcohol, was unhealthy and immoral. Brandt explains: "Embedded in the cigarette were the complex historical meanings of rebellion and idleness, independence and attraction. All kids were told smoking was bad—and was for adults—which created, in part, its impressive appeal."[18]

The cigarette industry exploded during the First World War. Until then attitudes towards cigarette smoking were ambivalent, in part because of its early associations with effeminacy, orientalism, and decadence.[19] Anti-tobacco reformers, which included such powerful individuals as Henry Ford, pushed legislators to establish smoking bans in numerous states. In comparison to the bodily and psychological injuries of war, however, the potential dangers to soldiers' health or morality by smoking seemed trivial. John J. Pershing, Major General of the United States National Army, during the war exclaimed: "You ask me what we need to win this war. I answer tobacco, as much as bullets."[20] American cigarette companies shipped vast numbers of their product overseas, securing a generation of smokers upon the soldiers' return from war.

By the 1950s, smoking was more popularly perceived as cool, masculine, and virile, as evident in the cigarettes dangling carelessly from the mouths of hard-living, hard-drinking, car-driving, motorcycle-riding, rebellious movie stars like James Dean and Marlon Brando. But by the 1950s, the tobacco industries were also well aware, as a result of numerous medical studies, that smoking was harmful to human health. More specifically, it was clearly evident that cigarettes, due to their high nicotine content, were addictive, and were likely to cause emphysema, diabetes, heart disease, and cancer. Like a bullet, a cigarette can kill you. Rather than modify its products, however, the tobacco industry dug in its heels to resist regulation and embarked on a decades-long campaign of public deception.[21]

Cigarette manufacturers continued to explore new markets, including children, with products, packaging, and advertising that were slickly designed and stamped with a disingenuous seal of approval by the medical industry itself. At that time, Philip Morris repositioned its filtered Marlboro brand, which had originally been marketed to women, as a masculine cigarette for men concerned about their health. The new advertising campaign, devised by the Chicago-based Leo Burnett advertising firm, featured a rugged cowboy to personify the Marlboro Man. A great commercial success, the Marlboro Man evoked romantic notions of the open range, rugged solitude, and the American West, though these feelings were certainly tinged with homoeroticism as well.

The erotic associations of the cigarette were not new; pin-up illustrators had been commonly employed throughout the first half of the twentieth century to design cigarette advertisements with pretty girls, in which smoking was identified with sexual arousal, if not a visual metaphor for sex itself. Lucky Strike's 1931 advertising campaign, "Do you inhale?," featured illustrations of couples in sexually suggestive positions, such as a scantily clad woman with bare legs, provocatively splayed, who lays her face in the lap of a sailor. In another, which mimics the style of a pulp romance, or pornographic novel, a woman exposes her décolletage; her slit skirt reveals the garter on her upper thigh as she smokes a cigarette: "While waiting for the fleet to come, nothing satisfies like a Lucky." Though Lucky Strike may have had its origin in the Victorian culture of gentlemanly comfort, elegance, and exclusivity of the men's club, signified by its appealing original green tin with gold medallion and red lettering, its new package design in 1942 was meant to appeal to both men and women who were interested in fashion, shopping, and maintaining a slim figure. With their sexually provocative packaging and presentation, cigarettes were particularly appealing to adolescent boys, our future soldiers.

In 1998, the tobacco companies Lorillard, Philip Morris Inc., R. J. Reynolds, and Brown & Williamson lost a major lawsuit. The resulting Tobacco Master Settlement Agreement forced big tobacco to contribute to tobacco-related health care costs, and to halt their advertising campaigns. In a disturbingly fitting conclusion to *Mad Men*, set a decade later, we learn that Don Draper's once glamorous former wife and mother of his three children will soon die of lung cancer. Despite its controversial history, which involves not only its entanglement with war, but also its manipulation of the public with aggressive advertising campaigns, enticing consumers to indulge a dangerous and potentially deadly pleasure, tobacco remains nevertheless an important element of American identity. It is memorialized in the classical Corinthian columns for the new U.S. Capitol building designed in 1816 by Benjamin Latrobe, who topped them with tobacco leaves, rather than the traditional acanthus, as a symbol of the new nation.

Targeted

The new woman of the belle époque was the target customer for many manufacturers in the late nineteenth century, including purveyors of tobacco. Art nouveau illustrator Alfonse Mucha's enticing graphic advertisements for all sorts of new commercial products in the 1890s, from baking powder to bicycles, often featured an attractive image of a young woman drinking coffee, preparing cocoa for her children, or sexily smoking a cigarette. These original Virginia Slims, Mucha's appealing young women with their slender bodies and unruly hair, signified a new spirit of liberation. Path breaking feminists in both Europe and North America had begun to organize for women's social, political, economic, and sexual emancipation in the first half of the nineteenth century. Their efforts culminated by the turn of the century, however, less in a new wave of educated women professionals and political leaders, than in the erotically enticing and sexually threatening images of single women that were ubiquitous in the public, urban spaces of modernity.[22] These transgressive new women, without chaperone, sexually liberated, and perhaps promiscuous, smoked cigarettes and rode bicycles, wore avant-garde fashions, and shopped. The purchasing power of the new woman was unprecedented in the 1890s when advertisements, illustrated by artists from Jules Chéret to William Bradley, began to feature them in graphic posters and illustrated journals. This new freedom evolved into the popular, masculinized image of the female flapper in the 1920s, with her bare legs, cropped hair, audacious spirit, and cigarettes.

"Ladies love their magazines," we learn from *Mad Men*. Cigarettes were just one of many products advertised to women with the explosion of print culture, in the form of posters and illustrated journals of the late nineteenth and early twentieth centuries. Many of the items advertised in women's magazines of the early twentieth century were things that could be purchased in department stores, a new institution that evolved from the early modern marketplaces and eighteenth-century covered arcades of Paris and other European cities. By the early twentieth century different types of retail spaces had emerged. At the high end of the spectrum, fashionable department stores and exclusive boutiques, such as Liberty's of London, La Maison Moderne, and Siegfried Bing's gallery, l'Art Nouveau, in Paris, sold the most stylish accessories for modern dress and home. Larger department stores catered to a wider clientele. Among the best-known companies established in the nineteenth century were Harrods (London), Le Bon Marché and La Samaritain (Paris), Macy's (New York), Wanamaker's (Philadelphia), and Marshall Field and Company (Chicago).[23] At the lower end of the spectrum were merchandisers of less expensive goods for a middle class audience. The Chicago-based Sears, Roebuck & Co. was the largest of these companies in the United States, selling all kinds of products, from clothing, furniture, and tools, to complete houses, through its mail-order catalogues.

The goods sold in these new retail spaces were first advertised inside the buildings themselves. The sumptuous marble palaces were arranged as spectacular bazaars with mountains of lace, walls of textiles, and cascades of colorful parasols and paper lanterns. Increasingly, toward the turn of the century, such visual displays were extended to the street-facing show windows of the department stores, where carefully staged arrangements of goods and clothing, sometimes worn by live mannequins, enticed shoppers to enter the store. One of the most influential innovators of show window design in the United States was L. Frank Baum, who, before writing the Oz books, published the trade journal, *The Show Window*.[24] Taking advantage of new innovations in lighting and plate glass, Baum promoted an aesthetic for colorful, enchanting displays of abundance. Nearly a half century later, Raymond Loewy would also begin his professional career by designing show windows in New York.[25]

The American retailer Target was first introduced in 1962 as an upscale discount outlet of the Minneapolis-based Dayton's department store. Stewart K. Widdess, Dayton's Director of Publicity, and his staff decided upon the name "Target" and the original bull's-eye concept for the store's signage. Widdess remarked: "As a marksman's goal is to hit the center bulls-eye, the new store would do much the same in terms of retail goods, services, commitment to the community, price, value and overall experience."

According to Associated Press reporter Mae Anderson, the company first considered using as its logo a bull's-eye with a few bullet holes in it, but decided that such an image was not appropriate for a family store, which was meant to be, rather, "fun to shop and exciting to visit."[26]

Today Target Corporation's more simplified red and white bull's-eye trademark, like the London Transport roundel, and Loewy's Lucky Strike package, is recognized as one of the most successful advertising designs of the late twentieth and early twenty-first centuries (see Fig. 3.3).

In 2006, the company received the AIGA (American Institute of Graphic Arts) Corporate Leadership Award for "changing the cultural under-standing and appreciation of design, communicating the importance of

Fig. 3.3 Retailers Begin Holiday Shopping Season Before Thanksgiving, Times Square, New York, November 24, 2004. Photo by Mario Tama. Getty Image News 51789984.

design to consumers, and its steadfast commitment to championing and advocating design." More specifically, Target was recognized by the AIGA for its promotion of "creativity, innovation, and technology," by working with contemporary designers to engineer useful, stylish, and socially responsible products. The company's "Design for All" campaign, launched in 2002, "made good design look indispensable—as much of a necessity as toothpaste."[27]

When Target opened outside Minneapolis in 1962, it was joined in the south by a competitor, Walmart, the first in the long line of successful businesses started by entrepreneur Sam Walton in Bentonville, Arkansas. Like Target, Walmart, as it is known today, sells a range of products from food, drugs, and toiletry items, and household furnishings, to office supplies, gardening equipment, toys, clothes, electronics, and sporting goods. *Fortune* magazine classifies Walmart and Target as "General Merchandisers," constituting one of America's top industries; in 2014, Walmart was ranked first in *Fortune*'s list of the 500 most profitable global businesses.[28] Unlike the elegant urban marble palaces of the belle époque, or the colorful strip malls of the 1950s commuter suburbs, Target and Walmart stores today are typically built in more recently developed suburban areas. These "big-box" retailers inhabit enormous single-story warehouse buildings, surrounded by vast parking lots, which are largely devoid of the colorful neon signage that made the first suburban shopping malls pioneered by Victor Gruen so lively and decorative.

Target's distinctive identity as a retailer today results not only from the company's collaboration with fashionable designers, including Michael Graves and Isaac Mizrahi, to produce affordable yet stylish lines of goods for the middle-class shopper, but also from its cultivation of a younger, more urban clientele—a relationship that has been developed by its opening of smaller stores in the heart of big cities, such as Chicago, Seattle, and Los Angeles. Target stores, large and small, suburban and urban, with their bright, spacious, orderly arrangements of goods, appeal to professional singles and young couples, as well as to middle-class family shoppers. In order to court these new urban markets, Target Corporation has been supportive of progressive legislation, such as the protection of unionized labor, and has fostered more sustainable design by adapting preexisting buildings for the new stores, which reduces the need to use new materials and undeveloped land.[29]

Though Walmart sells the same sorts of household items as Target, it appeals more readily to a working-class audience, with marketing campaigns featuring low prices and common sense, rather than style or pleasure. Walmart revised its logo in 2008 by updating the trademark's original blocky capital letters, WAL ★ MART, separated by a five-pointed star. In the new logo, only the "W" is capitalized, the letterforms are more rounded, and the star is replaced with a "sunburst," which moves to the end of the new name, Walmart*, like an asterisk. Typographer Tobias Frere-Jones, principal of the New York firm Hoefler & Frere-Jones, described Walmart's new design as looking more friendly, casual, and approachable, but not too radical. "Otherwise," he suggests, "it might look like they're trying too hard to play with the cool kids."[30]

The update coincided with Walmart's settlement in dozens of lawsuits against the company for violating labor laws when it forced employees to work extra hours off the clock.[31] Despite the update of its trademark, however, the new Walmart continued to fight its public image as an exploitative and unethical corporation, concerned only with its own profits. At the risk of oversimplification, we may conclude that Target's target audience is also likely relatively better educated, fashion savvy, urban, professional, and politically progressive than Walmart's more traditional, rural, and politically conservative one. But the politics are tricky to sort out. In 2011, progressive Democratic First Lady Michelle Obama enlisted Walmart as a partner in her campaign to bring healthier food to isolated poor urban communities.[32] Walmart has also made commitments in the past several years to using sustainable packaging and products as well as more energy efficient stores and fleets of trucks.[33]

Target's iconic logo evokes not so much the shooting range, as the Pop Art aesthetic of the 1960s, which was ushered in by Jasper Johns's memorable *Flag* and *Target* paintings of the 1950s. In an interview, archived by the San Francisco Museum of Modern Art, Johns explains that the flag painting (the idea for which, he elsewhere recounts, came to him in a dream) "made him think of a target."[34] Perhaps he meant that a flag, like a target, is meaningful not only as an object, but also, and more importantly, as a sign. We could also reverse this idea, with respect to the London Transport roundel, noting that the red, white, and blue roundel makes us think of the British flag, or, indeed, that the red, white, and blue trademarks of Standard Oil and its many descendants remind us of the American flag. Patriotism is inevitably linked to consumption in the realm of signs.

Target's trademark recalls the London Transport roundel, the archetypal corporate bull's-eye, but it also draws on the trendy appropriation of the British Royal Air Force emblem in 1960s London. The symbol was a hip signifier of knowing, urban style. The circular disc, flat and simplistic, is reminiscent of the clean-cut style of 1960s mod fashion, which featured sharp suits for men and short rectangular dresses for women in bold geometric patterns. For the mods, post-war British working class youth, shopping for clothes and records (likewise, we might note, in the shape of a bull's-eye), and listening to music may have been a way to escape the dreariness of their everyday, low-wage employment. But wearing stylish clothes from Carnaby Street or riding Italian motor scooters was more than just conspicuous consumption. Rather, the playful assembling of fashion elements articulated a metropolitan identity, and freedom through consumption, that overturned the outdated conventions of their parents' generation.[35]

One colorful Target advertisement campaign of the late 1990s featured fashionable, yet bland and anonymous models posed against modular backdrops of toilet paper and mouthwash.[36] The groups of identical products are linked by the blue color palette of their packaging, and hint at Andy Warhol's 1960s silkscreen prints of Campbell's soup cans and movie stars, which themselves evoke the postmodern glamour of the banal. A 2007 television commercial advertising a Thanksgiving Day sale cleverly animated the well-known pictographic athlete designed by Otl Aicher for the 1972 Munich Olympics, sending it running and leaping through the store with a cart, playfully rendering shopping as Olympic sport.[37] These advertisements, with their in-the-know sensibility, wink at the ironic and are delightful for the culturally educated shopper aware of her own complicity in the apparatus of late capitalism, with its anonymity and endless circulation of copies. Like so many other corporate logos of the 1960s, Target's target is an empty sign, which can be filled with myriad content. Today, Target's image is youthful, cheerful, stylish, and fun—qualities embodied by its miniature bull terrier mascot, Bullseye [sic]. If Widdess had chosen to adopt the bullet-riddled target as a logo for the company, however, the effect of Target's sign might have been closer to that of Julius Gipken's frightening 1917 poster for a German Air Force fundraiser to be held at the Berlin Zoo during the First World War, in which an imposing black silhouette of the imperial German eagle sits atop a British Royal Air

Force logo, talons clutching the destroyed target, shot through by German gunfire.[38]

Ready, Aim, Fire!

What then is the relationship between smoking, shopping, and shooting? Why do we hunt for bargains? Where are the links between corporate success, design, and violence? Despite its use of a shooting target as its emblem of corporate identity, Target Corporation does not sell firearms. This has led some in recent years to question whether or not the company is "anti-gun." Supporters of the Second Amendment to the U.S. Constitution defend with passion their individual right to bear arms, a right that has recently been upheld by the U.S. Supreme Court in two important decisions.[39] The Second Amendment states:

> A well regulated Militia, being necessary to the security of a free State, the right of the people to keep and bear Arms, shall not be infringed.[40]

The U.S. has been divided over what exactly the Second Amendment means since the late 1960s, with those on the political right supporting greater access to firearms, and those on the left advocating for more stringent gun control.[41] The loudest voice in the argument currently is that of the National Rifle Association (NRA), an organization founded in 1871, which today lobbies Congress for fewer regulations to be placed on the sale and possession of guns and ammunition, and which is fiercely opposed by civic leaders who favor community safety. In fact, Target Corporation does contribute to the National League of Cities, an organization that advocates for greater regulation of firearms in urban areas.[42] For gun rights proponents, it is not only the right to purchase guns that is important, but also the personal right to bring them into public places, such as restaurants, theaters, shopping centers, supermarkets, and even schools. While Walmart sells guns and ammunition, and allows concealed weapons to be brought into its stores, Target does not.

American feelings about gun ownership are as deep as those for tobacco and oil, and are equally entangled in notions of rebellion and conquest. Guns were crucial to the success of the American Revolutionary War (1775–83), and were central of course to the many bloody battles of the nineteenth century, including the Civil War (1861–5). They were used in the many Indian campaigns of that century, as well as in the settlement of the west by pioneers, lured by the prospect of gold, and the mission of manifest destiny.

Historian Frederick Jackson Turner proposed this interpretation in his 1893 lecture, "The Significance of the Frontier in American History," in which he claimed that westward expansion by farmers and pioneers was the formative element of American identity, calling the frontier a "military training ground" that kept alive the revolutionary spirit.[43] We also associate firearms in America with the violent period of prohibition, and with both organized crime and law enforcement in the 1920s and 1930s.

More recently, firearms have become symbols of the urban drug wars, and signs of violence brought about by the desperation of poverty. They also remind us constantly of war around the globe. All such phases in the life of firearms are vividly represented, and even celebrated, in the popular arts of television, cinema, music, and video gaming. Their representation in media has been widely studied by sociologists and psychologists.

The debate over U.S. gun rights and gun control is often stereotyped as a clash between rural and urban, white and non-white, southern and northern, religious and secular, progressive and conservative. In 2008, Barack Obama, at the time a senator from the state of Illinois, famously asserted, in his most memorable gaffe of the presidential campaign that year, that white rural voters were difficult for him to reach because they "cling to their guns and religion."[44] But the politicized roots of the gun debate in America are not exactly black and white.

The current political divide over firearms may be traced to the assassinations of American political leaders and activists in the 1960s, including President John F. Kennedy (1963), civil rights leader Dr. Martin Luther King, Jr. (1968), and New York Senator Robert Kennedy (1968), each of whom were progressive voices for social change. The precedent for this more modern use of firearms in the continuing American struggle to define itself culturally and politically was set, tragically, by the assassination of President Abraham Lincoln in 1865. Lincoln's presidency and murder were perhaps the most pivotal events in American history, marking the end of the Civil War, which dramatized the tension between pursuit of individual wealth and of universal equality, two different interpretations of freedom, between which the nation continues to vacillate today.

The 1960s' assassinations of the Kennedy brothers and Dr. King, like the assassination of President Lincoln, took place during a moment of heightened awareness of racial inequality. At that time, some white Americans feared that African Americans connected to the militant Black Panther Party for Self-Defense were actively organizing to arm themselves in resistance to white leadership. This anxiety fueled the transition of the NRA from an organization devoted to firearm safety to one prepared to protect Second Amendment rights in the midst of the 1960s culture wars.[45]

Black nationalist and civil rights leader Malcolm X made reference to the Second Amendment and his call for black citizens to arm themselves in self-defense drew attention to the issue. In his 1964 speech, "The Ballot or the Bullet," delivered in Cleveland, Ohio, Malcolm X urged African Americans to exercise their right to vote. In addition, referring to the 1955 murder in Mississippi of Emmet Till, a fourteen-year-old African American boy who was killed for purportedly flirting with a white woman, and the 1963 murders of four young girls aged from eleven to fourteen while they were attending Sunday school classes at church in Birmingham, Alabama, he cautioned: "in areas where the government has proven itself either unwilling or unable to defend the lives and the property of Negroes, it's time for Negroes to defend themselves."[46] Malcolm X was himself assassinated less than one year later.

In 1968, following the assassination of President John F. Kennedy, the U.S. Congress introduced legislation to restrict the purchase of guns by mail order. (Kennedy's killer had purchased his Italian military surplus weapon through the mail.) At that time, the new restrictions had full bi-partisan support, as well as the support, with some reservations, of the NRA. But, in 1986, the organization pushed forward the Firearm Owner's Protection Act, which overturned some of the 1968 legislation.

In 1993, President Bill Clinton signed into the law the Brady Handgun Violence Prevention Act, which mandated criminal background checks on all firearm purchasers in the United States. The bill was named after James Brady, the White House Press Secretary, who was wounded in the 1981 attempted assassination of then President Ronald Reagan. In 1994, Congress also passed a ten-year ban on "assault weapons," semi-automatic handguns and rifles designed for military use, which can fire multiple bullets in rapid succession. Assault weapons, the name of which derives from the Sturmgewehr military rifle used by Nazi soldiers during the Second World War, are meant to be used offensively, and were not designed for personal protection, nor for hunting animals. The ban expired in 2004 and has not been reinstated.

To "call shotgun," when getting into a car with many passengers, is to claim a seat next to the driver. American children just old enough to safely ride in the front seat of a car commonly use this figure of speech. The expression likely derives from the pioneer days, before the invention of automobiles, when teams of horses hauled wagons across the country. The passenger seated next to the driver was responsible for manning the shotgun to defend against dangerous foes, such as (real) panthers, bandits, or Indians. Today, presumably, the front-seated passenger in an automobile need not be armed with a shotgun, nor charged with this special responsibility, yet the front passenger seat *is* the choice place to sit. It is the best place to ride. "Shotgun!" today thus signifies hierarchy. The one who "calls shotgun" first is quickest thinking and beats the others to the punch. The peculiar and passionate American desire to arm oneself with a gun is not only a practical concern; it is also an expression of staking a claim.

In addition to stemming from the frontier culture described by Turner, the American passion for firearms results from their privileged position at the center of design and manufacture in the United States. As John Heskett and David Hounshell have shown, the firearm manufacturing industry was one of the first to rely upon standardization and the use of interchangeable parts, preceding by nearly a century Henry Ford's assembly line production in the manufacture of automobiles, which came to be known as the "American System."[47] Some would argue that the American economy has always been dependent on the production and use of military weaponry, not only for its own defense, but also for export to other nations. This is the military–industrial complex of which President Eisenhower warned in the 1950s.[48]

Samuel Colt's 1836 revolver, a handgun with a rotating cylinder holding several bullets that could fire more than one shot without having to be reloaded, quickly became a global export as well as a recognizable symbol of the frontier. The new gun was promoted at international exhibitions and romanticized in art and literature. By the mid-nineteenth century, Colt, together with Remington, Smith and Wesson, and Winchester, had become synonymous with romantic ideas of the American spirit as well as with the power of its industry. Today's Remington Arms Company dates from 1816, when the young Eliphalet Remington produced a flintlock rifle in his father's forge at Ilion Gulch, New York. By the 1870s, E. Remington & Sons was so successful that it had diversified to produce typewriters as well.

The romantic sway of firearms cannot be overstated. Despite our outward repudiation of their actions, a part of us admires the rebellious spirit and stunning feats of outlaws like Billy the Kid, Jesse James, John Dillinger, and Bonnie and Clyde, who robbed banks and escaped from prison—sticking it to the man. The crimes of the prohibition era inspired a genre of gangster films and many memorable characters, from Marlon Brando as Francis Ford Coppola's 1972 *The Godfather* to his latter-day television incarnation, Tony Soprano, played by actor James Gandolfini. We are drawn to these figures, both real and fictional, for their brash audacity, defiance, and power, characteristics we value and aspire to achieve. They dramatize the pioneer's inner desire for confrontation, as in Clint Eastwood's notorious dare, as vigilante police officer Dirty Harry Callahan, "Go ahead, make my day," a provocation later famously quoted by U.S. President and former Hollywood actor Ronald Reagan.[49] The stories of these violent criminals and the heroes who bring them to justice are entwined with stories of the American dream—of the success of immigrants, disaffected rebels, the working classes, and all those oppressed who overcome adversity. Such characteristics are magnified when combined with smoking, drinking, or driving. The hard-drinking, fast-driving, gun-toting heroes (or heroines) seduce us. The tragic aspects of these activities, including fatal car crashes, prison, lung cancer, and murder, do not sway us from the glamor of the image, a glamor that elevates the power of myth.

A photograph taken in 1934 by depression-era bank robber Clyde Barrow of his partner Bonnie Parker, in the midst of their notorious crime spree, depicts her posing stylishly by the side of their 1932 Ford V-8 B-400 convertible sedan, with a revolver in her hand and cigar between her teeth.[50] The picture captures the glamor and allure of crime and danger, bound inextricably to tobacco, alcohol, automobiles, and firearms. Though she presents herself as a gangster in this photograph, with the recognizable masculine cigar as prop, Parker was also known to have chain-smoked Camel cigarettes, an arguably more feminine habit in the 1930s. A second photograph, taken after the pair were ambushed and shot to death by federal marshals (134 times), reveals the arsenal of guns and ammunition that they had with them in their car. Among the weapons they used were a Colt .38 snub-nosed revolver, a .45-caliber Colt 1911 automatic pistol, a 12-gauge Winchester shotgun, and a .45-caliber Thompson submachine "Tommy" gun.[51] Parker clearly imagined herself as a film star, a femme fatale. From the stylish noir crime dramas and gripping, entertaining westerns of the 1940s and 1950s, to Alfred Hitchcock's psychological thrillers, to the Cold War glamor of James Bond, to Quentin Tarantino's darkly satirical aestheticization of violence at the turn of the twenty-first century, film and television entertainment can hardly be imagined without its blazing guns.

According to research conducted in 2008, small firearms kill approximately 1,000 people around the world every day, with millions more wounded or with lives disrupted as a result.[52] Many such deaths are the result of global war with its dreadful acts of violence, genocide, and terror, as well as its related structures for security and defense, especially today in the wars in Iraq, Afghanistan, and Syria, but also all throughout the Middle East, and in parts of Africa, Asia, Eastern Europe, Mexico, and Central and South America. The disproportionate majority of the gun-related deaths not directly related to military conflict, however, occur in the United States—about 30,000 per year.[53]

Often described as an epidemic of gun violence, U.S. gun-related deaths have been analyzed from the point of view of public health, and as the result of a deeply racially and economically divided society. Particularly frightening, though they account statistically for only a small proportion of gun-related deaths, are the mass shootings that have escalated in frequency since the 1990s. Although these incidents have occurred in many places around the world, from Australia, to Kenya, to Norway, again the majority of them have taken place in the United States.[54]

One of the first such mass shootings to cause widespread terror was the 1966 massacre at the University of Texas in Austin, during which a sniper, a former Marine and graduate student in architectural engineering, methodically killed sixteen people and wounded thirty-two others from his perch atop the campus clock tower. For many years the event that most gripped the public imagination was the 1999 mass shooting at Columbine High School in Littleton, Colorado, a suburb of Denver, in which two student gunmen murdered twelve of their fellow students and one teacher, wounding twenty-four others.

A similar school shooting happened in 2007 at Virginia Polytechnic Institute and State University in Blacksburg, Virginia, during which a college senior shot and killed thirty-two people and wounded seventeen others. Most heartbreaking was the 2012 shooting of six educators and twenty first-graders, no more than six years old, at Sandy Hook Elementary School in Newtown, Connecticut. In each case the heavily armed perpetrators had easy access to legally obtained guns and ammunition that allowed them to carry out their violent and terrifying acts. Remarkably, in the wake of such incidents in the United States, it has been ever more difficult to move toward stronger legislation to control access to guns. In fact, it is often immediately following such incidents that gun and ammunition sales are at their highest.[55]

American weapons still constitute a majority in the firearms market overall, despite the popularity of high-quality European guns such as the Austrian Glock and German Sig Sauer, and American gun manufacturers, like the big tobacco producers of the early twentieth century, are always looking for new markets. The Pennsylvania-based company, Keystone Sporting Arms, founded in 1996, produces a popular rifle marketed for young shooters. Called the Davey Crickett, or just Crickett, the single shot .22-caliber rifle is marketed to children. It is produced in a variety of colors, including pink, and features as its logo a cartoon cricket dressed in khaki hunting gear and carrying a rifle. He looks very much like a close relative of Walt Disney's Jiminy Cricket, a loveable cartoon character created for the 1940 animated film, *Pinocchio*. Actually, the Crickett rifle, also called "My First Rifle," was modeled on the even cuter Chipmunk rifle, first manufactured by the Oregon-based Rogue Rifle company in 1982, and later purchased by Keystone Sporting Arms. How old should a youth be to use the Crickett rifle? According to testimonials published on the company's website children aged nine, seven, or even four-and-a-half are often eager to begin shooting sports.[56] On April 30, 2013, a two-year-old girl in Burkesville, Kentucky, was killed by her five-year-old brother. He was playing with the Crickett youth model rifle that he received for his birthday when he accidentally shot her.[57]

Most striking about the testimonials submitted by Crickett's My First Rifle enthusiasts (whether they are authentic or not) is that they highlight an untapped market of little girls. There is certainly no dearth of gun-toting women in the mythical history of firearms; outlaw Bonnie Parker is one; Annie Oakley, the famous sharpshooter who performed with Buffalo Bill's Wild West show, is another. And there are plenty of sexy gun-wielding women criminals, police officers, or secret agents in television, film, and other popular media. But gun manufacturers understand that the market for new women gun owners still has potential for growth.

Following the tragedy in Newtown, Connecticut, much was made of the fact that the shooter had used a Bushmaster .223-caliber AR–15 style semi-automatic assault rifle, a weapon that upon closer examination serves as a potent example of the mythical meaning of firearms in the imagination.[58] Richard Dyke, recognizing the civilian market for military-style weapons, founded the Maine-based company, Bushmaster, in 1976. A bushmaster is a type of snake, a large venomous pit viper of the genus *Lachesis*, found in Central and South America, which can reach up to twelve feet in length. Lachesis is also the name of the second of the three Fates, or Moirai, in Greek mythology. She was responsible for measuring the thread spun by her sister, Clotho, and thus determining destiny, or the length of one's life. Bushmaster's name and logo, which depicts a coiled snake ready to strike, recalls not only the deadly pit viper, but also the name of the 158th Infantry Regiment of the Arizona National Guard. The Bushmasters, so-named during their training in the jungles of Panama during the Second World War, originated during the Indian campaigns of 1865, and the majority of its members are still today Native American.[59] The Bushmaster logo also features the image of an assault rifle, such that the coiling snake is imaginatively identified with a recoiling gun. The "bushmaster" in both name and form thus activates a range of meanings, from the tragedy of classical mythology, to the violence of the nineteenth-century Indian campaigns, to the danger and power of the poisonous pit viper, to the romance of twentieth-century war.

In 2006, Cerberus Capital Management, L.P., a private equity investment firm founded in the early 1990s, purchased Bushmaster. The firearms manufacturer had struggled following the infamous 2002 Washington, D.C., beltway sniper shootings, when it was discovered that the shooters, who murdered ten individuals and wounded three others in random shootings over a span of twenty days, had used a Bushmaster .223-caliber AR–15 rifle. Bushmaster was sued because it had continued to supply guns to Bull's Eye Shooter Supply in Tacoma, Washington, the store from which the shooters had stolen their guns, even though the company was aware of the store's pattern of failing to comply with the federal criminal background check law. (Cerberus, by the way, is the ancient Greek mythological three-headed dog that guards the entrance to Hades.) In addition to the struggling Bushmaster, Cerberus purchased several other firearms manufacturers, including Dakota Arms, DPMS Firearms, and the legendary Remington, consolidating them under the name Freedom Group.[60] Following the Newtown shooting in 2012, however, Cerberus announced its intention to sell Freedom Group, which was no longer a profitable investment. Some of Cerberus's biggest clients had already begun to talk about divesting.[61]

No

Perhaps the most unexpected transformation of the circular bull's-eye emblem is its use as the ubiquitous red circle with a diagonal slash, indicating a prohibited activity, as in "No Smoking" or "No Guns."

In 1974, Dan Shanosky and Roger Cook designed a set of thirty-four symbol signs, including the No Smoking sign, for the U.S. Department of

Transportation. In 1979, sixteen additional symbols were added to the lexicon, which has since been used around the globe, "at the crossroads of modern life."[62] It was not until the 1970s that No Smoking signs began to appear with frequency. By the late 1990s, however, particularly following the 1998 Tobacco Master Settlement Agreement, the stylized image of the burning cigarette encircled and slashed in red became commonplace. And the No Smoking signs, it seems, did play a role in shifting the public away from the smoking culture that had dominated for nearly a century. Allan Brandt notes that in the 1980s with the proliferation of No Smoking signs in public places, "the nonsmoker was deputized as an agent of the state." Smokers, he writes, became increasingly embarrassed or uncomfortable lighting up in public, and more reluctant to invite the non-smoker's criticism or outright hostility.[63]

In 2013, following the passage of a new law which allows one to carry concealed weapons in the state of Illinois (the last of the fifty states to allow it), many public places, such as stores, restaurants, and especially schools, began to post No Guns signs, with the silhouette of a pistol, encircled and slashed in red (see Fig. 3.4).

Although it is now legal to carry concealed weapons in the state of Illinois generally, individual businesses and institutions, whether private or public, including schools and college campuses, may still elect to prohibit them. Will the sudden proliferation of No Guns signs in the windows of restaurants and schools change the cultural acceptance of carrying firearms?

Fig. 3.4 "No Guns" window sign, 2013. Pursuant to 430 IL.CS 66/65. Author's collection.

Mad Men reveals the lack of corporate responsibility in the 1960s, but more uncomfortably, with an ambiguous blend of shame and highly eroticized guilty pleasure, it reveals our complicity, indeed our indulgence, in the unregulated manipulation of the consumer with advertisements for all kinds of products, from airlines, cars, cigarettes, and beer, to laxatives and pantyhose. The world is still reeling from the global economic crisis of the early twenty-first century, which in the United States necessitated a number of government bailouts, for banks and other institutions deemed "too big to fail." But while many individuals lost their jobs, homes, and retirement savings, many big corporations continued to thrive.

In 2011, the global tobacco trade as a whole generated $500 billion in sales, with $35 billion in profits.[64] In 2012, Target Corporation alone generated $72 billion in sales, ranking thirty-sixth on *Fortune*'s list of 500 most profitable businesses, while Walmart ranked first with $443.9 billion in sales.[65] Walmart was not obliged to share its profits, however, with its 1.6 million female employees who sued the company for sex discrimination. In 2011, the U.S. Supreme Court invalidated the employees' class action lawsuit on the grounds that the plaintiffs did not have enough in common to constitute a class, in effect ruling, as one reporter put it, that Walmart was "too big for justice."[66] In the first nine months of 2013, Freedom Group reported $677.3 million in profits. The portion of guns and ammunition manufactured by the various companies that make up Freedom Group, and sold at Walmart, accounted for 13 percent of Freedom Group's total sales. What a lucky strike.

Notes

1 Here are a few more expressions: in the crosshairs, shooting blanks, don't shoot the messenger, like shooting fish in a barrel, she's a loose cannon, straight shooter, high caliber, low caliber, he fired back, I'm gunning for you, it's a blast, don't jump the gun, stay on target, looking down the barrel, lock-n-load, rifling through someone's things, shoot!, half-cocked, loaded, lock stock and barrel, big shot, fire away, bullet proof, hired gun, make a killing.

2 Patrick Chaplin, *Darts in England, 1900–39: A Social History* (Manchester: Manchester University Press, 2009).

3 David Lawrence, *A Logo For London: The London Transport Bar and Circle* (London: Laurence King Publishing, 2013).

4 Lawrence, *A Logo for London*, 12.

5 Herbert Bayer, "Towards a Universal Type," in Michael Bierut, Jessica Helfand, Steven Heller, and Rick Poynor (eds), *Looking Closer 3: Classic Writings on Graphic Design* (New York: Allworth Press, 1999), 60–2, originally published in *PM* 4/2 (December 1939–January 1940).

6   "bull's-eye, *n.*," *Oxford English Dictionary Online* (June 2014), copyright Oxford University Press, available online: http://www.oed.com/view/Entry/24 594?redirectedFrom=bulls-eye& (accessed June 23, 2014).

7   Le Corbusier, *The City of To-morrow and its Planning*, trans. Frederick Etchells (1929; reprint, New York: Dover Publications, 1987), x.

8   Richard C. Overton, *Burlington Route: A History of the Burlington Lines* (New York: Alfred A. Knopf, Inc., 1965), cited in "The Burlington Zephyr," *Perspecta* 13/14 (1971): 194–5.

9   Jerry Siegel and Joe Schuster, "Superman: The Man of Tomorrow," DC Comics *Superman*, No. 3 (Winter 1941): front cover. The inside covers of *Superman*, No. 4 advertised blank cartridge guns, BB pistols, "pea-matic" shooters, and a "television rifle." The back cover featured a full-page advertisement for a Daisy Air Rifle with the caption, "3 Ways to Git a Carbine Fer Christmas [sic]," instructing readers to mail in the special "secret plan." Christmas coupon. Images reproduced in Jerry Siegel and Joe Schuster, *Superman Archives* (New York: DC Comics Archive Editions, 1989), vol. 1, 139, 206.

10 Greg Votolata, "Bullets and Beyond (The Shinkansen)," in Hazel Clark and David Brody (eds), *Design Studies: A Reader* (Oxford: Berg, 2009), 511–15.

11 Votolato, "Bullets and Beyond," 513.

12 Stephen Bayley, *The Lucky Strike Packet by Raymond Loewy* (Frankfurt am Main: Verlag Form, 1998; *The Designs of Raymond Loewy* (exh. cat., Washington, DC, Renwick Gallery of the National Collection of Fine Arts; Washington, DC: Smithsonian Institution Press, 1975), 50; Raymond Loewy, *Never Leave Well Enough Alone* (New York: Simon and Schuster, 1951), 145–9.

13 Loewy, *Never Leave Well Enough Alone*, 148.

14 Richard Elliott, "The Early History of Cigarettes in America," *Brandstand, quarterly newsletter of the Cigarette Pack Collectors Association*, 34 (Spring 2009), available online: http://cigarhistory.info/Cigarette_items/Cigarette-History.html (accessed June 23, 2014). For more on Pocahontas see Chapter 4.

15 Flannagan and Hooker, *The Story of Lucky Strike: The Romance of Tobacco and the Exciting Story of Cigarette Manufacture* (1938, reprint; Richmond: The American Tobacco Company, 1953), unpaginated.

16 Reavis Cox, *Competition in the American Tobacco Industry 1911–1932: A Study of the Effects of the Partition of the American Tobacco Company by the United States Supreme Court* (1933; New York: AMS Press, 1968), 381; Howard Cox, *The Global Cigarette: Origins and Evolution of British American Tobacco 1880–1945* (Oxford: Oxford University Press, 2000); Patrick G. Porter, "Origins of the American Tobacco Company," *The Business History Review* 43/1 (Spring 1969): 59–76; Tracy Campbell, *The Politics of Despair: Power and Resistance in the Tobacco Wars* (Lexington: The University Press of Kentucky, 1993).

17 Allan M. Brandt, *The Cigarette Century: The Rise, Fall, and Deadly Persistence of the Product that Defined America* (New York: Basic Books, 2007), 32.

18 Brandt, *The Cigarette Century*, 14.

19 Relli Shechter, *Smoking, Culture and Economy in the Middle East: The Egyptian Tobacco Market 1850–2000* (London: I. B. Tauris Publishers, 2006).

20 United States Army Major General John J. Pershing, quoted in Brandt, *The Cigarette Century*, 51.

21 Naomi Oreskes and Erik M. Conway, *Merchants of Doubt: How a Handful of Scientists Obscured the Truth on Issues from Tobacco Smoke to Global Warming* (New York: Bloomsbury, 2010), 136–68.

22 Griselda Pollock, "Modernity and the Spaces of Femininity," in *Vision and Difference: Femininity, Feminism, and the Histories of Art* (London: Routledge, 1988), 50–90; Andreas Huyssen, "Mass Culture as Woman: Modernism's Other," in *After the Great Divide: Modernism, Mass Culture, Postmodernism (Theories of Representation and Difference)* (Purdue: Indiana University Press, 1987), 44–64.

23 Rosalind H. Williams, *Dream Worlds: Mass Consumption in Late Nineteenth-Century France* (Berkeley: University of California Press, 1982); Michael B. Miller, *The Bon Marché: Bourgeois Culture and the Department Store, 1869–1920* (Princeton: Princeton University Press, 1981); William Leach, *Land of Desire: Merchants, Power, and the Rise of a New American Culture* (New York: Pantheon, 1993).

24 The name of the journal was changed to *The Merchants Record and Show Window* in 1900, and to *Display World* in the 1920s. Today it is known as *Visual Merchandising*. Leach, *Land of Desire*, 56. See also, L. Frank Baum, *The Art of Decorating Dry Goods Windows and Interior: A Complete Manual of Window Trimming, Designed as an Educator in all the Details of the Art, According to the Best Accepted Methods, and Treating Fully Every Important Subject* (Chicago: Show Window Publishing Co., 1900).

25 Loewy, *Never Leave Well Enough Alone*, 56–8.

26 Mae Anderson, "Your logo here: How a logo becomes an icon," *US News and World Report* online (July 20, 2012), available online: http://bigstory. ap.org/article/your-logo-here-how-logo-becomes-icon-0 (accessed July 20, 2014); See also "Through the Years," Target Corporation [website], available online: https://corporate.target.com/about/history/Target-through-the-years (accessed July 20, 2014).

27 "Target Corporation 2006 AIGA Corporate Leadership Award," AIGA [website], available online: http://www.aiga.org/cla-target-corporation/ (accessed July 21, 2014).

28 "Fortune 500 2014," *Fortune* (July 21, 2014), available online: http://fortune. com/2013/07/08/the-most-profitable-companies-in-the-global-500/ (accessed July 21, 2014).

29 Stephanie Clifford, "Retailers' Idea: Think Smaller in Urban Push," *New York Times* (July 25, 2012), available online: http://www.nytimes.com/2012/07/26/ business/retailers-expand-into-cities-by-opening-smaller-stores.html?_r=0 (accessed July 20, 2014).

30 Reena Jana, "Walmart Gets a Facelift," *Bloomberg Businessweek*, available online: http://www.businessweek.com/stories/2008-07-02/

walmart-gets-a-faceliftbusinessweek-business-news-stock-market-and-financial-advice (accessed July 20, 2014).

31 Steven Greenhouse and Stephanie Rosenbloom, "Walmart Settles 63 Lawsuits Over Wages," *New York Times* (December 24, 2008), available online: http://www.nytimes.com/2008/12/24/business/24walmart.html?_r=0 (accessed July 20, 2014).

32 Tahman Bradley, "Michelle Obama and Walmart Join Forces Promoting Healthy Food," ABC News [website], available online: http://abcnews.go.com/Politics/WorldNews/michelle-obama-walmart-join-forces-promote-,healthy-eating/story?id=12723177 (accessed July 20, 2014).

33 Erica L. Plambeck and Lyn Denend, "The Greening of Walmart," *Stanford Social Innovation Review* (Spring 2008), available online: http://www.ssireview.org/articles/entry/the_greening_of_wal_mart (accessed July 20, 2014).

34 "Jasper Johns Discusses His Target Paintings," San Francisco Museum of Modern Art [website] (October 2001), available online: http://www.sfmoma.org/explore/multimedia/videos/141 (accessed August 31, 2014); Jonathan Jones, "Star Turn: Is it patriotic? Subversive? Both? Jonathan Jones on how Jasper Johns made a provocative masterpiece out of the American flag," *Guardian* (April 22, 2003), available online: http://www.theguardian.com/artanddesign/2003/apr/22/artsfeatures (accessed July 21, 2014). See also Jasper Johns, *Jasper Johns: Writings, Sketchbook Notes, Interviews*, ed. Kirk Varnedoe and Cristel Hollevoet (exh. cat., New York: Museum of Modern Art, 1996).

35 Paul Jobling and David Crowley, *Graphic Design: Reproduction and Representation Since 1800* (Manchester: Manchester University Press, 1996), 212–13. See also, Dick Hebdige, *Subculture: The Meaning of Style* (London: Methuen, 1979); Stuart Hall and Tony Jefferson (eds), *Resistance Through Ritual: Youth Sub-Cultures in Post-War Britain* (London: Hutchison, 1976); Christopher Breward, *Fashion* (Oxford: Oxford University Press, 2003), 224–7.

36 Advertisements for household products sold at Target: Scope, Zest, Charmin, and Windex, with the caption, "Once in a blue room. Blue skies. Blue eyes. Cleanest. Keenest. Blue," *Vogue* (April 2001).

37 [Advertisement for Target Two-Day Sale], Target Corporation [website] (2007), available online: http://www.youtube.com/watch?v=FZf7TjGbaHA&feature=PlayList&p=8DD39DD8E19B3DA4&playnext=1&playnext_from=PL&index=9 (accessed August 31, 2014). For more on Aicher's design program for the 1972 Munich Olympics, see Chapter 8.

38 Image reproduced in Philip B. Meggs and Alson W. Purvis, *Meggs' History of Graphic Design* (fourth edition, Hoboken, NJ: John Wiley and Sons, 2006), 276.

39 District of Columbia v. Heller, 554 U.S. 570 (2008); McDonald v. Chicago, 561 U.S. 3025 (2010).

40 U.S. Const. amend. II.

41 Jill Lepore, "Battleground America: One Nation, Under the Gun," *The New Yorker* (April 23, 2012): 38–47, available online: http://www.newyorker.com/reporting/2012/04/23/120423fa_fact_lepore (accessed July 16, 2014).

42 "Target Corporation Trade Association and Policy-Based Organization Support January 1–June 30, 2012," Target Corporation [website], available online: https://corporate.target.com/_media/TargetCorp/csr/pdf/2012-July-Organization-Support.pdf (accessed July 18, 2014).

43 Frederick Jackson Turner, *The Frontier in American History* (New York: Henry Holt & Co, 1921), 16.

44 "Barack Obama: In Pennsylvania, people 'bitter, cling to guns, religion, anti-immigrant sentiment,'" [Transcript of speech given by Barack Obama during a private fundraiser in San Francisco, California, April 6, 2008, recorded by Mayhill Fowler], CNBC [website], available online: http://www.cnbcfix.com/obama-cling-guns-religion.html (accessed July 16, 2014).

45 Lepore, "Battleground America."

46 Malcolm X, "The Bullet or the Ballot," [Speech delivered on April 3, 1964, Cleveland, Ohio, chapter of the Congress of Racial Equality, and on April 12, 1964, King Solomon Baptist Church, Detroit, Michigan], published in *Malcolm X Speaks: Selected Speeches and Statements*, ed. George Breitman (New York: Merit Publishers, 1965), 23–44.

47 John Heskett, *Industrial Design* (London: Thames & Hudson, 1980), 50–67; David Hounshell, *From the American System to Mass Production, 1800–1932: The Development of Manufacturing Technology in the United States* (Baltimore: Johns Hopkins University Press, 1984).

48 The origin of the term "military–industrial complex" is attributed to the Farewell Address given by President Dwight Eisenhower, in which the former military general cautioned against the misplaced power resulting from the coordination between a government, its military, and its arms industry. Dwight D. Eisenhower, "Farewell Address" (January 17, 1961), transcript, PBS: Public Broadcasting System [website], available online: http://www.pbs.org/wgbh/americanexperience/features/primary-resources/eisenhower-farewell/ (accessed June 5, 2014).

49 George J. Church, Sam Allis, Barrett Seaman, "Go Ahead – Make My Day: With Second-Term Swagger, Reagan Throws Down the Gauntlet to Congress," *Time* (March 25, 1985), available online: http://content.time.com/time/magazine/article/0,9171,964091,00.htmlhttp://content.time.com/time/magazine/article/0,9171,964091,00.html (accessed July 20, 2014).

50 Jeff Guinn, "The Irresistible Bonnie Parker: A pistol-wielding, cigar-chomping bank robber hams it up shortly before she and Clyde Barrow met their violent end," *Smithsonian Magazine* (April 2009), available online: http://www.smithsonianmag.com/history/the-irresistible-bonnie-parker-59411903/?no-ist (accessed June 10, 2015).

51 An anonymous bystander photographed the arsenal, which was obtained after Bonnie and Clyde's death, May 23, 1934, available online: http://commons.wikimedia.org/wiki/File:BarrowDeathCarArsenal1934.jpg (accessed June 10, 2015).

52 "Global Impact of Gun Violence," Gun Policy [website], available online: http://www.gunpolicy.org/firearms/region (accessed July 20, 2014).

53 "About Gun Violence," Brady Campaign to Prevent Gun Violence [website], available online: http://www.bradycampaign.org/about-gun-violence (accessed July 20, 2014).

54 "The World's Deadliest Mass Shootings," *The Washington Post* (July 20, 2012, updated December 14, 2012), available online: http://www.washingtonpost.com/wp-srv/special/nation/mass-shootings-timeline/ (accessed July 20, 2014).

55 Peter Cohan, "The NRA Industrial Complex," *Forbes* (23 July 2012), available online: http://www.forbes.com/sites/petercohan/2012/07/23/the-nra-industrial-complex/ (accessed July 21, 2014).

56 "Testimonials," Crickett. My First Rifle [website], available online: http://www.crickett.com/crickett_testimonials.php (accessed September 13, 2014).

57 "5-year-old accidentally kills sister with his own rifle," *Chicago Tribune* (May 2, 2013), Section 1, 20.

58 Alec MacGillis, "A Buyer's Guide to the Bushmaster Company," *The New Republic* (December 18, 2012), available online: http://www.newrepublic.com/article/111237/private-equity-firm-cerberus-putting-sale-its-stake-freedom-group-maker-bushmaster (accessed July 20, 2014).

59 Anthony Arthur, *Bushmasters: America's Jungle Warriors of World War II* (New York: St. Martin's Press, 1987); Roy Lancaster, *The Story of Bushmasters* (Detroit: Lancaster Publications, 1945).

60 Natasha Singer, "How Freedom Group Became the Big Shot," *New York Times* (November 26, 2011), available online: http://www.nytimes.com/2011/11/27/business/how-freedom-group-became-the-gun-industrys-giant.html?pagewanted=all (accessed July 20, 2014).

61 Peter Lattman, "In Unusual Move, Cerberus to Sell Gun Company," *New York Times* (December 18, 2012), available online: http://dealbook.nytimes.com/2012/12/18/cerberus-to-sell-gunmaker-freedom-group/ (accessed July 20, 2014).

62 "Symbol Signs," AIGA [website], available online: http://www.aiga.org/symbol-signs/ (accessed July 22, 2014).

63 Brandt, *The Cigarette Century*, 288, 302–3.

64 Simon Bowers, "Global Profits for Tobacco Trade Total $35 billion as Smoking Deaths Top 6 Million," *Guardian* (March 21, 2012), available online: http://www.theguardian.com/business/2012/mar/22/tobacco-profits-deaths-6-million (accessed July 22, 2014).

65 "Target 2012 Annual Report," Target Corporation [website], available online: https://corporate.target.com/_media/TargetCorp/annualreports/content/download/pdf/Annual-Report.pdf?ext=.pdf (accessed July 22, 2014).

66 John Nichols, "Supreme Court Decides That Walmart's a 'Too-Big-For-Justice' Corporation," *The Nation* (June 20, 2011), available online: http://www.thenation.com/blog/161556/supreme-court-decides-walmarts-too-big-justice-corporation (accessed August 31, 2014); 10-277 Walmart Store, Inc. v. Dukes et al., 564 U.S. (2011), available online: http://www.supremecourt.gov/opinions/10pdf/10-277.pdf (accessed July 20, 2014).

CHAPTER FOUR

I Is for Indian

Learning to Read

As I read one of my favorite picture books, Nancy Larrick's 1959 *First ABC*, illustrated by René Martin, with its large, colorful drawings, I pause when I come to the letter "I."

"I is for Indian," it reads.

So I explain to my own children that we don't use the term "Indian" anymore, because it emerged from a discourse of conquest and is considered derogatory, and because it is imbued with the notion of the primitive. But does this make sense to a four-year-old?

The Indian in the book is beautiful, after all, stunning in his elegant and exotic costume, with an enchanting far-away look (see Plate 5).

The page is really no different from "D is for Dinosaur," or "Q is for Queen," or "H is for Horse. A lovely brown circus horse." My own world as a child was surely as distinct from that of dinosaurs, queens, or circus horses, as it was from the Indian, proud and wise in his native dress.

> I is for Indian, a tall stately Indian. This one is a chief of the Blackfoot tribe. The black-tipped feathers of his bonnet are from the tail of a golden eagle. They seem to flow back from his head. Today Blackfoot Indians live in Montana and nearby Canada.[1]

Larrick's text is both romantic and factual, combining the language of fantasy with that of the educational encyclopedia. The pedagogical strategy was in keeping with her program as president of the International Reading Association, an organization established in 1956 to improve children's literacy and reading instruction in school. The caption recalls Roland Barthes's analysis of "written clothing" in French fashion magazines from the 1950s with their disjunctive signification of image and text, in which a photograph of a model in a stylish outfit becomes "a leather belt, with a rose stuck in it, worn above the waist, on a soft shetland dress."[2] An oversized sans serif letter I, in both its capital and lower case form. Accompanying Martin's compelling full-page illustration of the chief (see Plate 5) is an oversized sans serif letter I, in both its capital and lower case form (see Fig. 4.1). The alphabet letters remind us that children learn to read by synthesizing text and image with the stories that they represent.

In the color plate, the chief gazes out beyond the viewer, his skin reddened, his brow furrowed, his lower cheek bearing a scar. His headdress is composed of a green and yellow decorated headband, to which are attached the long, graceful eagle plumes, their quills painted blue and yellow, set against a red backing. It is fastened by a length of white fur, attached to circular medallions at the temple, ornamented with blue and green dots. He wears a fringed buckskin tunic, painted with a green diamond pattern, a choker of alternating white shell and red stone, and eight strands of small turquoise beads in concentric rings across his chest, from one of which hangs a painted circular pendant with a radial sun or star motif. A larger and more elegant necklace of red, white, and blue stones is attached to the breast of the tunic with two leather buttons, laced with fringes.

Martin was born in Paris, and raised in Switzerland. His studies of art in Rome and Florence, as well as with his father, an engraver, prepared him for his career as a prolific illustrator of children's books about the natural world, on such diverse topics as *The Story of Electricity* (1961), *Let's Find Out About Snakes* (1968), *Your Brain and How it Works* (1972), *Sea Stars and Their Kin* (1976), and *The Sun, the Moon, and the Stars* (1979). His evocative portrait of the Blackfoot chief in *First ABC* belongs to the world of charming mid-century illustration that was popular in educational and scientific texts for youth, as well as in picture books, such as those illustrated by Richard Scarry for the Golden Books series in the 1950s and 1960s.[3]

Many possible sources for Martin's Blackfoot chief can be identified. In mood and compositional style, the illustration is similar to the luscious paintings of Native Americans by George Catlin in the early nineteenth century, and in color to the lithographic prints collected in the three-volume *History of the Indian Tribes of North America*, edited by Thomas McKenney and James Hall (1836–44) and illustrated by artist Charles Bird King.[4] Versions of these images were later popularized by print companies, such as Currier & Ives, toward the end of the nineteenth century.[5] The regal stance of Martin's Indian is reminiscent, for example, of Catlin's 1832 portrait of *Stu-mick-o-súcks, Buffalo Bull's Back Fat, Head Chief, Blood Tribe* (Blackfoot/Kainai) (see Fig. 4.2).

Many of Catlin's chiefs wear some form of feathered decoration in their hair, and a few wear similar plumed headdresses, such as that featured in his 1845 portrait of *A-wu-ne-wa-be, Bird of Thunder* (Ojibwe/Chippewa), but it is difficult to see any of Catlin's depictions of historical Native Americans as a precise model for Martin's illustration of the specific Blackfoot war bonnet.

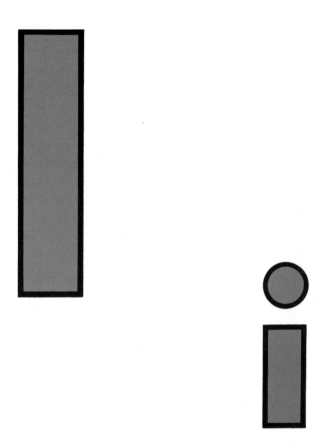

I IS FOR INDIAN, a tall stately Indian. This one is a chief of the Blackfoot tribe. The black-tipped feathers of his bonnet are from the tail of a golden eagle. They seem to flow back from his head. Today Blackfoot Indians live in Montana and nearby Canada.

30

Fig. 4.1 "I is for Indian," in Nancy Larrick and Rene Martin, *First ABC: An Educational Picture Book*, New York: Platt & Munk, Publishers, 1965. Reproduced with permission of Penguin Random House.

Fig. 4.2 George Catlin, *Stu-mick-o-súcks, Buffalo Bull's Back Fat, Head Chief, Blood Tribe*. 1832. Oil on canvas, 73.7 × 61 cm (29 × 24 in). Washington, DC, Smithsonian Institution. Gift of Mrs. Joseph Harrison, Jr.

More likely is the dependence of Martin's Blackfoot chief on the many popular representations of Native Americans in theater and film, dating to Buffalo Bill's Wild West shows of the 1880s.[6] A photograph of the troupe (1890), organized by William Frederick "Buffalo Bill" Cody, depicts native participants wearing similar feathered headdresses, with ribbon of quills attached by headbands.[7] Native performers in the show, representing different tribes, purportedly wore their own authentic dress; however, the consistency among the outfits, including those worn by children in the photograph, suggests the use of stock costume elements, such as tall, feathered headdresses and beaded shell breastplates. If stock costumes were, indeed, used, they may have been modeled on the elegant and ornamental attire of certain individuals, like the Lakota chief and holy man Sitting Bull, who performed in such shows.

Of the different Native American costume elements familiar to audiences through illustration, theater, photography, film, and eventually television in the first half of the twentieth century, the war bonnet of the Plains Indians is the most iconic. Photographer Edward Curtis captured it memorably in his documentary portfolio, *The North American Indian*, which appeared in multiple volumes from 1907 to 1930.[8] The Indian, signified most readily by his battle regalia, is a totem that lies deep in the American imagination, and embodies contradictory concepts, including the bounty and beauty of the new land, the fraught and fearful encounter between the white European and his Other, and the tragic destruction of both land and people in the name of progress. And we see this totemic representation of the Indian everywhere.

Noble Savage

As the phrase "I is for Indian" suggests, the Native American is a letter in the alphabet of our cultural vocabulary. The Indian is at the foundation of our verbal and imaginative language, not only in America, but in all ideas of the nation as well.

What is the Indian?

The term, which when used to refer to Native Americans today, is generally regarded as being in poor taste, since it arose from a basic misunderstanding of geography and ethnicity: in the late fifteenth century, European explorer Christopher Columbus mistook the islands of the Caribbean in the West Atlantic for the "West Indies" (that is, pertaining to India in Asia). As Europeans began to inhabit North America—the land of promise, the land of plenty, the land of new beginnings, dreams, and radical visions—the Indian came to signify a deep ambivalence toward civilization. America was not the heart of darkness for these European settlers, explorers, and entrepreneurs, but rather the domain of the noble savage, an intermediate state of being, between primitive and civilized, according to Jean-Jacques Rousseau.[9]

In 1853, Catlin's paintings of Native Americans were exhibited in London, much to the dismay of novelist Charles Dickens, who described them in a scathing review entitled "The Noble Savage":

> To come to the point at once, I beg to say that I have not the least belief in the Noble Savage. I consider him a prodigious nuisance, and

an enormous superstition. His calling rum fire-water, and me a pale face, wholly fail to reconcile me to him. I don't care what he calls me. I call him a savage, and I call a savage a something highly desirable to be civilized off the face of the earth [...] To conclude as I began. My position is, that if we have anything to learn from the Noble Savage, it is what to avoid. His virtues are a fable; his happiness is a delusion; his nobility, nonsense.[10]

Dickens's polemical response to Catlin's paintings reveals his distaste, not so much for the indigenous peoples of the Americas themselves (which he believed should be treated humanely), but rather for the romanticization of them by white Europeans in the face of industrialization. The nostalgic and aesthetic appreciation of native peoples living in a pre-industrial state in the visual arts and design of the mid-nineteenth century reflected an anti-industrial embrace of nature, the pastoral, and the agrarian. This romantic sentiment was especially politicized in French Realist paintings from around the time of the 1848–9 revolutions in Europe.

The relationship between white settlers and indigenous people in the Americas is defined by narratives of encounter, a term which means both "to meet unexpectedly," and "to meet in conflict."[11] Among the earliest stories of encounter were the discovery of the Americas populated by "naked savages," as recounted by Christopher Columbus during his voyages in the 1490s, and the tale of seventeenth-century native heroine Pocahontas. The first Thanksgiving meal in 1621, shared by Pilgrims at Plymouth with the indigenous Patuxet and Wampanoag peoples who had donated food to the starving colonists, is a tale often learned by American schoolchildren today. Meriwether Lewis and William Clark's accounts of the exploratory expedition to western America, in 1804, accompanied by their Shoshone guide, Sacagawea, built upon that romantic myth of friendly cooperation between white settlers and native peoples, but the many violent encounters that took place through much of the nineteenth century tell a different story. These powerful events include the brutal 1813 relocation of the Cherokee, Choctaw, Seminole, Muscogee (Creek), and Chickasaw Nations to the Indian Territory reservation in present-day Utah, along the Trail of Tears; the 1876 Battle of the Little Bighorn in the eastern Montana territory, which concluded with the death of U.S. Army General George Armstrong Custer, and the defeat of his army by the Lakota, Northern Cheyenne, and Arapaho peoples, including Lakota war leader Crazy Horse; and the bloody massacre of Lakota Sioux in 1890 at Wounded Knee, South Dakota, an event precipitated by the growing popularity of the Ghost Dance ceremony, a practice that combined visionary Christianity with indigenous resistance to white oppression. The killing of Sitting Bull prevented the Lakota holy man and former performer for Buffalo Bill's Wild West from supporting that resistance movement, and highlighted, instead, the settlers' ambivalent experience of "Indians" as both welcoming hosts and dangerous foes.

1. Parody of BP logo designed by Laurent Hunziker, 2010. Winner of Popular Choice in the Greenpeace UK Rebrand BP Competition. Reproduced with permission of the artist.

2. BP logo, redesigned by Raymond Loewy/Compagnie de l'Esthétique Industrielle, 1957. (www.RaymondLoewy.com)

3. Karlsplatz Stadtbahn Station, Vienna, designed by Otto Wagner, 1898. Detail of sunflower motif. Photo by author, 2009.

4. Poster designed for the West German Green Party (Die Grünen) election, 1979/80. Courtesy Museum für Kunst und Gewerbe Hamburg, Germany.

5. Blackfoot chief, illustrated by Rene Martin, for "I is for Indian," in Nancy Larrick and Rene Martin, *First ABC: An Educational Picture Book*, New York: Platt & Munk, Publishers, 1965. Reproduced with permission of Penguin Random House.

6. Embroidered patches with sports team logos. Clockwise from top right: Atlanta Braves, University of Illinois, Cleveland Indians, Chicago Blackhawks, Kansas City Chiefs, Boston Braves, Washington Redskins, Seattle Seahawks. Author's collection. Photo by author.

7. Map of the 2004 US Presidential Election Results by State. Copyright M. T. Gastern, C. R. Shalizi, and M. E. J. Newman. Creative Commons. https://creativecommons.org/licenses/by/2.0/

8. Map of the 2004 US Presidential Election Results by State. Population Cartogram made using the diffusion methods of Michael Gastner and Mark Newman. Copyright M. T. Gastern, C. R. Shalizi, and M. E. J. Newman. Creative Commons. https://creativecommons.org/licenses/by/2.0/

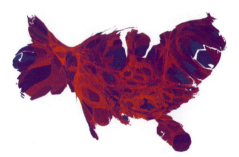

9. Map of the 2004 US Presidential Election Results by County. Population Cartogram made using the diffusion methods of Michael Gastner and Mark Newman. Copyright M. T. Gastern, C. R. Shalizi, and M. E. J. Newman. Creative Commons. https://creativecommons.org/licenses/by/2.0/

10. Shepard Fairey, *Barack Hussein Obama*. Hand-finished collage, stencil, and acrylic on heavy paper, 2008. Sheet: 175.3 × 115.6 cm (69 × 45 in). Copyright Shepard Fairey. National Portrait Gallery, Smithsonian Institution, Washington, D.C.

11. Nine-patch quilt, made by Margaret O'Leary, 2014. Hand-pieced cotton. 48.26 × 48.26 cm (19 × 19 in). Photo by Deborah O'Leary.

These early settlement, and later military, encounters between white Europeans and indigenous peoples in the Americas were followed at the end of the nineteenth century by the work of academic anthropologists and ethnographers, such as Frederic Ward Putnam and Franz Boas, who collected artifacts, and interviewed native informants, in order to better understand the development of human civilization, and to present such information to the public.[12]

By the early twentieth century, however, the revulsion toward the Native American as primitive, expressed so vividly by Dickens, had not disappeared, and the negative associations of the Indian as violent, savage, and uncivilized would now serve a different purpose, as a symbol of fierce determination and spirited competition for many sports teams in America. In part, because of Putnam and Boas's entertaining and scientific ethnographic exhibitions for the 1893 World's Columbian Exposition, held in Chicago, and viewed by thousands of spectators, the image of the Indian remained both romantic and frightening in the popular American imagination. The 1893 World's Columbian Exposition had been scheduled to open in 1892 in order to celebrate the 500-year anniversary of Christopher Columbus's arrival in the New World. As was the case with many world's fairs, however, the efforts to secure funding, to organize the event with various exhibiting nations, and to build display buildings took longer than expected. When it finally did open the exhibition was a sensation, featuring models of Columbus's ships, the Niña, the Pinta, and the Santa Maria, arriving in Chicago on the shores of Lake Michigan. Among the most sensational exhibits was the ethnographic department's staging of native dwellings, including a village of indigenous people from the Pacific Northwest, who performed a traditional Hamatsa dance, in which initiates in the Kwakwaka'wakw rite of passage simulated the cannibalistic eating of human flesh.

Brave, Chief, Warrior

There has been much controversy over the years about whether the use of Native American names, images, and personalities (historical or fictional) as mascots for schools and sports teams is appropriate.[13]

Among the earliest examples of such usage is that of the Boston Braves, the National League baseball team, which from 1912 used a logo on its uniforms featuring the profile image of a Native American with feathered headdress.[14] From 1953 to 1966, the team's later incarnation as the Milwaukee Braves and its manifestation as the Atlanta Braves, respectively, the logo took the form of a more expressively rendered Indian brave, featuring a fierce hairstyle and open mouth, we presume issuing a battle cry. Shortly thereafter, alternative logos of a single stylized feather and lone tomahawk were developed for that team.

Cleveland's American League baseball team was founded in 1901 as the Cleveland Bluebirds. It changed its name in 1915 to the Cleveland Indians, by some accounts, in honor of a former Penobscot Indian player on the team.[15] In 1928, the Cleveland Indians adopted as its trademark a profile image of a Native American in feathered headdress. Over the years this image evolved into the one currently used by the team – a distinctive caricature of the fictional mascot, Chief Wahoo, notable for its bright red skin and wide toothy grin. The Chicago Blackhawks (National Hockey League) and the Washington Redskins (National Football League), like the original Boston Braves, adopted stylized profile images of the Indian chief in feathered headdress in 1926 and 1937, respectively. Their team emblems represent the traditional "noble savage" rather than the "Indian" caricature adopted by the Cleveland Indians.[16]

A brief glance through several of the most prominent examples of Native American sports teams logos and mascots reveals a limited taxonomy of visual icons that signify in varying degree courage, valor, strength, tribal competition, masculinity, warfare, violence, humor, and carnivalesque impulse (see Plate 6).

There are at least four predominant types of logos used by sports teams and schools that make reference to Native American culture. These types include: the depiction of a Native American chief or warrior as "noble savage," usually with a stylized profile portrait that highlights key decorative features, such as plaited hair, face paint, or feathers; symbols of primitive weaponry, such as arrowheads, feathered spear, or tomahawk, used to signify the Native American in the abstract; depictions of specific Native American leaders or tribal peoples; and the depiction of the Native American as humorous or entertaining, which is sometimes presented as parody.

i   The generic "noble savage" in full, feathered headdress, or with plaited hair adorned with feathers, is often red, or illustrated as having red skin, and the silhouette features a sloping brow and prominent nose. Occasionally, the face is decorated with war paint or jewelry, as in the original logo for the Boston Braves, and in the ones currently used by the Chicago Blackhawks and Washington Redskins.

ii The second type is metonymic or synecdochic, in which the specific part, the weapon, represents the Native American more generally. These types of emblems are typically linked to team names that evoke battle and use the word "brave," "chief," or "warrior" as a part of the team name, as in the American NFL (National Football League) Kansas City Chiefs, a team that is signified by an arrowhead with interlocking KC (Kansas City) logo.

iii The third type, which identifies the team with a specific Native American tribe of local significance, can be illustrated by the Florida State University Seminoles and Central Michigan University Chippewas. Both teams are endorsed by the tribal leaders in their respective regions. Variations of this third type include the Chicago Blackhawks, named after Ma-ka-tai-me-she-kia-kiak, the eighteenth-century Chief Black Hawk of the Sauk tribe from the Great Lakes region; and the University of Illinois, whose recently retired team mascot, the fictional Chief Illiniwek, represented the Illini tribes native to the upper Mississippi River valley. (The logo of Chief Illiniwek varied from the standard profile image of the "noble savage," featuring instead a stylized frontal image of male Indian warrior in feathered headdress.) In some cases, these types are combined, as in the University of Illinois Fighting Illini, or the University of North Dakota Fighting Sioux, both of which conflate the image of Native American as inherently violent with that of authentic tribal peoples in the region.

iv Chief Wahoo is one example of the fourth, less common, type. The parodic representation of the humorous Native American sometimes renders the full body in dynamic motion rather than the isolated face or head. This more carnivalesque portrayal of the Native American is often affirmed by performances of the team mascot, such as Chief Illiniwek of the University of Illinois, or Chief Osceola of the Florida Seminoles, usually a student, but sometimes an indigenous tribesperson, dressed in native costume, who dances, parades, or gesticulates wildly as a form of entertainment and to generate fan enthusiasm at games.

The earlier Boston Braves logo, particularly after a more colorful version was introduced in 1929, differs in spirit from Martin's illustration of the Blackfoot chief in war bonnet (discussed earlier), although both ostensibly refer to the same idea. The logo, like Martin's illustration, relies not only on a naturalistic rendering of the bonnet itself, with plumes, headband, decorative trimming, worn over long plaited hair, but also on a particular physiognomic depiction of the Indian with sloped forehead, defined cheekbones, red skin, large nose, and scarred or decorated face. Whereas Martin's illustration is evocative and nostalgic, however, the Braves logo is devoid of emotional content. The physical characteristics of the Indian are easier to discern in profile, from which perspective they are also strikingly iconic. The profile silhouette serves to abstract the image of the Native American or Indian, translating him from a person into a sign. The sports logo, linear and schematic, is not romantic, but rather informative.

The reliance upon physical features as visual signifier dates to nineteenth-century anthropological studies of race.[17] Its usage in the sports logos, however, is complexly intertwined with the history of race-oriented performance, especially the minstrel show and blackface traditions that emerged before the American Civil War, and which persisted well into the twentieth century, where their legacy can be seen in early film animation.

One controversial animation of Native Americans is found in Walt Disney's 1953 adaptation of *Peter Pan*, based on the story by J. M. Barrie, in which Peter and the Lost Boys encounter a group of "native savages" in the forest. In the Disney version, the savages perform the musical number "What Makes a Red Man Red?," which reinforces a set of stereotypes, including a circle of dancing drummers around a fire, surrounding an imposing chief in feathered headdress, with arms folded across his chest. The chief orders the "squaw" (the white character, Wendy, in fringed buckskin dress) to gather firewood, while his daughter, the "Indian Princess," flirts romantically with Peter Pan. The chief utters "Ugg" and "How," while the drummers also sing a refrain describing the "Injun," and the rhythmic beat of the drums throbs to a melodic pentatonic scale. The Lost Boys dance around the fire circle while tapping their open mouths to utter percussive, yelping war whoops, including the phrase "Wahoo!"

Most striking in the film is the "Indians'" bright red skin, the visible physical evidence of the "red man's" difference. Although the first comical caricature of the Cleveland Indians' "Chief Wahoo" appeared a few years before Disney's *Peter Pan*, in 1946, its aesthetic clearly derives from that of the Disney animators who explored racial stereotypes in their cartoons extensively throughout the 1930s and 1940s, and who themselves were influenced by popular racist caricatures, especially of African Americans, dating back to the nineteenth century.[18]

Given the reprehensible history of ethnic stereotyping in America, which continues today with pointed attacks on the Mexican immigrant and the Arab or Muslim, the present-day socio-political focus of anxiety, it is not surprising that many have raised objections to the continued usage of such logos and mascots to represent sports teams.[19] But moving beyond such usage is no simple task. The controversy over the years has largely focused on whether such logos and mascots of Native Americans are "dignified" or not. Chief Illiniweck, for example, with his chiseled, stoic features, presumably represents the more respectful end of the spectrum, while Chief Wahoo represents the most ridiculous. Chief Wahoo, with his goofy appearance, draws upon racial stereotypes of the African American from the minstrelsy tradition, as much as he embodies notions of the Indian with bright red skin and feathered headdress. He emerges from a vast, and likely unconscious, database of diverse racial stereotypes. Although some traditional nations endorse the "respectful" usage of the Native American tribal name as mascot, it can also be argued that the adoption of a Native American tribe or person, regardless of its style of depiction, is inherently disrespectful, because it positions him as something less than human, like an object or animal. Chief Wahoo's persistence, despite the many thoughtful, rationalized, emotionally fraught, litigated examples of putting these sorts of mascots to rest (several teams previously used the name Savages, which is now largely rejected), indicates that he serves a necessary function as totem that keeps our tragic history of racial encounter and conflict actively present in our imagination, even while holding it at a safe and comfortable distance. At present the debate has been focused on the Washington Redskins, arguably among the least politically correct team names, but standing nevertheless for sports fans in the nation's capital. In a recent statement the team's owner defiantly pledged, "We'll never change the name. It's that simple. NEVER—you can use caps [capital letters]."[20]

How can we explain that the "respectful" Chief Illiniwek was decommissioned as a mascot in 2007, but that the "demeaning" Chief Wahoo still persists? Although certainly most Cleveland Indians' fans acknowledge the racist roots of the team logo, the image represents far more for them. Allegiance to one's local sports team, not only in the U.S. but also all around the world, is a powerful feeling and can be a source of deep rivalry, sometimes even erupting into violence. With its banners, pageantry, and dazzling uniforms, competitive sport serves as a localized version of the performance of national patriotism that is otherwise carried out in battle. The identification with a local team is deeply connected, for some, to a sense of personal identity and pride. One's team is "worth fighting for." For those who identify with a school sports team, that identification is furthermore connected to a formative period of development, during which youth find themselves, or individuate, to use more psychological language.

The symbolism of warfare, signified by the clash between cowboys and Indians, performed at Buffalo Bill's Wild West shows was ritualized into a routine that typically featured a reenactment of Custer's last stand, followed by an Indian attack on settlers' cabins. In the show's grand finale, Cody rode to the rescue of the settlers with his entourage of white cowboys. In sports competition, the ritual is reversed, with Native Americans as the triumphant warriors.

The identification of the Native American with warfare is ubiquitous in the U.S., and carries over to the usage of Native American tribal names for military helicopters, such as the Bell UH–1 Iroquois, the Boeing CH–47 Chinook, the Lockheed AH–56 Cheyenne, and the iconic Sikorsky UH–60 Black Hawk. The first U.S. Army helicopter that had a Native American name was the 1956 Korean War aircraft Bell H–13 Sioux (best known to audiences from the popular TV comedy M*A*S*H, 1972–83).

During the Korean War (1950–3), U.S. Army General Hamilton Howze, first Director of Army Aviation, felt that the helicopters needed tougher names than those typically given by the manufacturers, and so recommended the use of Native American tribal names for the aircraft as a general policy.[21] U.S. Army aviators were first trained in Fort Sill, Oklahoma, which had, since the 1860s, served as a prison for Native Americans captured in that century's Indian wars. (The Apache leader, Geronimo, who was captured and held at Fort Sill in 1894, inspired the U.S. Army paratroopers' tradition of yelling "Geronimo" as they jump from planes.) Though Howze's decision to use Native American tribal names for military aircraft may not have been directly related to the aviator training at historic Fort Still, it is none the less unsettling to note that the symbolic association of Native Americans with military warfare today was likely influenced by prior military conflict between the U.S. Army and Native Americans.

Less straightforward usages of Native American iconography as signifiers for virility and resistance are apparent in the adoption of the fierce mohawk hairstyle as a countercultural fashion statement of the punk movement in the 1970s. The hairstyle, which is actually derived from the Iroquois rather than the Mohawk people, is characterized by a ridge of hair running down the center of an otherwise completely shaved scalp. Because of the exposed scalp, as well as its generalized association with Native Americans, the hairstyle also evokes, in an oblique manner, the brutal practice of scalping, or removing the scalp as a war trophy, a practice that was not uncommon in the nineteenth century Americas. The hairstyle was likely appropriated by punk rockers because of its signification of pain and violence, as well as its shocking disruption of social conventions, much like ripped clothing and body piercings.[22]

Similarly complex and contradictory are the costumes of the New Orleans Mardi Gras Indians, whose masquerade tradition dates to the eighteenth century. Originally the Mardi Gras Indians were organized as neighborhood gangs (today called "clubs") of mixed race men who claimed both African and Native American ancestry. Their masquerade costumes even still today are decorated elaborately with feathers and beaded images of cowboys and Indians, drawn from popular culture. The purpose of the costume is to evoke the ancestral Native American as spirit guide. Though the original masquerades, which were organized as showy competitions between gangs, could at times be violent, today the parades, with leaders dressed in brightly colored garb, are opportunities to draw attention to an overlooked and underserved community.[23] Like the punk rockers of 1970s Britain, the New Orleans Mardi Gras Indians are admired for the unique combination of implied violence and ornament, which is symbolized by their fierce and decorative costumes.

Indian Princess

Let us return briefly to Larrick's text:

> I is for Indian, a tall stately Indian. This one is a chief of the Blackfoot tribe. The black-tipped feathers of his bonnet are from the tail of a golden eagle. They seem to flow back from his head. Today Blackfoot Indians live in Montana and nearby Canada.

This passage is loaded with reference, not just to the Noble Savage, as identified by his "tall and stately" appearance, and decorative, detailed war bonnet, but also to the identification of the Indian with native fauna and geography.

The descriptive phrases, "The black-tipped feathers of his bonnet are from the tail of a golden eagle. They seem to flow back from his head," recall the language of the costume album or fashion magazine. But the more matter-of-fact statement, "This one is a chief of the Blackfoot tribe ... Today Blackfoot Indians live in Montana and nearby Canada," recalls the rhetorical style of a field guide. Why Blackfoot? Why Montana and Canada? This is not just a generic Indian, we read, but is rather a species indigenous to western North America. Our tendency to read it as a "species," like a species of native plant or animal, results from the ethnographic and anthropological approach of the late nineteenth century which set out to classify and organize all beings, including human beings, within the context of natural and biological sciences.

The golden eagle (*Aquila chrysaetos*) was first described in the eighteenth century by Swedish biologist Carl Linnaeus, and is found in Europe, Asia, and Africa, though it is most populous in North America. A large and powerful bird of prey, it has a mythical and sacred status within many Native American belief systems. It is a dark brown raptor with a golden sheen around the neck and broad wings marked with a band of white and black tipped feathers. Naturalist John James Audubon painted the golden eagle for his portfolio, *The Birds of North America* (1840–4) (see Fig. 4.3).[24]

Audubon's "portraits" of North American birds require some mention within the context of nineteenth-century images of Native Americans. Both Audubon and Catlin frame the subjects of their paintings in a similar manner: they are excerpted, except for minimal, key hints of natural surroundings, and depicted in enlarged detail, focusing on their most decorative features. In Catlin's case, these are costume elements, including dress, jewelry, hair styles, face and body paint, and accessories uniquely worn by the native peoples portrayed; in Audubon's, feathers and colorful, identifiable markings of the birds, their eggs, or the plants they inhabit and feed upon appear. Beyond these features, each artist portrays his subject in a naturalistic, illustrative style, and composes a graceful harmonious arrangement of forms that imbues the image with a certain dignity that elicits reverence. The arms of Catlin's chief are folded quietly across his lap; the bodies and wings of Audubon's birds form linear arabesques.

It should come as no surprise that Catlin approached his illustrations of the native peoples of North America much like a naturalist. Catlin trained as a portrait painter, and channeled into his artwork his enthusiasm for Native Americans, whom he first encountered in unfamiliar and ornamental dress while he was a child in Pennsylvania. This experience mingled with the allure of stories told to him by his mother of her own

Fig. 4.3 Golden Eagle, *Aquila chrysaetos*. Female adult, Northern Hare. 1833. In John James Audubon, *The Birds of America*, 4 vols, London, 1827–38, vol. 2, pl. 181. Photo courtesy University of Pittsburgh.

capture by native tribes on the western frontier, as a young girl. Catlin's curiosity led him to travel westward across America, documenting various individuals, particularly native chiefs and their families. Audubon, a native of Haiti, followed his childhood interest in birds to pursue a career as self-taught ornithologist, and, like Catlin, traveled westward to document new and unfamiliar species. The accuracy of his drawings stems, in part, from the fact that he often hunted and collected the birds as specimens for close study.

It is possible to read Catlin's representations of Native American peoples like one reads Audubon's contemporaneous depictions of North American birds. Both men documented the surprising treasures of the New World, and implicitly warned of their extinction. I suggest that we can also find another gendered layer of meaning within the identification of native land as bird or savage: that is, its representation as female. Not only were Catlin and Audubon's depictions graceful, reverent, colorful, primitive, mysterious, and decorative; they were also, by extension, feminine. To understand this we must turn back to the many myths of encounter between European explorers and native peoples. One of the most suggestive is Columbus's assertion that the globe, newly assessed as a result of his voyage, must not be spherical as previously thought, but rather pear-shaped, and more specifically, that the New World resembled the nipple of a woman's breast.[25]

Jackson Lears and others have demonstrated that the New World was understood in terms of the fertility of its land, as well as in the erotic availability of its resources, mineral, vegetable, animal, and human. The image of America as a formidable Indian Queen, naked, muscular, and sometimes emasculating, Lears points out, was common as early as the sixteenth century. Later, the image was softened to that of a seductive Indian Princess, often depicted with naked breasts and wearing a skirt of wheat or corn.[26] The association of America as Indian with food is suggested in the story of Thanksgiving, with its cornucopia of plenty, as well as in food products such as Red Man chewing tobacco and Land O'Lakes butter. The original butter package, featuring an Indian maiden, was designed by Brown & Bigelow illustrator Arthur C. Hanson, in 1928. The logo was updated, in 1939, by Jess Betlach, and again in the 1950s, by Ojibwa artist Patrick DesJarlait. Notoriously, if one cuts little windows in the cardboard butter package, and folds it strategically, the appearance of the maiden's knees, seen through the open windows, transforms, erotically, into that of bare breasts.

The Indian Princess is an important motif, arguably as powerful, if not more so, than that of the Brave, Chief, or Warrior. She likely evolved from descriptions and images of Pocahontas, daughter of the local Chief Powhatan (and a "princess" in the eyes of the white settlers), which originated from the seventeeth century. According to lore, she halted the execution of captive colonist John Smith, founder of Jamestown, Virginia, by physically intervening with her body, and laying her head atop his so that he could not be put to death.[27] Central to the legend of Pocahontas is her baptism and conversion to Christianity upon her marriage to Virginia tobacco farmer John Rolfe, at which time she adopted the biblical name "Rebecca."[28] In other words, Pocahontas signifies the benevolent native, willing and available for both conversion and consumption. It is too simple, however, to see Pocahontas merely as the passive, submissive, or enabling native participant in the settling of North America by white Europeans. Today it is tempting to interpret her rather more complexly as the mother of a mixed race child, an ethnically blended new American who signifies the plural American identity.[29]

Sacagawea (1788–1812), a Shoshone girl, was enslaved by the Hidatsa tribe at age ten and purchased a few years later by her husband, French trapper Toussaint Charbonneau. Both Sacagawea and Charbonneau accompanied Lewis and Clark to the Pacific coast in 1804. In the story of Sacagawea, as in that of Pocahontas, the fact that she bore a son to a white man has particular meaning. Both girls were young, innocent, helpful, and fertile. Their romantic, consensual (we assume), sexual, procreative partnerships symbolize, or suggest the possibility of a peaceful and productive rather than violent encounter with "the Other." They resemble the archetype of the Virgin Mary, a young girl of humble background, who bears a son, and who, as a result, is imbued with divinity. The complex and powerful archetype represents not only the nurturing mother, but also the uncorrupted virgin, the woman as fertile field of creativity and fruit, and the attentive partner.

In addition to the images of Pocahontas and Sacagawea, the fictional Minnehaha, wife of Chief Hiawatha, described in Henry Wadsworth Longfellow's 1855 poem *Song of Hiawatha*, was influential in shaping the image of the desirable young Indian girl as a sign for romantic encounter, primitive past, nature, and peace. Illustrations of Minnehaha proliferated in the second half of the nineteenth century. Though fictional, these images were imbued with complex ideas of race and gender that continued to resonate in many public institutions for girls through the twentieth century.[30] In the 1950s, for example, the YMCA (Young Men's Christian Association) organized the Indian Princesses program for fathers and daughters. It was an offshoot of the YMCA's Indian Guides program for fathers and sons, which had been founded in 1926 to encourage parent–child bonding with activities such as camping, hunting, fishing, and learning about Native American heritage. The Indian Princesses program (which later became known as "Indian Maidens" and which exists today in various chapters as the "Adventure Guides") involved similar kinds of outdoor activities. It served to reinforce the imagined relationship between Native American communities and nature, combining it with notions of responsible womanhood and patriarchal familial structure.

The identification of earth with an archetypal female creative force, divinity, goddess, or sacred figure is found in many belief systems, such as the Navajo Changing Woman, Asdzaa nádleehé, and can be traced to ancient fertility cults as well as to classical antiquity.[31] Environmentalists in the 1960s and 1970s, including James Lovelock and Lynn Margulis, authors of the Gaia hypothesis described in Chapter 1, often described planet earth as a life-giving and nurturing entity with the procreative power of the female body.

Is there a more complex gendered aspect to the names of men's sports teams featuring Native American Indians (braves, chiefs, and warriors) as mascots? The identity of the virile and masculine warfaring Indian in this context is exaggerated by its contrast to the equally prominent association of the Indian with femininity, fertility, and peace. The carnivalesque impulse, made visible in the donning of war paint and performing as savage, suggests a ritual of reversal whereby the masculine sportsman is momentarily transformed by dressing in drag into the feminized Other.[32] The appearance of the Native American within the context of the male sports arena rehearses the structural pairing of masculine cowboy and feminine Indian central to the imagining of the Native American in wild west popular culture, including television, theater, film, and comics. The Indian, after all, wears a *war bonnet*, a strange linguistic conflation of masculine military uniform with a feature of feminine dress that is associated with the life of the pioneer woman on the western frontier. Women's sports teams in the U.S. tend not to adopt concrete mascots such as braves, chiefs, or warriors (or Indian Princesses), so much as abstract or environmental phenomena, as in the WNBA (Women's National Basketball Association) Atlanta Dream, Chicago Sky, Indiana Fever, and Tulsa Shock.

One of the most iconic images of the ecological Native American in popular culture is the Crying Indian who appeared in public service announcements denouncing litter on the interstate highways in the 1970s. Keep America Beautiful, a non-profit consortium dating to 1953, comprising business partners Philip Morris, Anheuser Busch, PepsiCo, and Coca Cola, launched the campaign on Earth Day, 1971. The poster announcement was composed of a three-quarter-length portrait of a Native American (with requisite plaited hair, jewelry, and buckskin tunic), a heart-rending tear running down his cheek, while he implores the viewer to keep America beautiful.[33] The wise, proud, and peaceful Indian, the embodiment of the Noble Savage, is saddened and disappointed by the disrespectful and irresponsible motorist, who sullies and destroys the land with garbage, unthinkingly, with no regard for the future. The image is a powerful one that evokes a need for preservation, conservation, and a recognition that the land is, in fact, not ours, but rather belongs to the Native American, from whom it has been violently and unjustly taken. The Crying Indian also became widely and frequently parodied in the subsequent decades, much in the way that Dickens had rejected as anti-progressive the romantic ideas of the Noble Savage in the nineteenth century.

"Indian Giver"

When I was a child in elementary school there was a popular urban legend that if one found a Tootsie Roll Pop candy wrapper with an image of an Indian on it, one could win a million dollars. More reasonable variations of this legend, which dates to the 1930s, include being able to win a free Tootsie Roll Pop, or perhaps a whole bag of them, by redeeming the wrapper. According to lore, the image of the Indian on the wrapper was very rare, and therefore valuable. Tootsie Roll Pop wrappers are cut from paper with a pattern of children engaged in various sports, such as riding bicycles, skateboards, or playing football. Each wrapper is slightly different. The Indian is actually an image of a child wearing a feathered headdress, shooting a bow and arrow, an image that appears on about a third of all Tootsie Roll Pop wrappers. The allure of the treasure hunt, like Willie Wonka's search for the golden ticket in a chocolate bar, was compelling for fourth graders on the playground. But this particular equation of the Indian with monetary value is not merely an anomalous child's game, whose other play stereotypes of the Indian include sitting "Indian style" (cross-legged) and issuing a war whoop by tapping the open mouth with the hand while making a loud, yelping cry. These games are related to a deeper cultural structure in which the Indian is a form of currency. His image appears quite literally on the buffalo nickel and hers on the more recent Sacagawea Golden Dollar coin (see Fig. 4.4).

The Indian buffalo nickel with the feathered head of a Native American in profile on one side and an image of an American bison on the reverse was designed in the early twentieth century by American sculptor James Earle Fraser and issued between 1913 and 1938, roughly contemporaneously with the popularity of the same type of icon in sports teams logos. Fraser provided several inconsistent stories about his influences for the design of the coin. The image of the Native American was likely based on an amalgam of several prominent models, including Dewey Beard (Wasu Maza), also known as the Minneconjou Lakota Chief Iron Hail, General Custer's opponent at the Battle of Little Big Horn; a chief named Two Moons; an individual named Two Guns White Calf, who was the son of the last Blackfoot tribal chief; a Kiowa chief; Sam Resurrection, a Choctaw; and John Big Tree, a Seneca Indian, and also a Native American Hollywood actor.[34]

Sculptor Glenna Goodacre designed the Golden Dollar coin, featuring the portrait of Sacagawea on its obverse, in 1999. Unlike Fraser's stoic profile of the Native American on the buffalo nickel, Goodacre's image is a three-quarter view of Sacagawea looking over her shoulder, with a sleeping baby strapped to her back. Goodacre, who was inducted in 2003 into the National Cowgirl Museum and Hall of Fame in Fort Worth, Texas, and who is also known for her design of the Vietnam Women's Memorial in

Fig. 4.4 Native American $1 Coin Obverse © 1999 United States Mint. All rights reserved. Used with permission.

Washington, D.C. (1993), describes herself as a figurative sculptor in the naturalist tradition. Her expressive pieces recall sculptures by French artists Edgar Degas and Pierre-Auguste Renoir in the late nineteenth century. No known images of Sacagawea were recorded during her lifetime, thus Goodacre decided to use as her model a young Shoshone woman, Randy'L He-dow Teton, whom she met at the Institute of American Indian Arts Museum in Santa Fe, New Mexico.[35] Goodacre's design, chosen from a competition organized by the U.S. Mint, represents a shift in twenty-first-century imaginings of the Native American, not as a stoic war chief who turns away from his audience, but rather as a self-assured woman, mother, and leader who looks us in the eye, as we pull her out of our pocket. The coin also represents a new era in which the work of women artists and designers such as Goodacre has a place in the national discourse of American identity.

On the one hand, Sacagawea's image on the coin signifies the westward expansion initiated by Lewis and Clark's journey, and implies that native peoples endorsed that expansion, in that she seems to have served willingly as their guide. On the other, her come hither look, self-assured as it may be, is likely derived from the older European iconography of the erotic and seductive "odalisque." This contemporary Sacagawea seduces the viewer not so much to the bedroom, as does the Indian princess in nineteenth-century academic paintings and sculptures, but more explicitly to the pleasures and treasures of the new land and its profits. This image also emerges in popular film portrayals of the sexually available Indian princess, from the young native girl in Walt Disney's 1953 animated *Peter Pan*, to the white woman gone native in actor–director Kevin Costner's *Dances With Wolves* (1990), to the more updated Disney production of *Pocahontas* (1995), and even to director Terrence Malick's *New World* (2005), in which Pocahontas is an erotic object of consumption, as much as she is a symbol of homage to the land and its people.

From their first encounter with them, Europeans attempted to profit from Native Americans, with whom they famously traded slaves, food, furs, firearms, beads, raw materials, livestock, sugar, alcohol, and disease. Even the ostensibly more scientific investigation of Native Americans by ethnographers such as Boas, and documentary photographers such as Curtis, were intertwined with the profitability of entertainment, and with business more generally. Boas's work with Putnam for the Peabody Museum and Smithsonian Institution was closely connected to the public educational entertainment of the world's fairs; financier J. P. Morgan sponsored Curtis's lavish portfolio of photographs. The barter system established by white settlers and Native Americans gave rise to the trading posts throughout the western frontier. These were important locations of contact and community, socialization and exchange of language as well as goods. One who changes his mind in this honor system of exchange and demands the return of his goods (once he realizes he's gotten a poor deal) has been called, pejoratively, an "Indian giver."

The idea of Indian as currency is also encoded within the American system of production and manufacture, from food products to automobiles. Tobacco and corn, New World crops, may seem to be logically signified by the image of the Native American in their packaging and marketing, but the association of them with the railroad, and later with automobiles, is less obvious. The railroads were constructed during the nineteenth-century period of industrialization, as a way to traverse the continent more easily and to transport its natural timber and mineral resources for manufacture. They followed from the exploration and westward settlement of the continent that began in the eighteenth century, and that is recounted in tales from Meriwether Lewis and William Clark's expedition of unknown territory in 1804–6, to writer Laura Ingalls Wilder and her family surviving the wilderness of the Midwestern prairie, as portrayed in her books.

Settlers were drawn to the west coast of North America, like the Spaniards before them, in search of gold. And while they traveled to look for treasure many found fortune not in glittering minerals extracted from the earth but rather in the construction of the railroad, with train lines such as the Ojibway, Mohawk, Big Chief, Arrowhead Limited, Chippewa, Choctaw Rocket, Hiawatha, Illini, Iroquois, Seminole, Shawnee, Sioux, Superchief, Southwestern Chief, or Tomahawk. The ubiquitous Native American tribal names lend the trains an air of authenticity. Like the indigenous peoples whom they are named after, the massive industrial vehicles traverse the continent with a deep and reassuring grasp of its geography and terrain. We can rest assured that, in traveling across the unfamiliar continent by rail, we can be as confident in our journey as had we been led by Native American guides.

Later the railroad was replaced by the manufacture of automobiles and system of interstate highways that snake across the continent. Cars with names like Pontiac and Jeep Cherokee explicitly connect the idea of technological bounty to the landscape itself, and signify the romantic, erotic, and destructive appropriation of land by Europeans. The fraught encounter is captured in the story of Spanish explorer Francisco Vasquez de Coronado's invasion in 1540 of the southwestern Pueblo territories. According to one account, a conquistador raped a Zuni woman; when Coronado refused to punish him, the local people retaliated by stealing the Spanish horses. The sexual violence of warfare was thus equated in this incident with the theft of valuable property used for transportation. Could the destructive intrusion of the modern, industrial railroad into the feminized native landscape of North America be seen in similar terms?

In 1997, the Syracuse Chiefs, a minor league baseball team in Syracuse, New York, changed their mascot from a Native American to a flying baseball bat with angry shark-like face; in 2007 the logo was transformed into a train engine. Though the updated team name, mascot, and logo ostensibly no longer offends its Native American heritage, its signification remains the same. The erotic consumption of the virgin landscape and fetishism of the masculine automobile or steam engine is replayed today in countless advertisements that feature a driver in a lone vehicle that speeds swiftly through a remote and sublime landscape of forest, mountains, and streams apparently untouched by human civilization.

One of the more troubling examples of this relationship between Native American and currency is in the establishment of casinos on the Native American reservations, where alcoholism, diabetes, unemployment, and economic depression are endemic among indigenous populations, and gambling is a problematic vice for many who participate in this form of exchange. Casinos represent the most irrational component of the American dream, the fantasy of immediate wealth. American casinos tend not to be glamorous places, however, and are most popular among the working classes who are willing to risk what little they have for the dream of lucky success. For these gamblers wealth will not likely come as a result of privilege, power, or even hard work. In fact it will likely not come at all, and yet this fact does not dissuade them from the pleasure of participating in the leisure, escape, and reckless abandon of money. The casinos today in many ways take advantage of their less powerful or disenfranchised users, just as did the early European encounters with native peoples.

The racist stereotype of the "Indian giver" describes a person who may demand back a gift that he has given, or demand back an article given in trade, when such exchange is found to be unsatisfactory. The person is then regarded as disingenuous, as one who does not fully understand the rules of civilized society, or who has a tendency towards dubious and unsanctioned forms of exchange—like that signified by the Tootsie Roll Pop on the playground. The practice of "scalping"—that is, reselling tickets to concerts or sporting events at greatly inflated prices to those who were not lucky or industrious enough to secure them in advance— is likewise a form of exchange that circumvents the rules. Scalpers can usually be found outside sports arenas, peddling their expensive wares for desperate fans hoping to see a game at the last minute. Among many Native American peoples, by contrast, an elaborate system of gift giving does exist, the most notable being the potlatch system of the Northwest coast, in which a family's wealth and status is demonstrated through the ceremonial giving away of goods. In the exchange between native people and European interloper, it is indeed the Indian who has given away his land, his artifacts, and in many cases his language, customs, lifestyle, and people.

Bird of Prey

The American Football team, the Seattle Seahawks, uses a logo that departs from the taxonomy of Indian sports icons described above. Instead, a bird of prey, the "seahawk," otherwise known as an osprey, is rendered in a style that recalls the predominant aesthetic of the Northwest Coast tribes, including the Kwakwaka'wakw, Haida, Coast Salish, Chinook, and Tlingit. It is a version of the stylized depictions of eagles, ravens, and thunderbirds, seen in carved and painted ceremonial masks by twentieth-century native artists such as Mungo Martin and Willie Seaweed, decorative wooden chests, totem poles, painted longhouse motifs, woven blankets, and more recently in a variety of tourist art, from paintings and sculptures, to prints and drawings (see Fig. 4.5).

The distinctive visual style of the Northwest Coast formline design is characterized by symbolic abstraction of iconic features, such as eye, bill, paw, claw, tail, fin, and feather.[36] Of all of the sports logos evoking Native Americans or indigenous culture today, the Seahawks' logo is perhaps the least controversial, and yet the most primitivist, in that it seeks not to emblematize an imagined personification of a Native American so much as

Fig. 4.5 Kwakwa̱ka'wakw transformation mask. Cedar. Late nineteenth–early twentieth century. HM5521, William P. Palmer II Collection, Hudson Museum, University of Maine.

to identify, shamanistically, with the aesthetic mode of the mythical world with which the Northwest Coast cultures are associated.

Although the Seahawks' logo itself dates only to the 1970s, its primitivist origins lie in the expressionistic and surrealist explorations of native Northwest Coast artifacts by anthropologists, artists, and writers in the late nineteenth and early twentieth centuries. Many, if not the majority of historical indigenous objects from the Northwest Coast today reside not in the Pacific Northwest, but rather in The Field Museum of Natural History in Chicago, The Peabody Museum of Archaeology and Ethnology at Harvard University, and the National Museum of the American Indian, with collections in New York and Washington, D.C. Claude Lévi-Strauss was among the many twentieth-century anthropologists influenced by Franz Boas, who had collected many of the Native American objects for the 1893 World's Columbian Exposition in Chicago. Lévi-Strauss later demonstrated his structural study of myth with an extended analysis of the Xwéxwé (Dzonokwa) masks used by the native peoples of British Columbia and Alaska.[37]

Of the many popular exhibits there was a Kwakiutl (Kwakwa̱ka'wakw) Indian Village organized by Boas with the help of his native informant, George Hunt. The birth of an adorable Inuit baby girl, Marie Ahnighito Peary, known as Miss Columbia, in the Eskimo Village likewise was a source of delight for the visitors to the fair, as were the enormous Northwest

Coast totem poles, cut from single old-growth trees, well over one hundred feet tall.

The indigenous peoples of the Northwest Pacific Coast are very different in appearance, attire, language, architecture, diet, ceremony, and lifestyle, from the tribes of the Midwestern plains, which had become the face of the American Indian by the late nineteenth century. Martin's Blackfoot war bonnet represents one manifestation of the Indian in our imagination, but the carved wooden totem pole, awe-inspiring in its sheer height, and covered with magical, mythical symbols of the animal world, represents another. Boas and Putnam, in fact, attempted to distance their own scientific work from the entertainment oriented Wild West shows by banning Buffalo Bill from participation at the 1893 World's Columbian Exposition, a restriction that Cody circumvented by simply setting his troupe up outside the official fair grounds. Despite the academic aspirations of Boas and Putnam, the anthropological exhibits of native peoples in 1893 were likely experienced as carnivalesque attractions at the fair, just like the camels in the streets of Cairo, erotic belly dancers, and German beer halls along the Midway. These sorts of events were sanctioned inside the fairgrounds while the unofficial sideshow entertainment of cowboys and Indians carried on outside.

Children's books are often overlooked, and yet their significance to our cultural development is profound. Texts such as Larrick's *First ABC* are formative for young people learning to communicate through both word and image. When questioned about their personal ethnic heritage, a popular preoccupation for Americans, many will answer in terms of proportion, such as, "I am one quarter Irish, two-thirds Italian, and three-fifths German." Frequently, these fractions do not add up to a whole, and often tossed into the mix is a vague assertion of Native American ancestry as well, as in, "My great, great grandmother was Cherokee." Americans invariably imagine themselves as an amalgamation of something else. Postcolonial theorists would argue that both colonizer and colonized remain forever changed by their mutual fraught encounter.[38] And so, perhaps, the American "I" will always be part Indian.

Notes

1   Nancy Larrick, *First ABC. An Educational Picture Book*, illustrated by René Martin (New York: Platt & Munk Publishers, 1959), 30–1.

2   Roland Barthes, *The Fashion System* (1967), trans. Matthew Ward and Richard Howard (Berkeley: University of California Press, 1990), 3.

3   The illustrations by Richard Scarry in Ole Risom's *I am a Bunny* (New York: A Golden Book, 1963), featuring naturalistic, identifiable depictions of butterflies, birds, fall leaves, and spring flowers, are similar to the work he did for the Golden Books field guides for children.

4 George Gurney and Therese Thau Heyman (eds), *George Catlin and His Indian Gallery* (exh. cat., Washington, DC: Smithsonian Museum of American Art, 2002); Thomas Loraine McKenney and James Hall (eds), *History of the Indian Tribes of North America*, with color lithographic illustrations from original paintings by Charles Bird King, 3 vols (Philadelphia: Edward C. Biddle, 1836–44).

5 Bryan F. LeBeau, *Currier & Ives: America Imagined* (Washington, DC: Smithsonian Institution Press, 2001).

6 Louis S. Warren, *Buffalo Bill's America: William Cody and the Wild West Show* (New York: Alfred A. Knopf, 2005); William Cody, "The Great West That Was: Buffalo Bill's Life Story," *Hearst's International Magazine*, published in serial form from August 1916 to July 1917.

7 The photograph, first published in 1890, is attributed to the Italian photo studio of Vuillemenot Montabone, Rome, available online: http://commons. wikimedia.org/wiki/File:Buffalo_Bills_Wild_West_Show,_1890.jpg (accessed June 11, 2015).

8 Edward Curtis, *The North American Indian; being a series of volumes picturing and describing the Indians of the United States and Alaska*, 20 vols (Cambridge: The University Press, 1907–30).

9 The idea of the "noble savage" is frequently attributed to Rousseau, although the term may have been used first in John Dryden's seventeenth-century play *Conquest of Granada* (1672) by the character of a Christian prince, disguised as a Muslim, to refer to himself. Ter Ellingson, *The Myth of the Noble Savage* (Berkeley: University of California Press, 2001), 390. The concept of man existing in a state of nature dates to classical antiquity; however, it was during the Enlightenment period of the seventeenth and eighteenth centuries that thinkers from Denis Diderot and Thomas Hobbes to Benjamin Franklin, provoked by the accounts of explorers and their encounters with unfamiliar peoples, began to discuss the morality of the savage in relationship to the civilized. See Benjamin Franklin, "Remarks Concerning The Savages Of North-America," in Benjamin Franklin, *The Bagatelles from Passy*, ed. Claude A. Lopez (New York: Eakins Press, 1967); Hoxie Neale Fairchild, *The Noble Savage. A Study in Romantic Naturalism* (1928; reprint, New York: Russell and Russell, 1961); Steven A. LeBlanc and Katherine E. Register, *Constant Battles. The Myth of the Peaceful, Noble Savage* (New York: St. Martin's Press, 2003); Jean-Jacques Rousseau, "Discourse on the Origin of Inequality" (1754), in Jean Jacques Rousseau, *The First and Second Discourses Together With the Replies to Critics and Essay on the Origin of Languages*, ed. and trans. Victor Gourevitch (New York: Harper and Row, 1986), 117–238; and Arthur O. Lovejoy, "The Supposed Primitivism of Rousseau's Discourse on Inequality," *Modern Philology* 21/2 (November 1923): 165–86, reprinted in Arthur O. Lovejoy, *Essays in the History of Ideas* (1948; reprint, Baltimore: Johns Hopkins University Press, 1960).

10 Charles Dickens, "The Noble Savage," *Household Words* 7/168 (June 11, 1853): 337–9. See also Grace Moore, "Reappraising Dickens's 'Noble Savage'," *The Dickensian* 98/458 (2002): 236–43.

11 Warren Sears Nickerson, *Early Encounters. Native Americans and Europeans in New England. From the Papers of W. Sears Nickerson*, ed. Delores Bird Carpenter (East Lansing: Michigan State University Press, 1994), 1.

12 George W. Stocking, Jr., *Race, Culture and Evolution. Essays in the History of Anthropology* (New York: The Free Press, 1968); George W. Stocking, Jr., *Objects and Others. Essays on Museums and Material Culture* (Madison: University of Wisconsin Press, 1985). See also Anthony Pagden, *The Fall of Natural Man. The American Indian and the Origins of Comparative Ethnology* (Cambridge: Cambridge University Press, 1982).

13 S. L. Price, "The Indian Wars," *Sports Illustrated* (March 4, 2002): 68–72. The article with provocative subtitle, "The campaign against Indian nicknames and mascots presumes that they offend Native Americans—but do they? We took a poll, and you won't believe the results," elicited much criticism. See C. Richard King, Ellen Staurowsky, Lawrence Baca, Laurel R. Davis, and Cornel Pewewardy, "Of Polls and Race Prejudice: *Sports Illustrated*'s Errant 'Indian Wars'," *Journal of Sport and Social Issues* 26/4 (November 2002): 381–402.

14 The team was founded in 1871 with the name Boston Red Stockings. In 1912, it changed its name to the Braves. Many of the sports logos discussed in this chapter can be seen on Chris Creamer's Sports Logos [website], available online: http://www.sportslogos.net/ (accessed August 31, 2014).

15 Before its American League team was established in 1901, Cleveland's professional baseball team, which dated to the late 1860s, was known variously as the Forest Citys [sic], the Bluebirds (or Blues), and the Spiders.

16 The Washington Redskins was founded as the Boston Braves in 1932 and known as the Boston Redskins from 1933–6.

17 Sander Gilman, *Difference and Pathology: Stereotypes of Sexuality, Race, and Madness* (Ithaca, NY: Cornell University Press, 1985).

18 The animators for Walt Disney studios in the 1950s included Les Clark, Marc Davis, Ollie Johnston, Milt Kahl, Ward Kimball, Eric Larson, Jon Lounsbery, Wolfgang Reitheman, and Frank Thomas. For more on race in the American film industry, see Michael Rogin, *Blackface, White Noise: Jewish Immigrants in the Hollywood Melting Pot* (Berkeley: University of California Press, 1998). John Strausbaugh writes that MGM (Metro-Goldwyn-Mayer) studios featured widespread racial stereotypes in films before the Second World War. See John Strausbaugh, *Black Like You. Blackface, Whiteface, Insult and Imitation in American Popular Culture* (New York: Penguin, 2006), 240.

19 The anxiety surrounding Mexican immigration and Islamic or Arab communities in the United States today has intensified in recent years. Such anxiety is especially prominent in political discourse. Republican party candidates for presidency in 2015, for example, frequently dwell on this topic in public statements and debates. Front-running Republican party candidate Donald Trump also started a firestorm of media commentary, with his statement that Mexican immigrants to the United States are "criminals" and "rapists." Close behind Trump in popularity in prospective voter poles,

Republican party candidate Ben Carson stated that he would not support a Muslim as President of the United States. Donald Trump, "Full Text: Donald Trump Announces a Presidential Bid," *Washington Post* online (June 16, 2015), available online: https://www.washingtonpost.com/news/post-politics/wp/2015/06/16/full-text-donald-trump-announces-a-presidential-bid/ (accessed October 24, 2015); Jonathan Martin, "Without Calming Voice, G.O.P. is Letting Divisive Ones Speak on Muslims," *New York Times* online, September 21, 2015, available online: http://www.nytimes.com/2015/09/22/us/politics/without-calming-voice-ben-carson-gop-is-letting-divisive-ones-speak-on-muslims.html (accessed October 24, 2015).

20 "Dan Snyder: Redskins Name Will Never Change," *Huffington Post* (May 9, 2013), available online: http://www.huffingtonpost.com/2013/05/09/dan-snyder-redskins-name-change_n_3248542.html (accessed August 31, 2014). (*The Huffington Post* cites reporting that day by Erik Brady in *USA Today*.) In June 2014, the U.S. Patent and Trademark Office ruled that the Washington Redskins could no longer own the name as a trademark, which according to federal law is not allowed if it belittles other groups. Though the ruling does not prevent the NFL from continuing to use the logo or name, the organization is not protected from other companies who can now produce counterfeit merchandise with the team's name. It seems only a matter of time before the name will be officially retired. Gregory Karp and Robert Channick, "Redskins Lose Name Trademark," *Chicago Tribune* (June 19, 2014), Section 1, 1, 10.

21 Crispin Burke, "Everyone Relax—The Army's Native American Helicopter Names Are Not Racist. There's a difference between honor and exploitation," War is Boring [weblog], available online: https://medium.com/war-is-boring/everyone-relax-the-armys-native-american-helicopter-names-are-not-racist-d21beb55d782 (accessed June 11, 2015).

22 Though Dick Hebdige wrote in 1979 that it was still "too early to provide any comprehensive or confident evaluation of exisiting accounts of the punk subculture," he wrote extensively about youth appropriation of "revolting style." See Dick Hebdige, *Subculture: The Meaning of Style* (London: Routledge, 1979), 106–12.

23 George Lipsitz, "Mardi Gras Indians: Carnival and Counter-Narrative in Black New Orleans," *Cultural Critique* 10, Popular Narrative, Popular Images (Autumn 1988): 99–121.

24 John James Audubon, *The Birds of North America. From Drawings Made in the United States and Their Territories*, 7 vols (Philadelphia: J. B. Chavallier, 1840–4).

25 "Third Voyage of Columbus," in Christopher Columbus, *Four Voyages to the New World: Letters and Selected Documents*, ed. and trans. R. H. Major (New York: Corinth Books, 1961), 130, 131, 135, 137. Recounted in Jackson Lears, *Fables of Abundance. A Cultural History of Advertising in America* (New York: Basic Books, 1994), 27–8.

26 Lears, *Fables of Abundance*, 28–9, 36. See also Clare Le Corbeiller, "Miss America and Her Sisters: Personification of the Four Parts of the World," *Bulletin of the Metropolitan Museum of Art* 19 new series, (1961): 209–23;

E. McClung Fleming, "The American Image as Indian Princess, 1765–1783," *Winterthur Portfolio* 2 (1965): 65–9.

27   William Watson Waldron, *Pocahontas, Princess of Virginia, and Other Poems* (New York: Dean and Trevett, 1841); Grace Steele Woodward, *Pocahontas. Biography of a Young Powhatan Indian Princess* (Norman, OK: University of Oklahoma Press, 1969); Walt Disney pictures, *Pocahontas* (1995); and *The New World* (2005), directed by Terrence Malik.

28   *Baptism of Pocahontas* (1839) by artist John Gadsby Chapman hangs on the wall of the United States Capitol building rotunda alongside depictions of George Washington, the Pilgrims, Christopher Columbus, and the Declaration of Independence. The story of Pocahontas is thus clearly among the central symbols of American government.

29   Some prominent Americans claim to be descended from Pocahontas, including Edith White Bolling Galt Wilson, second wife of U.S. President Woodrow Wilson, and Nancy Reagan, wife of former U.S. President Ronald Reagan.

30   Henry Wadsworth Longfellow, "Song of Hiawatha" (1855), in *Poems and Other Writings*, ed. J. D. McClatchy (New York: Literary Classics of the United States, 2000), 141–279. An 1868 portrait bust of Minnehaha by African American sculptor Edmonia Lewis may be seen within the broader context of neoclassical sculpture that rehearsed ideas of America as eroticized Indian Princess by Hiram Powers and others. See, for example, Hiram Powers's sculpture, *The Last of the Tribes*, 1877.

31   On Changing Woman, see Gladys A. Reichard, *Navaho Religion: A Study of Symbolism* (Princeton: Princeton University Press, 1950, 1977), 13–25.

32   Mikhail Bakhtin, *Rabelais and His World*, trans. Hélène Iswolsky (1968; Bloomington: Indiana University Press, 1984). See also Marjorie Garber, *Vested Interests: Cross-Dressing and Cultural Anxiety* (New York: Routledge, 1992).

33   Actor Iron Eyes Cody played the Crying Indian. Cody enjoyed a long career performing Native American roles, though his own ethnic heritage is disputed. He claimed to be of Cherokee–Cree ancestry, while others believe that Cody, originally named Oscar DeCorti, was from an Italian–American Louisiana family. Iron Eyes Cody and Perry Collin, *Iron Eyes: My Life as a Hollywood Indian* (New York: Everest House, 1982). See also Gretchen M. Bataille and Charles L. P. Silet (eds), *The Pretend Indians. Images of Native Americans in the Movies* (Ames, IO: Iowa State University Press, 1980).

34   Walter Breen, *Walter Breen's Complete Encyclopedia of U.S. and Colonial Coins* (New York: Doubleday, 1988), 256; Roger W. Burdette, *Renaissance of American Coinage, 1909–1915* (Great Falls, VA: Seneca Mill Press, 2007), 219.

35   Thomas Fields-Meyer, "No Small Change. Glenna Goodacre Coins a New Phase in Funds: the Sacagawea Dollar," *People Magazine* 51/22 (June 14, 1999): 137.

36   Bill Holm, *Northwest Coast Indian Art: An Analysis of Form* (Seattle: University of Washington Press, 1965).

37   Claude Lévi-Strauss, "The Structural Study of Myth" (1955), in *Structural Anthropology,* trans. Claire Jacobson and Brooke Grundfest Schoepf (New York: Basic Books, 1961), 207–31; Claude Lévi-Strauss, *The Way of the Masks*, trans. Sylvia Modelski (Seattle: University of Washington Press, 1975).

38 Homi K. Bhabha, "The Other Question: Difference, Discrimination and
    the Discourse of Colonialism," in Russell Ferguson, Martha Gever, Trinh
    T. Minh-ha, and Cornel West (eds), *Out There: Marginalization and
    Contemporary Culture* (New York: The New Museum of Contemporary Art,
    1990), 71–88.

CHAPTER FIVE

The False Mirror

Uncanny New Media

The distinctive Eyemark used by the American television network CBS (Columbia Broadcasting System) is considered by designers and design historians alike to be an exemplary symbol of corporate identity, reflecting the "corporate virtues of economy, efficiency, adaptability, and recognizability."[1] Designed in 1951 by CBS Creative Director, William Golden, the encircled almond shape resembles a stylized human eye (see Fig. 5.1).

Its iconic simplicity, clarity, and legibility are characteristic of the mid-century corporate design style. But these rational interpretations of the CBS trademark do not fully explain its effectiveness and longevity, which result as much from its unconscious associations as from its economy of form. The eye is less a propagandistic demand than a provocative invitation with an aura of the magical, which, Golden reports, he was inspired to design after reading a story about Shaker simplicity and hex signs, talismanic symbols painted on barns in Pennsylvania Dutch communities in eastern Pennsylvania (see Fig. 5.2).[2]

An Eye for an Eye

In Golden's initial version of the design, the eye floats in the foreground of a cloud-filled sky. It recalls René Magritte's evocative 1929 painting, *The False Mirror*, which likewise isolates and magnifies a single human eyeball, the iris of which is a blue sky, interrupted by soft white clouds (see Fig. 5.3).

It is possible that Golden would have known this painting. In 1936, Magritte's work was exhibited at the Julian Levy Gallery in New York, an important venue for the promotion of Surrealism, which had exhibited the work of Max Ernst, Salvador Dalí, Marcel Duchamp, and others. Golden was employed at the time at *House & Garden* magazine, produced by Condé Nast publications in New York, where he apprenticed with art

Fig. 5.1 William Golden, logo for CBS television, original on-screen design, 1951. Published by permission of CBS Broadcasting Inc.

director Mehmed Fehmy Agha, and where he met his future wife, Austrian–American designer Cipe Pineles.

Anne Umland, curator of the 2013 Magritte retrospective at the Museum of Modern Art in New York, writes that the painting "seems to insinuate limits to the authority of optical vision: a mirror provides a mechanical reflection, but the eye is selective and subjective." Magritte's friend and collaborator, the Belgian surrealist poet Paul Nougé, chose the painting's title. Umland continues, "Magritte's single eye functions on multiple enigmatic levels: the viewer both looks through it, as through a window, and is looked at by it, thus seeing and being seen simultaneously."

From 1933 to 1936 Levy's friend, the surrealist photographer Man Ray, owned *The False Mirror*. In a 1933 letter to the Belgian surrealist writer E. L. T. Mesens, Man Ray wrote: "Tell Rene Magritte that I'm delighted he wants a photograph of mine, and I await with great curiosity the drawing he is sending me. His 'eye of the sky' is hanging in my apartment, and it sees many things! For once, a picture sees as much as it is seen itself."[3]

Magritte's paintings, like those of his surrealist contemporaries, evoke odd and disconcerting dream worlds. He began his career as a commercial artist in Belgium in the 1920s, and became friends with André Breton, leader of the Surrealist circle in Paris. While there, Magritte produced some of his best known works, including *The Treachery of Images* (1928–9), an

Fig. 5.2 Sarah Bates, Untitled (Shaker Inspirational Drawing), c. 1840–60, pen and brush and colored inks over graphite on paper, 38.4 × 53.2 cm (15⅛ × 20¹⁵⁄₁₆ in). Philadelphia Museum of Art, Gift of Mr. and Mrs. Julius Ziegert, 1963.

Fig. 5.3 René Magritte, *The False Mirror,* Le Perreux-sur-Marne, 1928, oil on canvas, 54 × 80.9 cm (21¼ × 31⅞ in). Museum of Modern Art, New York, MoMA 133.1936. © C. Herscovici / Artists Rights Society (ARS), New York.

illusionistic image of a pipe, like a tobacco store signboard, with the cheeky, perplexing caption, "Ceci n'est pas une pipe" (This is not a pipe). Like Dalí, Magritte later fell out of favor with Breton, who had little patience for commercial art, and for whom illusionistic, painted representations seemed less authentic than the immediate manifestation of the unconscious he attributed to automatism. By contrast, as Rosalind Krauss has demonstrated, Breton favored the realism of the photograph itself, which for him was more akin to the indexical marks of automatic drawing than the illusionism of painting.[4]

Throughout the 1930s both Dalí and Magritte produced commercial illustrations and advertisements, a medium that surely contributed to the strangeness of their compositions, which evoke the world of commerce, with its jarring disjunctions of fantasy and reality, as much as they do the depths of the unconscious, mapped by Sigmund Freud.

Alexey Brodovitch, art director of *Portfolio* (the short-lived graphic design journal that purportedly inspired Golden to design his eye) and of the prominent fashion magazine, *Harper's Bazaar*, was an important facilitator of Surrealism during that period, as was Dr. Agha, artistic director for *Vogue* and *Vanity Fair*; both were émigrés from the former Russian Empire. Under the direction of editor Carmel Snow at *Harper's Bazaar*, Brodovitch collaborated with photographers Man Ray and Martin Munkácsi to produce cinematic layouts that combined ghostly photographs with dynamic type in kinetic essays, which unfolded over time as the reader turned the pages of the magazine.[5] Over the years Brodovitch also worked with renowned photographers Irving Penn, Richard Avedon, and Hiro, shaping the direction of not only fashion photography, but also fashion itself. Salvador Dalí was a frequent contributor to *Vogue*. His commercial work may have led him to be shunned by the more literary Surrealists, but his orbit of celebrity, which included such well-known and glamorous figures as the Surrealist Italian fashion designer, Else Schiaparelli, kept him at the front of the art world. Jean Carlu, A. M. Cassandre, and Erté were among the European artists recruited to enliven the stylish ladies' magazines with modernist photography, illustration, and graphic design. Cassandre illustrated giant eyes on several covers of *Harper's Bazaar* in the late 1930s, which recall similar images produced by Surrealist photographers and painters during the period. His October 1938 cover in particular recalls the fetishistic photographs taken by Man Ray of his partner Lee Miller's eyes and lips between 1928 and 1932.[6]

Both Brodovitch and Agha understood the fashion magazine as an expression of modern sensibility with rapid, urban energy.[7] Drawn to fantasy, the new art directors at the cutting edge were frustrated with the signature Bauhaus style that they felt had come to be unthinkingly overused. Agha disparaged the formulaic, rectangular stamp of modernity at a 45-degree angle. By contrast, the lively integration of diverse avant-garde approaches in *Vogue* and *Harper's Bazaar*, from Bauhaus, De Stijl, and Constructivism to Surrealism, made the magazines into laboratories for modernist design.

The Surrealists, like the avant-garde artists connected to the Dada and Constructivist movements that preceded them, were particularly interested in the possibilities of new media, especially photography and film, which seemed to possess something of the supernatural. Experimental photographers in the late nineteenth and early twentieth centuries attempted to capture on film the physical presence of spirit matter, which would have been invisible to the naked eye.

Holding séances and documenting images of "ectoplasm" in the ether, their photographs gave way to even more enticing film experiments that provided a portal into the fourth dimension, time.[8] Dada artist Hans Richter's film *Ghosts Before Breakfast* (1928) is a humorous example that features unexpected effects, including characters that vanish into thin air as they round a light post. Salvador Dalí and Luis Buñuel's film *Un Chien Andalou* (1929) is a more sophisticated exploration of the uncanny, drawn from Sigmund Freud's studies that so captivated them.[9]

In 1924, French poet André Breton published his first "Manifesto of Surrealism," a project that coincided with the translation of Freud's *Interpretation of Dreams* into French the following year.[10] Breton, building upon the term's first use by the proto-surrealist French poet Guillaume Apollinaire, defined *sur-realité* as a contradictory state that gave rise to new and unexpected associations.[11] For Breton the phrase described a heightened state of being, simultaneously conscious and unconscious, in which two distinct realities converge.

The most memorable image in *Un Chien Andalou* is the film's opening scene in which a man who appears to be a barber (played by Luis Buñuel) sharpens a razor and proceeds to slice through the eyeball of a young woman. The woman, played by Simone Mareuil, stares straight ahead while Buñuel holds her eye wide open. In a series of alternating film cuts, the vitreous humor that oozes from Mareuil's eye is equated with the clouds that pass across the moon in the night sky, much as they do across Magritte's eye of *The False Mirror*, painted that same year. The film's narrative is fragmented and irrational with shocking, disconcerting, and comically absurd scenes that hint at the erotic and violent impulses, which, Freud believed, were submerged in the unconscious, and which revealed themselves in the nonlinear, compressed, and fragmentary narratives of dreams.

Freud described the "uncanny" in his 1919 essay of that name as an experience of something both familiar and unfamiliar, which can be frightening and disorienting. It is an effect that is produced "when the distinction between imagination and reality is effaced."[12] Wax dolls can be uncanny, as can automata and epileptic seizures, both of which lend the impression of automatic processes at work behind the ordinary appearance of mental activity. The word *heimlich* (of the home) in German describes something familiar and agreeable, as well as that which is concealed and kept out of sight. *Unheimlich* (in its adjective form), or *das Unheimliche* (the uncanny, as Freud described it, in its nominative form), by contrast describes what ought to have remained secret and hidden, but which has come to light. Hidden parts of the body, such as private sexual parts, can be either *heimlich* or *unheimlich*. The uncanny (*das Unheimliche*) is something that is secretly familiar (*heimlich*), but which "has undergone repression and then returned from it."[13]

Central to Freud's understanding of the uncanny was the German Romantic writer E. T. A. Hoffmann's 1816 fable, "The Sand-Man." The tale's protagonist, Nathaniel, learns from his nurse that the Sand-Man is:

> a wicked man who comes when children won't go to bed, and throws handfuls of sand in their eyes so that they jump out of the heads all bleeding. Then he puts the eyes in a sack and carries them off to the half-moon to feed his children. They sit up there in their nest, and their beaks are hooked like owls' beaks, and they use them to peck up naughty boys' and girls' eyes with.[14]

In Freud's interpretation of the story, Nathaniel's experience of the uncanny is "directly attached to the figure of the Sand-Man, that is, to the idea of being robbed of one's eyes." Freud explains:

> We know from psycho-analytic experience, however, that the fear of damaging or losing one's eyes is a terrible one in children. Many adults retain their apprehensiveness in this respect, and no physical injury is so much dreaded by them as an injury to the eye. We are accustomed to say, too, that we will treasure a thing as the apple of our eye. A study of dreams, phantasies and myths has taught us that anxiety about one's eyes, the fear of going blind, is often enough a substitute for the dread of being castrated. The self-blinding of the mythical criminal, Oedipus, was simply a mitigated form of the punishment of castration – the only punishment that was adequate for him by the *lex talionis* [an eye for an eye].[15]

Freud finds evidence for the centrality of the myth of Oedipus, and its related castration anxiety, in the fact that Nathaniel's encounter with the Sand-Man, who threatens to destroy his eyes, always coincides with the destruction or frustration of his love relationships in the story. The events involving the Sand-Man are also intimately connected to the death of Nathaniel's father.[16]

For Freud, the experience of the uncanny was wide-ranging, and included the narcissistic experience of "the double" as represented through reflections in mirrors, shadows, and the encountering of one's doppelgänger, as well as the dread of the "evil eye," in which is feared a secret intention of and power for doing harm, as well as the blurring of boundaries between life and death. What would be uncanny to us in life, however, Freud explains, such as the sudden opening of Snow White's eyes in the familiar fairytale by the Brothers Grimm, we are willing to accept in art and literature in a suspended state of disbelief, because we know that a story is already unreal.

Apple of My Eye

The isolated, fetishized eye is a key feature in the innovative title sequence designed by Saul Bass for the beginning of director Alfred Hitchcock's 1958 film *Vertigo*, a story, like "The Sand Man," of love and obsession.[17]

The film opens with a close-up view of a woman's lips (those of lead actress Kim Novak); the camera pans slowly upward over her face to focus on her eyes, and comes to rest more closely still upon her right eye. The words on screen emerge from the depths of her pupil, which transforms into a spiraling graphic design that spins slowly throughout the opening sequence.

Set to a jarring, mysterious soundtrack, the abstract, mathematically-generated form resembles a dilating and contracting pupil, which recedes again into the woman's real eye as the final opening credit, "Directed by Alfred Hitchcock," appears on screen. Bass's title sequence sets the mood for the psychological thriller, which explores several of Freud's richest ideas, including neurotic phobia (the fear of heights and sensation of vertigo experienced by detective John "Scottie" Ferguson, played by actor James Stewart); obsession; the uncanny (as experienced through the double character Madeleine/Judy played by Novak); and the fetish (manifested through lingering views of Novak's spiraling knot of blonde hair, jewelry, grey suit, and fragments of her face—lips and eyes). Though it was produced several years later than Golden's design for CBS, *Vertigo* similarly draws upon a surrealist iconography of the eye.

Bass was trained as a commercial artist in New York, where he studied at Brooklyn College with Hungarian artist György Kepes, who introduced him to the experiments of the European avant-garde, new cinema, and innovative design. Kepes immigrated to the United States in 1937 to teach at the New Bauhaus in Chicago, founded that year by his fellow Hungarian émigré, László Moholy-Nagy. Kepes's influential 1944 book, *Language of Vision*, established a theory of universal design based on Gestalt psychology, a theory of perception in which it is believed that the human mind considers objects in their entirety before, or simultaneously with, its perception of their individual parts. The theory, which dates to German studies of philosophy and psychology in the late nineteenth century, asserts that international visual communication outside of verbal language structures is possible.[18] Kepes's writings set the stage for a number of subsequent publications in the 1940s, including Paul Rand, *Thoughts on*

Design (1946), László Moholy-Nagy, *Vision in Motion* (1947), and Rudolf Arnheim, *Art and Visual Perception* (1954). It was from this context, in addition to the Surrealist milieu, that both Golden's eye design for CBS and Bass's title sequence for *Vertigo* emerged.

Paul Rand (born Peretz Rosenbaum) likewise absorbed the work of European designers during his training as a commercial artist at the Pratt Institute, Parsons The New School for Design, and The Arts Students League of New York. He began his career in the 1930s at *Apparel Arts* (the predecessor to *GQ*) and subsequently took a position as artistic director at *Esquire–Coronet* magazines.

Before he established his reputation as a designer of memorable corporate identities, including those for IBM, ABC television, and Westinghouse Electric, Rand had become known in the 1940s for his expressive cover designs for *Direction* magazine. The white cover of the December 1940 issue appears to be wrapped in barbed wire and sprinkled with droplets of blood, an image that can be read ambiguously as both ornamental Christmas package and *memento mori*.[19] The wire "crucifix," as Rand described it, is multivalent—a feature of Rand's work that was noticed by Moholy-Nagy, who described Rand as both idealist and realist, conversant in "the language of the poet and the business man ... He is able to analyze his problems but his fantasy is boundless."[20]

It may seem logical at first to align the mid-century modernist designs of Paul Rand and others, including Chermayeff and Geismar, and Unimark, cofounded by Massimo Vignelli, with a rational, anti-ornamental aesthetic. The Swiss or International Typographic style that became popular in the 1950s and 1960s did emerge from scientific and sociological theories of visual communication in the first half of the twentieth century, from the industrial world of the machine, Gestalt psychology, and logical positivism, theories that eschewed fantasy, decoration, and the feminine. From this point of view it is easy to understand the modernists' rejection of a postmodern aesthetic and ideology in the late twentieth century. But though Massimo Vignelli and Paul Rand may have bristled at such an interpretation, it is clear that fantasy was still very much at work in their mid-century modernist designs, a fact that Moholy-Nagy noticed right away in Paul Rand's covers for *Direction* magazine, and that is even more evident in the work of Saul Bass, who was more directly engaged with film. We remember Bass & Associates' graphics for the logos of Continental Airlines, Bell Telephone, and the Girl Scouts of America, and Paul Rand's striated IBM logo, not only because we can perceive them in Gestalt, but also because they activate our unconscious.

Rand, who disapproved of postmodern "eclecticism, historicism, and activism," warned against the seductiveness of postmodern theory, but his own visually elegant designs, like Golden's eye, are also tantalizing and seductive.[21] The CBS Eyemark, which Golden felt was so evocative because it suggested the television network "seeing the world around us," also signifies our uneasy pleasure in news media that reports sensationally on celebrity and tragedy. The eye symbol anticipated the new format of "eyewitness news" that emerged in the 1960s, in which news coverage began to rely increasingly on visual material, such as film footage and live reports from the field.[22] This tendency dramatically increased beginning in the 1980s with the introduction of 24-hour international cable and satellite television stations, which provided continuous, live visual coverage of dramatic world events, such as the protests in Tiananmen Square, Beijing, and the fall of the Berlin Wall, both in 1989, and the first Gulf War in 1990–1. CNN (Cable Network News), first launched in 1980, today uses a variety of marvelous special effects, from three-dimensional maps to simulations and holograms, which evoke the *Society of the Spectacle*, described in 1967 by Guy Debord.[23]

Artist Andy Warhol captured well the erotic violence of news photography in his silkscreened paintings, with enlarged, repeated images of car crashes and screen idols. Just weeks after Marilyn Monroe's tragic death in August 1962, Warhol painted the actress. In a series of canvases, including the *Marilyn Diptych* and *Gold Marilyn Monroe*, Warhol replicated her image from a set of publicity stills from the 1953 film *Niagara*. Such images reflect our tendency to worship visual manifestations of celebrity, but also, as Warhol's serial paintings reveal, our numbness to the visual, which results from our desensitization to the sheer number of images we see. Just as a word begins to lose its meaning when spoken quickly many times over, signifiers become detached from that which they signify in Warhol's work. Labels of Campbell's soup cans, like Marilyn's red lips, blue eyelids, and blonde hair, are free-floating. Though Warhol's paintings converse directly with print photographs, which he took from newspapers and magazines, they also deal implicitly with film and television, newer forms of mass media through which such images likewise circulated in the 1960s.

The erotics of looking and being looked at, suggested by Golden's television eye, were of course present throughout the history of modern print culture, and of painting before that. Man Ray captured this sensation in his 1933 photograph, *Veiled Erotic*, a portrait of artist Meret Oppenheim, standing nude and smeared with ink, leaning against a printing press, which suggests something explicitly sexual about the medium of print itself. The sensual pleasure of looking or being looked at through a camera is evident, for example, in erotic postcards, one of the earliest uses of the new medium of photography in the nineteenth century. But such pleasure is elevated and heightened in the glossy fashion magazines of the 1930s, which indulged fantasy in their rich juxtapositions and evocative photographs as well as in the tactile sensation of turning the paper pages. The fashion magazine's stimulation of desire is similar to erotica in this respect.

The Shock of the New

New media is inherently disconcerting and alienating, because it is unfamiliar. German psychiatrist Ernst Jentsch, whose 1906 essay, "On the Psychology of the Uncanny," provided the foundation for Freud's later study of the topic, found that we often "incorporate the new and the unusual with mistrust, unease and even hostility."[24] Television, like print, photography, and film, the new media that preceded it, is uncanny because it mystifies the technology of its reproductive mechanism and appears natural. In 1951 television was still a relatively new medium, having evolved from innovations in radio communication and electronics at the end of the nineteenth century. The earliest experiments with what would become television technology date to the 1880s, when Thomas Edison discovered a way to record moving visual images on photosensitive film around a rotating drum, and when German inventor Paul Gottlieb Nipkow developed a perforated rotating disk that could be used to scan images.

While Edison's "kinetograph" led to the development of the movie camera in the 1890s, Nipkow's disk (which the young student devised because he longed to see a picture of his mother over the Christmas holiday) was not fully exploited for another generation.[25]

Several individuals, working independently in the 1920s, attempted to transmit visual images by using versions of the Nipkow disk to scan an image, line by line, translating it into points of light, which could be projected onto a photoelectric cell located behind it. The cell then converted the light into electrical voltages that corresponded to varying degrees of brightness in the picture. As the electrical information was projected back again through a second rotating disk, the image was recreated. Scottish inventor John Logie Baird used a mechanical process by which he shone light through the surface of the rotating disk to record a moving image, which he was then able to save on wax cylinders. The first image captured on Baird's "televisor" was a ghostly, grainy human face (the face of Baird's business partner who happened to be in the office) that seemed to shift in and out of its scan lines. Baird demonstrated the process to a fascinated public at Selfridge's London department store in 1925. Around the same time the American Philo Farnsworth, the Germans Max Dieckmann and Rudolf Hell, and the Russian–American Vladimir Zworykin, each developed similar methods for transmitting images by sending an electronic impulse through a cathode-ray tube to a central receiving station. The station would then send the electronic signals into the air via radio waves, where individual television antennas within the transmission range could receive them and recreate the image. Farnsworth called his version an "image dissector." Zworykin's was the "iconoscope."[26]

What exactly is television? Is it a kind of radio? Is it a movie? Is it science fiction? How does it work? With its photoelectrons, magnetic fields, selenium cells, and cathode-ray tubes, television in the early 1950s was like something from another planet; something aliens might use to invade us as they beamed down into our livings rooms from their flying saucers. Even the smooth, rounded shape of the first television sets in the medium's early days were prescient of the future space age. Though all media were at one time new, Lev Manovich writes, that which we call "new media" today is something that can be described mathematically and is subject to algorithmic manipulation. New media, he explains, synthesizes two nineteenth-century developments: computing, which began with Charles Babbage's invention of the Analytic Engine in 1833, and photography, which began with the first daguerreotypes produced by Louis Daguerre in 1839.[27]

But many of the aesthetic characteristics of new media, Manovich points out, such as its use of layering and collage, and even its "database" form, were already present in early film.[28] In the inventive 1929 film, *Man With a Movie Camera*, for example, Dziga Vertov equates the camera with the human eye of the cameraman. Vertov (the Russian filmmaker's pseudonym for Denis Arkadievitch Kaufman) used superimposed imagery, as well as quick film cuts that alternated between the camera lens/eye and that which the lens/eye sees, with shifting focus and intermittent close-ups of the mechanical lens opening and closing. The film's evocative isolation of the single open eye is similar to the famous scene from Dalí and Buñel's film *Un Chien Andalou*, as well as Magritte's painting *The False Mirror*, both of which were also produced in 1929. The Surrealists' explorations of the unconscious in painting, illustration, photography, and film coincided with the experiments of the Russian and German avant-garde in the 1920s, studies in the techniques of photography, film, and graphic design, which Moholy-Nagy described as the "new vision" of twentieth-century technologies.[29]

In 1964, Saul Bass and his wife, Elaine, produced the film *The Searching Eye* for the Eastman Kodak pavilion at that year's New York World's Fair. Like Vertov's *Man With a Movie Camera*, the film equated the eye of the camera with the human eye, a window onto the external world, as opposed to the Surrealist eye, a window into the unconscious. Golden's eye is rather the "silent eye" of the television camera, "an electronic eye that has no moving parts, and that can see in the dimmest light."[30]

Canadian intellectual Herbert Marshall McLuhan called the media "extensions of man." Just as the wheel is an extension of the foot, the book an extension of the eye, and clothing an extension of the skin, he wrote, so, too, is electrical circuitry an extension of the central nervous system.[31] McLuhan, writing about communication theory in the late 1960s, understood that television, as a new medium, moved beyond the sense of sight to produce a more immersive, multi-sensory, non-linear, and indeed more primitive experience, which he believed was closer to the "acoustic" world of classical antiquity than to the visual world of the enlightenment.

"Television completes the cycle of the human sensorium," he wrote. "With the omnipresent ear and the moving eye, we have abolished writing, the specialized acoustic-visual metaphor that established the dynamics of Western civilization."[32]

Today, the mechanical eye has extended yet further. Envisioned in the 2002 film, *Minority Report*, directed by Steven Spielberg (based on a short story by sci-fi writer Philip K. Dick), is a future dominated by individually tailored advertising and government surveillance, in which the eye plays a central role, that eerily foreshadows the use of personally-directed advertisements on the Internet, and even the not quite perfected invention of Google Glass.

"No good can come of it"

The word "television" was coined in 1900 by Russian scientist Constantin Perskyi, in a paper that he presented to the First International Congress of Electricity, at the Paris Exposition universelle. The word combined the Greek *tele-* (far) with the Latin *vision* (sight). In 1921, C. P. Scott, British journalist and editor of the *Manchester Guardian*, wrote, tongue in cheek: "Television? The word is half Greek and half Latin. No good can come of it."[33]

Indeed, when television was first introduced to the public in the 1920s, some viewers were wary and anxious that the BBC (British Broadcasting Corporation) would be able to see them from the television sets in their living rooms, as if the apparatus were a human eye. One woman, rather anticipating the ominous telescreen of writer George Orwell's dystopian 1949 novel of the future, *1984*, worried that the television might have X-ray-like vision that could see through her walls into the bathroom.[34]

Beyond the public's immediate anxiety about the disconcerting mechanical–electrical processes of television intruding into the most intimate parts of their private lives, many critics also worried about the longer-term effects of the new medium upon viewers. Frankfurt School theorists Max Horkheimer and Theodor Adorno criticized television, "a synthesis of radio and film," for its potential to drive the "culture industry" to new heights.[35] Like Hollywood film and popular music, television, they believed, would be used to reinforce the formulaic clichés of entertainment. Mass culture, the antithesis of avant-garde, when numbed by entertainment, they wrote, is eager to consume and easy to control. "Real life," they warned, "is becoming indistinguishable from the movies."[36]

Writing in 1944, Adorno and Horkheimer were keenly aware of the dangers of television as a tool of propaganda used by the Nazi Third Reich in Germany. Television debuted there with a public broadcast of the 1936 Olympic games in Berlin under the supervision of Joseph Goebbels,

Minister of Public Enlightenment and Propaganda under Adolf Hitler. Walter Benjamin also observed the close relationship between fascism, mass movements, and the reproductive technologies of photography and film.[37]

In the United States, early television was dominated by RCA (Radio Corporation of America), organized post-1918 through a collaboration between General Electric, the U.S. government, and numerous other companies that had been involved with radio production, broadcast, and electronic telecommunications during the First World War, including Westinghouse Electric and AT&T (American Telephone and Telegraph Company). RCA gained early control of television technology as well when its general manager, savvy and powerful businessman David Sarnoff, acquired the patent for Zworykin's iconoscope in 1936. Zworykin developed the technology, while working as a research engineer at Westinghouse Electric, during which time, according to some accounts, he was sent to the west coast by Sarnoff to spy on Philo Farnsworth, who was simultaneously developing similar technology. The clouded origins of television in corporate espionage, which remain disputed to this day, only added to the mystique of the new technology as a mechanism for secret spying.

Television was first introduced to the American public in 1939 when RCA broadcast the dedication of its pavilion at the New York World's Fair. RCA's broadcast division, NBC (National Broadcasting Company), would also be the first network to introduce color television to the public in 1951, beating out its competitor CBS, which had devised a less practical system.

CBS's color television broadcasts required special, more expensive color television sets for display whereas NBC developed a compatible technology for receiving color television broadcasts on black-and-white sets. NBC art director John J. Graham designed the company's peacock trademark, introduced in 1956, to emphasize the richness in color of the new medium. With eleven rainbow-colored feathers, the stylized peacock drew on associations of luxury, exoticism, and pride—an appropriate image for the powerful media empire. At the same time the image cleverly resembled a colorful painter's palette, the tips of its wings like paint-filled brushes. The new trademark, with radiating feathers, was also similar in composition to NBC's original 1920s trademark, in which streaks of electricity radiated from a circular radio receiver, and unconsciously demonstrated the transition from radio to television, from the acoustic to the visual.

While Sarnoff dominated the radio and television broadcasting industry, William Paley, wealthy heir to a family cigar business, built CBS, from his fashionable NBC building at 30 Rockefeller Plaza. A worldly, well-traveled, and sophisticated art collector, who served on the New York Museum of Modern Art's Board of Trustees, Paley surrounded himself with a creative, innovative staff with "good taste." In 1934, Paley hired American modern architect William Lescaze to develop new radio studios for the company with attention to acoustics, style, and signage. Lescaze's designs, according to Dennis Doordan, were more technologically and stylistically progressive than the suite of art deco buildings designed by Raymond Hood for John D. Rockefeller, Jr., in midtown Manhattan.[38]

CBS's Los Angeles studio was designed, in 1951, by William Pereira and Charles Luckman. The new New York headquarters was built in the mid-1960s by Eero Saarinen, during which period Paley also hired the innovative graphic designer Lou Dorfsman to work on multiple projects, from CBS advertisements and the interior of the building to the appearance of the news anchors on screen.

Before that, concepts man Paul Kesten, followed by Frank Stanton, President of CBS, shaped the direction of the company. Stanton was responsible for adopting Golden's eye design. The CBS trademark first aired in 1951, during station identification breaks between programs. Despite the attribution of the logo to Golden, alternate origin stories emerged over the years, which traced the onscreen graphic not to Golden, but rather to the CBS design executive Georg Olden. Olden's name may have been easy to confuse with that of Golden when he signed his name with first initial only: "G. Olden."[39] Olden was the first African American to achieve a place of prominence in the world of American design. His career began with his unexpected success in a previously exclusively white profession on the cusp of the Civil Rights Movement. In 1963, he was commissioned to design a U.S. postage stamp celebrating the centennial of the Emancipation Proclamation. His career ended, by contrast, in relative anonymity, financial loss, and a humiliating defeat in a racial discrimination lawsuit against the world-renowned McCann Erickson advertisement agency, from which he was let go only three years after being hired as its vice president.

The award-winning Eyemark was almost certainly designed by the auspiciously named William Golden, whose name suggests brilliance and wealth, rooted in the mythical triumph of striking or winning gold, a triumph that was realized by his professional success. But the misattribution of the CBS eye design seemed plausible, since the division of onscreen graphics was actually Olden's domain at that time. The confusion may have arisen from the fact that Olden had designed several title cards for programs that aired concurrently with the introduction of the new logo.[40]

ABC (American Broadcasting Company) entered the field to become television's third largest competitor in the United States in 1944. Its well-known circular logo, designed by Paul Rand, was not introduced until 1962. Rand's design, which was used in both color and black-and-white versions, employed a letterform modeled on Herbert Bayer's universal alphabet, developed at the Bauhaus in 1925.

In the animated color version of Rand's logo, the looping circular forms of the letters dance across the screen to resolve in an arrangement of red, green, and blue, alluding to the new technology of the color television, which used filters to produce three superimposed images in different hues.

In 1939, the FCC (Federal Communications Commission) had forced RCA to sell one of its two NBC broadcasting divisions, NBC Red and

NBC Blue, to prevent its monopolization of the market. RCA elected to keep its flagship network, NBC Red, which was the home of its more upscale programming and strong sponsorship. It sold NBC Blue, a network for lower-market sponsorship and more experimental public service programming, to financier Edward John Noble, under whose leadership it was renamed ABC (American Broadcasting Company) in 1944.

Although ABC remained in third place among the top television news networks in the United States, it made significant leaps into entertainment programming, especially for children, partnering with Disney in the 1950s, when it aired the *Mickey Mouse Club*, and in the 1960s, when it broadcast several popular cartoons, including *The Flintstones*, *The Jetsons*, *Bugs Bunny*, and *Looney Tunes*. In 1959, after CBS turned down the crime drama series, *The Untouchables*, due to its violent content, ABC was happy to add it to its growing list of programming, which included by then the soap opera *General Hospital*, the detective series *The Fugitive*, and ABC's signature program *Wide World of Sports*. Though the content of the two channels' programming is more homogenous today, it seems that in television's first decades CBS identified as a high-style network, noted for its contemporary graphics and architecture, whereas ABC led the way with popular and children's programming. Could the original station's reputation also account for the longevity and enduring appeal of the iconic CBS Eyemark?

Rand's cheerful abc signifies less the ominous and all-knowing eye of news media, with its connotations of voyeurism and surveillance, than the happy world of childhood—a children's abc. By the 1960s the television set was not so much the uncanny eye of Orwell's Big Brother as an entertaining box of delights to absorb the eyes and minds of viewers. It was a completely successful alien invasion.

Seeing is Believing

Electrical information was for McLuhan both exciting and menacing, with great potential for revolutionary change as well as the threat of "tyrannical womb-to-tomb surveillance." Children today, he wrote, live "mythically and in depth," no longer constrained by the rational, visual world, in which they are told not to believe what they hear, and where wise men are referred to as "visionaries."[41] But, in 1951, public perception of television or electronic media had not yet reached that moment. Golden's Eyemark dispelled any confusion about television's mystifying technology, or notion of it as the product of eccentric tinkerers, and reassured its viewers of the continuing authority of the visual. It reminds us too, more troublingly, of the authority of the tightly coordinated interests of government, media, and telecommunication. CBS has evolved immeasurably since 1951, yet the Eyemark is still a powerful symbol of its corporate identity. Indeed it has taken on new meanings, or rather, its original signification has become magnified.

The single, open eye, which was so fascinating for the avant-garde of the 1920s, is an image that has been used historically in many cultures to signify omniscience. The ancient Egyptian Eye of Horus, the sky god, is one of the most familiar versions. Often used as an amulet, the Egyptian symbol was believed to have protective, healing, and restorative qualities, as well as the power to ward off evil. The all-seeing eye, or Eye of Providence, when used in a Christian context, is often framed by a triangle and surrounded by clouds or rays of light, symbolizing the celestial aspect of the Holy Trinity. One of the best-known versions appears on the reverse of the Great Seal of the United States, the nation's official emblem, designed in 1776, and codified in 1782, and also appears on the back of the one-dollar bill. When Golden noticed the Shaker eye design in the first issue of *Portfolio*, he likely associated its magical content with the much broader range of talismanic, official, technological, and Surrealistic meanings embodied in the symbol.

Like Magritte's "eye of the sky," as Man Ray called it, Golden's Eyemark can be interpreted in two ways: as representing both the omniscience of the new medium, which sees all; and as the eye of the spectator that watches the images as they float across the screen, beamed from the exterior public world into the interior private space of one's living room. It is both an apparatus of surveillance, and a secret keyhole through which we voyeuristically watch the world. We are ever more concerned with voyeurism and surveillance today. Indeed, we can be, and often are, watched through the cameras in our Orwellian telescreens and by the GPS (Global Positioning System) in our cellular telephones. We know that others may invade our privacy or even steal our identities, and that larger forces beyond our control, like the government's intelligence apparatus, can intrusively record our activities or watch us secretly.[42] At the same time, we are anxious that we are volunteering too much information about ourselves, freely giving away our privacy with social media activities and online financial transactions. We worry about the safety of our children who naively navigate about this new world of voyeurism and surveillance.

And yet, there is also a narcissistic pleasure in imagining that someone else might want to look at us, that we may be important enough to be surveilled, or that someone should want to know the details of our private identities. We become the stars of our own movies. This narcissistic symptom of the surveillance culture was evident in the popularity of television "reality" shows at the turn of the twenty-first century, programs in which we watch a day in the life of a game show contestant, aspiring performer, ordinary family, or celebrity chef, following the minutiae of their banal activities and emotions with the rapt fascination we would bring to a carnival side-show. There is an erotic, exhibitionist element as well—the secret desire that one's most intimate activities will be available for all to see (hence the prominent motif of the revealed nude photographs or sex tape in contemporary culture). Social media networking sites like Facebook, in which one stages one's identity for public view, fuel the narcissistic pleasure of exhibition.

Jacques Lacan explored the work of Sigmund Freud, as well as that of the Surrealists, in France in the 1920s and 1930s, reinterpreting many of Freud's psychoanalytic principles. Among his many influential theories that would later shape analysis of film and photography in the later twentieth century was his concept of the "mirror stage," which he first presented in a paper to the Congress of the International Psychoanalytic Association in 1936.[43] An infant between the ages of six and eighteen months, he noted, will begin to recognize his own reflection in the mirror. More specifically he will recognize the image as separate from himself, as other. But even as adults, as Sherry Turkle writes: "We come to see ourselves differently as we catch sight of our images in the mirror of the machine."[44]

We are confronted with reflections of ourselves as we gaze into our screens—the screen of the cinema, upon which our unconscious is projected, the screens of our televisions, on which our worlds are beamed back at us, and the computer screen in which we see reflected our very movements as we touch it. Far beyond the reflection of our faces in the mirror, we see ourselves reflected in our online identities, our social media profiles in which those identities are constructed and performed. Are these mirrors false? Are surfaces deceptive? Are we easily misled by appearances?

The Eyemark remains a powerful symbol today, but it no longer refers just to television—the original analog medium. More broadly, it signifies CBS digital channels, websites, and our increasing intimacy with this world of new media. The complexity and depth of visual media—a long century of innovation in photography and film, followed by the introduction of television—is made simple in the icon, which insinuates the continued centrality of vision and privileging of visual information as the most important form of communication. The proliferation of television programming in the age of the Internet has given rise to some new genres and has elevated some forms of drama, satire, and documentary, but for the most part, as Horkheimer and Adorno predicted, television entertainment relies upon formulaic clichés, replicating its most popular and profitable shows with minute variations ad infinitum, such that it can be possible to find "nothing worth watching" from among hundreds of channels. More and more, we stream stored content, watching it on our computers and other electronic devices.

Is the CBS Eyemark a talisman to ward off evil, or is it in fact the evil eye? As we enter the storm of cloud computing—the storage of data on massive external servers—perhaps it is not the eye that is the most suggestive part of Golden's original design, but rather the cloud-filled sky. What do the clouds signify? With the introduction of computers over the course of the past generation, our materials have become more and more ethereal. We no longer write on paper, nor capture images on film, but rather generate media electronically. Now we do not even retain the content of this media, which exists as memory, but rather send it into the air, the "cloud," where it is overseen by powerful giants of the telecommunication industry. Media no longer lives on earth, in the world of three dimensions, but rather in the air. Or does it? As the cloud grows, massive data centers (on the earth) search for more sustainable sources for the increasingly large amounts of energy they need to run.[45] While the term "cloud" was chosen for its descriptive element, suggesting ethereality, vaporousness, and an expansive calm, can't it also signify the great plumes of carbon pollution emitted from gargantuan data servers around the world, the byproduct of our greedy, narcissistic desire for ever quicker data and media to be at our fingertips? If the cloud signifies something of our future, might it not be useful at this point to ask a simple question: Does this cloud have a silver lining?

Notes

1   Dennis Doordan, "Design at CBS," *Design Issues* 6/2 (Spring 1990): 4–17.

2   "The Gift to Be Simple," *Portfolio*, 1/1 (1950), unpaginated. You can also view the entire issue, edited by Frank Zachary and Alexey Brodovitch, online at http://www.designers-books.com/portfolio–1-frank-zachary–1950-usa/ (accessed June 13, 2015).

3   "Selections from 'Magritte: The Mystery of the Ordinary, 1926–1938'," New York Museum of Modern Art [exhibition website] (2013), available online: http://www.moma.org/interactives/exhibitions/2013/magritte/#/additional/5/1 (accessed July 4, 2014); See also Anne Umland (ed.), *Magritte: The Mystery of the Ordinary, 1926–1938* (exh. cat., New York: Museum of Modern Art, 2013).

4   Rosalind Krauss, "Photographic Conditions of Surrealism," in *The Originality of the Avant-Garde and Other Modernist Myths* (Cambridge, MA: MIT Press, 1985), 87–118.

5   See, for example, Beatrice Mathieu, "Paris 1935," with photography by Man Ray and layout design by Alexey Brodovitch, *Harper's Bazaar* (September 1934), pages reproduced in Philip B. Meggs and Alston W. Purvis, *Meggs' History of Graphic Design* (fourth edition, Hoboken, NJ: John Wiley & Sons, 2006), 340.

6   See, for example, A. M. Cassandre's covers for the October 1938, September 1939, and October 1939 issues of *Harper's Bazaar*; Terence Pepper and Marina Warner (eds), *Man Ray Portraits* (exh. cat., London: National Portrait Gallery, 2013).

7   Alexey Brodovitch, "What Pleases the Modern Man?" in Michael Bierut, Jessica Helfand, Steven Heller, and Rick Poynor (eds), *Looking Closer 3: Classic Writings on Graphic Design* (New York: Allworth Press, 1999), 50–2, originally published in *Commercial Art* (August 1930); M. F. Agha, "What

Makes a Magazine 'Modern'?" in Bierut et al. (eds), *Looking Closer 3*, 53–5, originally published in *Advertising Arts* (October 1930).

8 Tatiana Kontou and Sarah Willburn (eds), *The Ashgate Research Companion to Nineteenth-Century Spiritualism and the Occult* (Farnham: Ashgate Publishers, 2012).

9 Briony Fer, "Surrealism, Myth and Psychoanalysis," in Briony Fer, David Batchelor, and Paul Wood, *Realism, Rationalism, Surrealism: Art Between the Wars* (New Haven: Yale University Press, 1993), 171–249.

10 Sigmund Freud, *La rêve et son interpretation*, trans. Hélène Legros (Paris: Gallimard, 1925). The original version was first published in Vienna in 1900.

11 André Breton, "Manifesto of Surrealism" (1924), in *Manifestoes of Surrealism*, trans. Richard Seaver and Helen R. Lane (Ann Arbor: University of Michigan Press, 1972), 1–47.

12 Sigmund Freud, "The 'Uncanny'" (1919), in *The Standard Edition of the Compete Psychological Works of Sigmund Freud*, trans. James Strachey, 24 vols (London: The Hogarth Press, 1953–74, 1995), vol. 17, 217–56.

13 Freud, "The 'Uncanny'," 245.

14 Freud, "The 'Uncanny'," 228.

15 Freud, "The 'Uncanny'," 231. *Lex talionis*, the law of retribution, or the principle of an "eye for and eye," is drawn from Exodus 21:24.

16 Freud discussed the ancient Greek myth of Oedipus Rex in the context of "typical dreams," in "The Interpretation of Dreams" (First Part) (1900), in *The Standard Edition*, vol. 4, 261–4.

17 Pat Kirkham, "Reassessing the Saul Bass and Alfred Hitchcock Collaboration," *West 86th* 18/1 (Spring–Summer 2011): 50–85; Jennifer Bass and Pat Kirkham, *Saul Bass: A Life in Film and Design* (London: Laurence King Publishing, 2011). See also Laura Mulvey, "Visual Pleasure and Narrative Cinema," *Screen* 16/3 (1975): 6–18; Kriss Ravetto-Biagioli, "*Vertigo* and the Vertiginous History of Film Theory," *Camera Obscura: Feminism, Culture, and Media Studies* 25/3 (issue 75) (2011): 101–41.

18 Ellen Lupton and Abbott Miller, *Design Writing Research: Writing on Graphic Design* (London: Phaidon, 1996), 62–5.

19 Meggs and Purvis, *Meggs' History of Graphic Design*, 374.

20 László Moholy-Nagy, quoted in Steven Heller, "Thoughts on Rand," *Print* 51/3 (May–June 1997): 106–9.

21 Paul Rand, "Confusion and Chaos: The Seduction of Contemporary Graphic Design," in Steven Heller and Maria Finamore (eds), *Design Culture: An Anthology of Writings from the AIGA Journal of Graphic Design* (New York: Allworth, 1997), 119–24, originally published in *AIGA Journal of Graphic Design*, 10/1 (1992).

22 Craig Allen, "Eyewitness News," in Michael D. Murray (ed.), *Encyclopedia of Television News* (Phoenix, AZ: Oryx Press, 1999), 73–4.

23 Guy Debord, *The Society of the Spectacle*, trans. Donald Nicholson-Smith (New York: Zone Books, 1994).

24 Ernst Jentsch, "Zur Pyschologie des Unheimlichen," *Psychiatrisch-Neurologische Wochenschrift* 8/195 (1906): 219–21, 226–7; cited in Freud, *The Standard Edition*, vol. 17, bibliography, 284.

25 Albert Abramson, *Electronic Motion Pictures: A History of the Television Camera* (Berkeley: University of California Press, 1955), 15–24.

26 Abramson, *Electronic Motion Pictures*, 35–50.

27 Lev Manovich, *The Language of New Media* (Cambridge, MA: MIT Press, 2001), 21–7.

28 Manovich, *The Language of New Media*, xiv–xxxvi, 50–1, 275–6.

29 Maria Morris Hambourg and Christopher Phillips (eds), *The New Vision: Photography Between the World Wars* (exh. cat., New York: Metropolitan Museum of Art, 1987).

30 Abramson, *Electronic Motion Pictures*, 1.

31 Marshall McLuhan, *The Medium is the Massage* [*sic*] (1967; Corte Madera, CA: Ginko Press, 2001), 26–40; Marshall McLuhan, *Understanding Media: The Extensions of Man* (New York: McGraw-Hill, 1964).

32 McLuhan, *The Medium is the Massage*, 125. See also Jonathan Crary, *Techniques of the Observer: On Vision and Modernity in the Nineteenth Century* (Cambridge, MA: MIT Press, 1990); Martin Jay, *Downcast Eyes: The Denigration of Vision in Twentieth-Century French Thought* (Berkeley: University of California Press, 1993); Nicholas Mirzoeff, *An Introduction to Visual Culture* (London: Routledge, 1999).

33 C. P. Scott, "A Hundred Years," *Manchester Guardian* (May 5, 1921).

34 "The Race for Television," a television documentary produced by Granada Television (UK), 1985. For this spectator the television was potentially as menacing as Jeremy Bentham's eighteenth-century panopticon, a circular prison in which all inmates could be watched simultaneously from a central tower, described by Michel Foucault, *Discipline and Punish: The Birth of the Prison*, trans. Alan Sheridan (New York: Vintage Books, 1979), 195–228.

35 Max Horkheimer and Theodor W. Adorno, "The Culture Industry: Enlightenment as Mass Deception" (1944), in *Dialectic of Enlightenment*, trans. John Cumming (New York: Continuum Publishing Company, 1994), 120–67.

36 Horkheimer and Adorno, "The Culture Industry," 126.

37 Walter Benjamin, "The Work of Art in the Age of Mechanical Reproduction" (1936), in *Illuminations*, trans. Harry Zohn (New York: Schocken Books, 1968), 217–52. See 241, 251, and n. 21.

38 Doordan, "Design at CBS."

39 Julie Lasky, "The Search for Georg Olden," in Steven Heller and Georgette Balance (eds), *Graphic Design History* (New York: Allworth Press, 2001), 115–28, originally published in *PRINT* (March–April 1994).

40 Georg Olden appeared on the May 20, 1963, episode of the CBS game show, *I've Got a Secret*, in which he explicitly denied having designed the CBS eye, available online: https://www.youtube.com/watch?v=McKpP3PkIks (accessed May 25, 2015).

41 McLuhan, *The Medium is the Massage*, 100. See also W. Terence Gordon, *McLuhan for Beginners* (New York: Writers and Readers Publishing, Inc., 1997), 7.

42 Following the attacks of September 11, 2001, Congress passed a statute (Public Law Pub. L. 107–56) enabling the federal government to trace possible terrorist threats through a wide-ranging program of surveillance. The Uniting and Strengthening America by Providing Tools Required to Intercept and Obstruct Terrorism Act of 2001, otherwise known as the USA Patriot Act, authorized federal wiretaps on private telecommunications, review of private records, and surveillance of individuals suspected of terrorist-related activities, broadly defined. Though questions had been raised about the program's violation of privacy since its inception, the controversial legislation was put in the spotlight in 2013 when Edward Snowden, former systems administrator for the CIA (Central Intelligence Agency) and contractor for the NSA (National Security Agency), leaked thousands of classified documents to the press, which revealed the far-reaching nature of the United States' surveillance programs. Glenn Greenwald, "NSA Collecting Phone Records of Millions of Verizon Customers Daily," *Guardian* (June 5, 2013), available online: http://www.theguardian.com/world/2013/jun/06/nsa-phone-records-verizon-court-order (accessed July 27, 2013).

43 Kaja Silverman, *The Subject of Semiotics* (Oxford: Oxford University Press, 1983), 157–62. Silverman refers to Jacques Lacan, *Écrits: A Selection*, trans. Alan Sheridan (New York: Norton, 1977), 2.

44 Sherry Turkle, *Life on the Screen: Identity in the Age of the Internet* (New York: Touchstone, 1995), 9; Sherry Turkle, *The Second Self: Computers and the Human Spirit* (New York: Simon and Schuster, 1984).

45 Nicholas Jackson, "Greenpeace Argues That Apple is the Dirtiest Tech Company," *The Atlantic* (April 21, 2011), available online: http://www.theatlantic.com/technology/archive/2011/04/greenpeace-argues-that-apple-is-the-dirtiest-tech-company/237674/ (accessed August 31, 2014).

CHAPTER SIX

Red State, Blue State

Totem and Taboo

The somewhat odd colloquial expressions "red states" and "blue states" recall the title of Dr. Seuss's popular reader for young children, *One Fish Two Fish Red Fish Blue Fish*. Theodore Seuss Geisel, the author of many beloved children's books, wisely observed in that story: "From there to here, from here to there, funny things are everywhere."[1] Dealing with themes near and dear to the hearts of progressive activists of the 1960s and 1970s, such as social justice, civil rights, and the environment, Dr. Seuss captured not only the surreal imagination of children with his musical, nonsensical poetry, teaching many to read along the way, but also the strangeness and absurdity of the human experience. This strangeness is captured in the totemic Red State, Blue State map of the United States that emerged at the turn of the twenty-first century.[2] What does this map signify? And why has it become fixed in the collective imagination? In what ways are ideological messages designed, mythologized, and communicated visually? This chapter explores the trouble with information graphics, especially those that proliferate in the news media today. It asks if there is a better, more productive, way to understand how we perceive ourselves, and our political differences.

On July 27, 2004, Barack Obama, then a U.S. senator from the state of Illinois, delivered a memorable keynote address at the Democratic National Convention, which selected Senator John Kerry as its presidential nominee that year. In that speech, which launched him into the public eye, the young politician drew attention to his own unlikely name and family background. Explaining the union of his black father from Kenya with his white mother from Kansas, who met while students at the University of Hawaii, "a magical place," Obama claimed that "only in America" could be written such a story.[3]

The rousing speech, delivered with what would become the future president's characteristic rhetorical style, introduced the seeds of his own mythic identity, and was designed to move beyond partisan divisions, an effort that President Obama has continued during his subsequent two terms in the White House.

> Now even as we speak, there are those who are preparing to divide us, the spin masters and negative ad peddlers who embrace the politics of anything goes.
>
> Well, I say to them tonight, there's not a liberal America and a conservative America; there's the United States of America.
>
> There's not a black America and white America and Latino America and Asian America; there's the United States of America.
>
> The pundits, the pundits like to slice and dice our country into red states and blue states: red states for Republicans, blue states for Democrats. But I've got news for them, too. We worship an awesome God in the blue states, and we don't like federal agents poking around in our libraries in the red states. We coach little league in the blue states, and, yes, we've got some gay friends in the red states.[4]

Contrary to Obama's view that the nation could move beyond partisan division, however, the 2004 presidential election proved to be one of the most divisive in recent history.[5]

The 2004 U.S. presidential election generated numerous graphic maps, illustrating the outcome of electoral votes in the various states. In what had become a general consensus by news media across the spectrum, following the previous presidential election four years earlier, those states whose electoral votes went to the winning Republican Party candidate George W. Bush were typically colored red, while those whose votes went to the losing Democratic Party candidate, John Kerry, were colored blue. The symbolic color-coding system of red states and blue states, with each color representing certain characteristics and political ideologies, appeared to be fixed. The widely used map, with its clear outline depicting the contours of the contiguous American landmass, and its division into clearly demarcated red or blue states, contributed to the impression that such states are in fact discrete and homogenous units (see Plate 7).

How did this color coding system evolve and what does it mean?

Since the explosive growth of print culture in the nineteenth century, graphic representations of political information in the form of charts, maps, posters, signage, illustrative cartoons, and satire, have been particularly important, functioning much like commercial advertisements that propagandistically convey political messages.[6] With the introduction of television and, later, digital media in the twentieth century, such graphic representations of political information took on even more complicated characteristics.

Color-coded political maps have been used for centuries. Once hand-drawn, illustrated, and colored by skilled cartographers or scribes, today they are produced using complex algorithms for data analysis. Though such maps have many purposes they are especially important tools for understanding the shifting borders of conquest and empire over time.[7] At first glance, the colors blue and red on the map of the 2004 presidential election results seem to be legible descriptors for "progressive" or "conservative" politics in the United States, rigidly aligned with the Democratic or Republican Parties, respectively. Mythically codified, red and blue signify both geographical region and political ideology.

Challenging his listeners' expectations, Senator Obama caught his audience off guard. "We worship an awesome God," he exclaimed, and "coach little league" in the blue states. "We don't like federal agents poking around in our libraries" and "yes, we've got some gay friends" in the red states.

These assertions came as a surprise, because the color red at that time had come to signify the "heartland," located in the geographical center of America, and at the heart of the American imagination. Red states embrace "traditional" and "family" values, defined, for example, by some conservative and religious organizations as supporting the institution of marriage between "one man and one woman."

Visually the red states dominate the map, appearing to represent by far the majority of the country, from Idaho to Texas, and from Ohio to Florida, but traditionally the heartland is located in the geographical center of the country—Iowa, Missouri, Nebraska, and Kansas. The notion of the heartland evokes a sentimental nostalgia for the mid-century culture of the patriarchal, nuclear, close-knit family, which was portrayed on television shows in the 1950s like *Leave it to Beaver* and *Father Knows Best*, set in the fictitious cities of "Mayfield" and "Springfield," that could be anywhere, and are, of course, also nowhere.[8] It is the "all-American" place of baseball (see Obama's reference to little league) and (red) apple pie, of small-town celebrations, with fireworks and American flags, (red) cherry sodas, and (red) strawberry milkshakes, and young children playing in suburban cul-de-sacs with their (red-painted) scooters, tricycles, and wagons.

The heartland is the nation's breadbasket, one of its most important agricultural regions, producing beef, pork, poultry, dairy, and eggs, as well as wheat, soybeans, corn, and sorghum—a plant used in the production of ethanol fuel. Red state farmers, however, are sometimes also referred to disparagingly as "red necks," a description of their skin, sunburned from working in fields, on tractors, and out of doors. The term is used pejoratively, and denotes a lack of sophistication, education, or taste, a penchant for country and western music, cowboy boots, and driving big trucks with hunting rifles mounted on the back. As the stereotype goes, those living in red states are practical, economical, and self-sufficient. They are patriots; they go to church; they eat meat; they drink popular and inexpensive brands of beer; and they passionately follow sporting events, especially American football, hockey, and NASCAR racing; and they own guns.

The blue states, on the other hand, are constellated on the East and West coasts, as well as around the Great Lakes. The central U.S. industrial rust belt grew in population during the Great Depression of the 1930s, a period also known as the Great Migration, when African Americans from the southern states moved northward to find employment in such places as factories in the cities of Chicago, St. Louis, Detroit, Cincinnati, Cleveland, Pittsburgh, and Buffalo.

On a basic level the red–blue dichotomy seems to indicate a difference between urban and rural places and culture in the United States, as well as a racial or ethnic divide. Though the heartland is geographically larger, there are fewer people living in it than in the big cities of New York, Chicago, and Los Angeles. Cities, more crowded, with greater concentrations of poverty and crime, are also plagued by problems, such as overcrowded schools with dwindling resources, inadequate housing, unemployment, and gun violence, which are perhaps less visible in more sparsely populated rural regions, although such problems certainly exist in all parts of the country.

Big urban areas are also generally much less white. They are often the first places settled by newly arrived immigrants, frequently the catalysts for flowerings in the arts and literature. By the 1960s, Detroit and Chicago were bustling metropolises, with wealthy and thriving African American communities, some of whose members made fortunes in the recorded music industries, through successful companies like Motown. Soul music traces its roots to gospel church singing, old Negro spirituals, and the blues, a genre that derives its name from a melancholic emotional state, the lyrics of which often deal with heartbreak, disappointment, sadness, and poverty, but which also have their origins in the historic enslavement of African Americans in America.

The blue states, in contrast, are seen to be home to the very wealthy, sometimes referred to disparagingly as the "liberal elite," who, like the color blue itself, may be perceived as cold and removed from the concerns of the real world, unlike their warm, friendly, red-blooded neighbors in the heartland.[9] The blue-state wealthy represent a wide range of backgrounds, from the old moneyed "blue blood" families of New England, some of whom trace their ancestry to the arrival of the Pilgrims from Plymouth, England, in 1621, to the new money of young Silicon Valley entrepreneurs and entertainers in the film and music industries. Such wealth is visible in the venerated cultural and intellectual traditions of the American Ivy League universities as well as in the glitz and glamor of Hollywood.

The stereotypical member of the liberal blue-state elite—the counter-point to the red neck—is the highly educated young urban professional ("yuppie"), or upwardly mobile family, both environmentally conscious and politically correct, who drives an energy efficient hybrid or stylish European car, and uses Apple devices, while drinking expensive coffee. The blue-state liberal shops at organic grocery stores, listens to public radio, eats trendy and unusual vegetables, and drinks biodynamic wine or artisan-crafted beer. The cultured blue-state family takes its children to the museum, and sends them to music lessons and expensive day camps where they can exercise their creativity by performing plays and building robots. In reality, however, while financially influential on politics, only a fraction of the blue-state liberals are actually wealthy or upper middle class. The vast majority are blue-collar workers.

"Blue-collar," referring originally to the indigo-dyed uniforms worn by factory workers, is an expression that denotes the working class, and can describe those in the lower tiers of manufacturing, such as assembly line workers. These workers may be employed as electricians, plumbers, or in the cleaning, hospitality, and construction industries, protected by powerful unions. More and more, however, in terms of income, the working class encompasses even those with higher levels of education, such as office or hospital workers and teachers. Postal or sanitation workers, police, firefighters, bus drivers—the folks who keep things running—and who once may have been the middle-class families' primary breadwinners, have seen their wages decline over time as the divide between rich and poor grows wider in the United States. Despite the attribution of patriotism to the red states, many young blue-state residents at the lower end of the economic spectrum choose to enlist in the military, which does offer a limited source of income, and some educational and economic family benefits. There, they have served and suffered for the past decade in Iraq and Afghanistan, alongside their red-state compatriots.

In the 2004 book *What's the Matter with Kansas? How Conservatives Won the Heart of America,* cultural critic Thomas Frank asks why an unemployed factory worker, or struggling farm worker living in the heartland would choose to support a political party with policies that did not benefit his economic interests.[10] The reason he is out of work is that the company, which once employed him, has found a cheaper way to make profits by moving its manufacturing sector overseas. The reason that his family farm is failing is that giant food corporations are eating up all of the federal subsidies for agriculture. A Republican representative in Congress, for whom the unemployed farm worker has voted, supports the interests of powerful and well-funded special interest groups armed with lobbyists. That farmer could choose not to vote for the candidate, but continues to do so. Why? Frank demonstrates the historical shift to social conservatism that underpins this political phenomenon with conservative politicians focusing on hot-button social issues, such as abortion and gay marriage, in order to direct the political conversation away from economic questions, and to stoke a conservative anger toward the liberal elite.

Roses Are Red and Violets Are "Kind of Blue"

But politics are not always based on rational or economic self-interest. More often, political decisions reflect feelings of identity. It is not a particular tax policy or piece of legislation that motivates voters, but rather a less tangible sense of belonging. Am I urban, rural, or suburban? Am I progressive or conservative? Do I drink beer or wine? Do I prefer bowling or basketball? Do I eat potato chips or arugula?[11] Of course, such generalizations are absurd, as Dr. Seuss's fable reveals.

Senator Obama pointed out in the speech from which I have quoted that we need not be divided as a nation along these sorts of arbitrary lines, and that individual states are not discrete, homogenous units, but rather comprise a blend of ideologies and positions. They are not red or blue, but rather, varying shades of purple. But the generalizations and stereotypes are reified in the color-coded map. In the familiar nursery rhyme, "Roses are Red, Violets are Blue, Sugar is Sweet, and So Are You," popularized in the nineteenth century by "Mother Goose" (the imaginary author of nursery rhymes and fairy tales, likely dating to the seventeenth century), roses and violets are identified by their colors, and metaphorically signify qualities that have to do with feelings. Though not explicit in the poem, the red-hot rose represents passion, while the true-blue violet symbolizes fidelity. These color associations are woven into cultural politics in surprising ways and have only become more fixed today.[12]

A set of maps indicating the same outcome of the 2004 presidential election, but visualized according to different criteria, reveals vividly the myth of the red and blue state. In maps redrawn by population, for example, we can easily see that, in fact, the majority of the map is blue (see Plate 8).

The more heavily populated urban centers of New York, Chicago, and Los Angeles are surrounded by swollen areas of traditionally democratic voters on the East and West coasts, and around the industrial Great Lakes region. When the map with its traditional configuration of land mass is further redrawn by reported results in each county, however, it appears generally purple, with a surprisingly blue southern Florida, the location of populous Miami–Dade County, and of its many Democratic voters. Our eye combines the small points of red or blue, lending the impression that the country is rather more equally divided politically. Once the reports by county are redrawn according to population again, however, the map appears primarily blue along the East and West Coasts, as well as the central Great Lakes region, surrounded by a sea of purple (see Plate 9). Just a few geographical areas remain predominantly red—those of the relatively sparsely populated ranching and farming states of Wyoming, Montana, and parts of Colorado. Kansas is also mostly red.[13]

This visual distortion of the data results from the peculiar practice in the United States of representation by electoral college. Each state, according to population, is allotted a certain number of official votes. Once all of its residents have voted during a presidential election, the popular vote, which can vary greatly from one district to another, is translated into an overall majority. For example, in Florida, the Republican candidate, George W. Bush, received more votes by just a small margin in the 2004 presidential election, due in part to the large number of voters in its southern counties. But *all* of Florida's electoral votes went to Bush, despite the fact that many people had actually voted for the Democratic candidate, John Kerry. More Floridians, in fact, voted for Kerry than residents of Wyoming, Montana, Colorado, and Kansas combined had voted for Bush.[14] The visualization of the data in 2004, when coded red or blue to correspond to the geographical area of state, based on electoral votes, rather than population or individual district reporting, lends the impression not only that George W. Bush won the election, but moreover, that he won by a landslide, particularly in America's heartland, the red center of the United States.

The graphic representation of data, particularly numerical data, when illustrated in the form of bar charts, pie charts, chronological timelines, Cartesian coordinate systems, pictograms, or shaded maps, implies scientific accuracy and objectivity, as noted humorously by Huckleberry Finn in Mark Twain's 1894 novel, *Tom Sawyer Abroad*. On the second day of their voyage to Africa by hot air balloon, Tom's friend, Huck, remarks that they must still be above Illinois. When Tom asks why, Huck responds, "I know by the color. We're right over Illinois yet. And you can see for yourself that Indiana ain't in sight." Tom, baffled, asks, "You know by the *color*? [...] What's the color got to do with it?" Huck answers, "It's got everything to do with it. Illinois is green, Indiana is pink. You show me any pink down here, if you can. No, sir; it's green." Tom is confused, "Indiana *pink*? Why, what a lie?" Huck retorts, "It ain't no lie; I've seen it on the map, and it's pink [...] what's a map for? Ain't it to learn you the facts? [...] It don't tell lies."[15]

The official and authoritative nature of such information is often aided by the use of modernist typefaces and clearly legible, grid-like tables that appear detached from any particular political agenda. Cartographers, statisticians, political scientists, and psychologists have noticed this problem and have been wary of the ideological manipulation of data—sometimes unintentionally—through its visual illustration, a phenomenon that geographer Mark Monmonnier calls "selective truth."[16] Though the origins of data visualization and statistical mapping date to antiquity, it is a practice that was particularly well developed in the eighteenth and early nineteenth centuries, with the introduction of new tools for measuring during the industrial period.[17] In the later nineteenth and twentieth centuries, the visualization of statistical information in the form of colorful maps and charts spread more widely in the form of printed journals and newspapers, and later television and digital media.[18]

In the United States, the complexities and contradictions of such color-coding systems are especially evident in the groups at either end of the political spectrum, which defy the stereotypes. Both the far left-leaning progressive greens and far right-wing libertarians tend to oppose war and support the legalization of marijuana. Many like to grow their own food and advocate for the use of alternative energy sources. Sometimes they educate their children at home, avoid city water supplies, and choose not to vaccinate their babies against dangerous diseases like measles or mumps, past epidemics that (thanks to longstanding public health policies of the past) are largely invisible in more affluent communities today. Likewise in a quandary are Roman Catholics, who though concerned with social justice and with the alleviation of poverty and suffering, an activity more often aligned with the blue state political left, may be more socially conservative when it comes to issues such as gay marriage, family planning, or women's reproductive rights—positions that are more closely connected to the red states' political right.

The most peculiar aspect of the early twenty-first century red state–blue state color-coding system was the rebranding of the color blue to represent labor, which historically has been signified by the color red.

Color-coded maps reporting election results were used in the United States beginning with the introduction of color television in the 1950s, yet for years networks did not rely upon a single system in order to convey their results. In 1996, presidential election Democratic Party candidate Bill Clinton beat the Republican Party candidate, George H. W. Bush. In that case, some media, including *Time* magazine and the *Washington Post*, illustrated the winning Democratic states in red and the Republican states in blue.[19] Is red seen as a more winning color? If so, this would seem to contradict the tradition of the blue ribbon, often awarded to winners of contests and competitions, or presented as an honorary recognition of merit. Second place usually receives a red ribbon.

Likely the most famous example of color-coded political propaganda in the history of art and design is Russian constructivist El Lissitzky's 1919 poster, *Beat the Whites with the Red Wedge*.[20] Designed to promote the political platform of the 1917 Russian Revolution, the poster portrays the workers' party, the Bolsheviks, as a dynamic, dagger-like, triangular shape, sharply thrust into the heart of the static, white Czarist regime. Red is the color traditionally associated with socialism, communism, and labor, seen for example in the red flags of China and the former Soviet Union, as well as on the cover of Chinese communist leader Mao Zedong's *Little Red Book*, which was widely distributed during China's Cultural Revolution (1966–76).

During the particularly intense period of "McCarthyism" from 1950 to 1956, so-named after Republican Senator Joseph McCarthy, who accused thousands of Americans of communist affiliations or sympathy, "reds" or "pinkos," as the press sometimes referred to them, were often blacklisted. Spied upon and harassed, those with socialist leanings, or those who may have been outspoken in their criticism of capitalism, and the class disparity that it spawns, were often prevented from working and sometimes jailed or deported on suspicion of their traitorous collaboration with America's communist enemies.

The coding of communism, or left-wing politics more generally, as "red" was common not only in the United States, but also in many other countries throughout the twentieth century. Around 2009, the British Labour Party, however, attempted to rebrand Labour as blue, suggesting that voters who deserted it in the late 1990s might be won back by the adoption of a more conservative stance on certain policies, such as immigration and crime, and by moving more toward local management, and away from the traditional welfare state with which it was associated. In part, the strategy may have been a response to the similarly awkward idea of the Red Tory, a progressive conservative position that rejects large, bureaucratic government, and advocates community-led services and the alleviation of poverty.

Political theorist and Labour peer Maurice Glasman, who coined the phrase "Blue Labour" and was a key figure in the British Blue Labour Party, described the movement as "a deeply conservative socialism that places family, faith and work at the heart of a new politics of reciprocity, mutuality and solidarity ... It's also 'blue' because it's a sad moment – in a Miles Davis kind of way."[21] For Glasman, the modern British welfare state had failed. He called for a return to moral and ethical social institutions, including trade unions and churches, which, he believed, had been swept away over the years because they undermined the government's power structure.

Hope and Change

Barack Obama dismissed the idea of red and blue states in his inspiring 2004 speech, which largely paved the way to his winning the Democratic party's nomination for U.S. President four years later. The "historic" election season that year, as it was deemed by many pundits, was one of the most exciting in recent memory, with many younger voters energized by Obama's progressive platform, and many older voters, who came of age during the Civil Rights protests of the 1950s and 1960s, believing that the African American candidate represented the fruits of their labor.[22] Still others were drawn to his charismatic rhetoric, dazzling back story, and handsome star presence.

A savvy program of visual communication complemented the array of supporters who came by the thousands to attend rallies and who volunteered for the campaign by answering phone calls and registering new voters. Posters, stickers, buttons, and other ephemera in the cool Gotham typeface, designed by Tobias Frere-Jones for the Hoefler & Frere-Jones foundry, dotted the visual landscape, as did interesting vintage-style posters that recalled the progressive New Deal of Franklin D. Roosevelt's 1930s administration, which had put into place many of the nation's most important social services following the Great Depression.[23] The campaign's organizing arm, Obama for America, orchestrated an impressive social media presence, which was modeled on the form and success of Facebook, while also raising money by selling limited edition collectibles.

Most popular during the 2008 campaign was graphic and conceptual artist Shepard Fairey's poster, featuring a portrait of Senator Obama in shades of red, white, and blue, above the bold word "HOPE," all in capital letters (see Plate 10).

Fairey initially designed and printed a run of 700 posters, which he sold and distributed freely on the street because he liked the candidate and supported his run for presidency. When the poster was officially approved by the Obama campaign Fairey printed thousands more, and devoted the proceeds, he reported, to producing more posters, some with the word "PROGRESS" or "CHANGE" inserted, instead of "HOPE." Fairey based the image on a press photograph of Obama, which he said reminded him of portraits of President John F. Kennedy, as well as Abraham Lincoln as he appears on the five-dollar bill.[24] In 2009, he settled out of court, however, after the Associated Press sued him for having used the original photograph without permission, though Fairey claimed all along that his transformation of the image into its artistic printed poster form constituted fair use.[25]

The HOPE poster, which inspired many parodies, has been compared on the one hand to the Social Realist graphic design of the WPA (Works Progress Administration, later Work Projects Administration; 1935–43) era, and, on the other, to iconic images of Che Guevara, the Marxist Argentine military leader who fought in the Cuban Revolution of 1953–9. With regard to the former, the style is reminiscent, for example, of official government posters for the Rural Electrification Administration, designed by Lester Beall in the 1930s, which combine avant-garde geometric abstraction and photomontage to communicate the progressive new programs of the FDR administration which included building dams, and bringing electricity and running water to poor, rural areas. It also recalls the graphic clarity of illustrated posters promoting the natural beauty of the U.S. National Parks, which underwent unprecedented preservation by Roosevelt's Civilian Conservation Corps at that time. The CCC, a massive federal jobs program, employed workers to build trails, bridges, and other structures in the parks in the midst of the Great Depression, in order to promote travel and tourism and to boost the struggling economy.

Also conspicuous in Fairey's poster image is the Obama campaign logo, a circular blue ring that rises above a curving field of red and white stripes. The image is rich and evocative, recalling the rising sun, maybe on a new day in American politics, or indeed a new America, above the waving American flag, which doubles as well for the landscape of the American heartland, with its "amber waves of grain."[26] Most importantly, the circular rising sun is also the letter "O" for Obama. In the portrait, the logo seems to rest on Obama's left jacket lapel, an ironic reference, perhaps, to the flag pin controversy that dogged his presidential campaign.[27] Despite its ironic, anti-establishment, countercultural references, the poster is also chic and commodifiable.

Like one of the pop art portraits of celebrities silkscreened by Andy Warhol in the 1960s, valued for its superficial cultural cachet as much as for its challenging content, Fairey's posters were snapped up quickly by collectors. Just as the image of a communist beret-clad Guevara, looking into the distant future, became a collectible countercultural symbol of resistance and rebellion throughout the 1960s, Fairey's poster of Obama, a visionary leader with the potential to transform America, was commoditized regardless of its transgressive associations.[28]

Despite the euphoria of the political left over the success of the Obama campaign, certain troubling aspects lingered. With its powerful, totalizing, indeed corporate aesthetic, or at least aesthetic strategy, was not this visual campaign dangerously similar to those of other mass political movements in history, most notably those of Nazi Germany, Communist Russia, and China? But disregarding its visual or aesthetic kinship with the stylish and streamlined graphics, rallies, crowds, speeches, flags, branding, and related art and architecture of fascism or communism, the surge of popular support for Obama seemed somehow entirely different—better, more legitimate, authentic, transformative, and morally good in the most positive way.[29] After all, not only was this the first African American candidate for the United States Presidency, but Obama was a professor in the University of Chicago's Law Faculty, raising a young family with his lawyer wife. In addition he hadn't had the easiest of upbringings, raised by his hard-working grandparents, and, at times, by his single mother, who had been a poor, struggling anthropology graduate student, in the 1960s, when she met, fell in love, conceived a child with, and married a fellow student, a black man from Africa. She, then, reared her mixed-race children in the rather exotic locations of Hawaii and—almost incomprehensibly—Indonesia.

One of the most interesting visual elements of the campaign was the effort by grassroots supporters to emulate the otherwise corporate signage at rallies in decidedly non-corporate, idiosyncratic ways, such as wearing red, white, and blue t-shirts with the Pepsi, Superman, or NASA logos. These trademarks, ostensibly having nothing to do with the Obama campaign, nevertheless evoked a patriotic spirit, as well as the consumer-oriented associations of fun, cosmic exploration, or superhuman power of these products through their visual similarities to the official logo, or to the Fairey portrait. Others in the heterogeneous crowds of all ages and races, of young parents with strollers and children on their shoulders, aging activists, businessmen in suits and ties, the homeless, the disabled, and veterans in wheelchairs, wore images of Dr. Martin Luther King, Jr., or t-shirts with unofficial inspirational references to hope, change, progress, and dreams of social and economic justice, to identify with one another and to share in the spirit of the event.[30]

This worldly, metropolitan leader, with such an unusual and transcendent background, seemed to have some element in his past with which all democratically aligned voters could connect, whether they had attended an Ivy League college, or were poor, went to church, smoked marijuana, wrote novels, were white, or of color, lived in the city, were struggling, or wealthy, were raised on food stamps, had young children, came from an international background, or had an extensive knowledge of poststructuralist feminist theory. Voters were flattered to see themselves reflected in his image. Beyond this self-identification with the candidate, however, many voters projected onto him a messianic quality, in which he came to signify the promise of racial equality embodied by Abraham Lincoln as well as by Dr. King.

In March 2008, at the height of the presidential campaign, Obama presented what has since been regarded as his most important speech, and possibly one of the most significant in American history, "A More Perfect Union."[31] The title of his speech, drawn from the Preamble to the U.S. Constitution, framed a heavy discussion about the history of race in America. In part, the speech was timed to quell the growing tensions concerning Obama's relationship with Jeremiah Wright, a Chicago pastor who had made incendiary and, to some, offensive remarks during his Sunday sermons, one of which had been recorded. Not only were the Obamas members of Wright's church, it was discovered, but Obama had openly credited Wright as mentor in his conversion to Christianity, and in the forging of his own identity as a black Chicago politician. The speech, a disavowal of Wright's insistence upon white racism, was a necessary and pivotal point for a candidate who wanted to reach beyond the black community, and beyond the bitter legacy of racism, to the national forum that had been addressed in the past by great leaders, including Lincoln and King. It was also clear, however, that Obama was of a different generation than Wright, and that he represented not a Moses leading his people to the Promised Land, as King had signified, but rather a Joshua—the inheritor of that legacy. As journalist David Remnick wrote, he was not a prophet, but the prophesied.[32]

Fairey's portrait, as the artist pointed out, drew upon associations with John F. Kennedy, a socially progressive president, yet also a fashionable figure who looms large in the American imagination. It also recalled similar portraits of King. Throughout the campaign, often with fearful anxiety for his own personal safety, Obama was compared to Lincoln, Kennedy, and King, the fallen martyr–leaders who furthered the dream of social equality, but who did not live to see its outcome in their own lifetimes. Voters projected onto Obama a range of promises: to raise the poor out of poverty, to restore equal status to women, to extend civil rights to the LGTBQ community, to rebuild the economy, to end the wars in Iraq and Afghanistan, to stop domestic violence, to repair America's damaged reputation in the international community, to reinvest in education, to reverse nuclear armament, to stop global warming, and to bring together red and blue states in harmonious brotherhood.[33] Voters breathlessly wondered: is this our savior?

Obama's win on election night 2008 was, for his supporters, a joyful, tearful celebration—a dramatic release of tension after months (and, for some, decades) of labor and anxiety.[34] *The New Yorker* magazine published a number of covers in the subsequent weeks, illustrating the win in a highly spiritualized manner, pointing to the next step along the new leader's mythical journey. The November 10, 2008, cover by Brian Stauffer, featured rather ominously a dark red corridor, with a small blue light at the end of the tunnel; while the following week, the November 17, 2008, cover by Bob Staake, illustrated a nighttime view of the Lincoln Memorial on the Washington, D.C. mall, the "O" in "New Y-O-rker" glowing celestially, like a moon gazing at its own reflection, and hovering like a guardian presence over the democracy.

The Politics of Fear

As the Obamas were ushered into office, thousands of supporters were euphoric, especially young people and African Americans, amazed that such a transformation, which seemed to offer the possibility of a "post-racial" society, could have taken place.[35] The joyous international community seemed ready to graciously forgive the United States for all its imperialistic sins in recent history, having redeemed itself by choosing a leader with a decidedly un-Anglo-Saxon name, non-white skin, and unconventional international background. Within America, however, cynical ultra-progressives remained skeptical. While some Democrats grudgingly celebrated the victory, they nevertheless lamented Obama's triumph over his Democratic rival for candidacy, Hillary Clinton, wife of former Democratic President Bill Clinton, leading some to ask which was worse, racism or sexism? As conservative Republicans licked their wounds, fury boiled over.

Obama's most articulate detractors were the Cold Warriors of the 1940s and 1950s. These individuals, most of them white men who came of age in the late 1930s and 1940s, would, at all costs, protect American democratic freedom, especially that of laissez-faire capitalism. The power of the Soviet Union during the Cold War, like the power of China today, represented for them a specter of communism that they had most feared in the wake of the Second World War. In order to preserve democracy in the world, and as the benefactors of capitalism, they believed that no use of military force was too great. Their ideas were at odds a half century ago with those of the generation that followed them, which put an end to the contentious U.S.

military intervention in Vietnam, and which turned attention to protecting the rights of the disenfranchised at home, especially women and African Americans. The current internal debates in the United States, triggered, so to speak, by the Obama presidency, have the strange feeling of reliving the past, not only by relitigating the social issues that many thought had been resolved thirty or forty years ago, but in some cases even returning to an antebellum fantasy of white supremacy.

The contingent of Americans who were shocked and outraged by the election of a mixed race president, if only in their collective unconscious, elicited a narrative of protest that has since emerged as a simmering cultural war constellated irrationally around a host of social taboos. Those on the right have panicked about what some perceive as weaknesses in U.S. foreign policy, from the new practice allowing gay and lesbian soldiers to serve in the military, to President Obama's refusal to intervene in Syria's civil war, which began in 2011, or Russia's 2014 invasion of Ukraine. They also express anxiety about what they perceive as erosion in the constitutional right to bear arms (arguably protected by the Second Amendment), in changes to immigration policy, and above all, what many see as an overstepping of federal responsibility to provide citizens with social services, such as education, health care, and a living wage.

Newly elected representatives to the U.S. Congress have worked hard to reverse civil rights legislation which protects women's reproductive choices, as well as the right to vote, especially among poor and non-white communities, groups which historically tend to favor Democrats. By contrast, they have sought to protect the financial interests of large corporations in the oil, chemical, and banking industries.

On the left, opponents have criticized the Obama administration for allowing to continue, or indeed for escalating, the controversial foreign military programs of the previous presidential administration, including the incarceration of terror suspects at the U.S. military prison in Guantanamo Bay, Cuba; the use of unmanned drones to carry out warfare well beyond America's borders; secret surveillance; and the deportation of an unprecedented number of illegal immigrants, while not acting quickly enough to reform immigration policies—each of which, they argue, has stripped away civil rights.

Despite the gentility of the gracious upper middle-class, handsome and stylish Obama family, with their impeccable manners and charming daughters, the presence of a black family in the White House has fueled a bizarre frenzy among the administration's most vociferous protesters, some of whom insist that the President is actually not an American citizen at all, demanding relentlessly that he reveal his birth certificate (which he has done, in fact, repeatedly), and fervently asserting that he is secretly Muslim (though he avowed his Christian faith on numerous occasions). These irrational fears have stemmed partly from Obama's obvious blackness, as well as his exotic name, and from a more general fear of the Other, especially the Arab or Muslim in America, but they also have deeper roots in the nation's internal divisions over racial equality, property, and the states' rights, which were, and are, at the heart of what is arguably still an ongoing "civil war."

Illustrator Barry Blitt mocked these anxieties notoriously during the 2008 presidential campaign in a *The New Yorker* cover titled "The Politics of Fear," depicting Michelle and Barack Obama in the Oval Office of the White House. Barack Obama is dressed in middle-eastern attire, including long tunic, white turban, and sandals, while the First Lady wears camouflage-print military fatigues, sports a large Afro hairstyle, and has an automatic rifle with magazine of bullets strapped junta-style across her chest. A portrait of Osama bin Laden hangs above the mantel and an American flag burns in the fireplace. The two share a conspiratorial fist bump. Michelle Obama, clearly channeling, in Blitt's interpretation, Black Panther leader Angela Davis, is freed in the illustration to be an "angry black woman," an image that she worked hard to assuage during the campaign.

Tall, strong, smart, and sharp-witted, Michelle Obama has a formidable presence. She has claimed that her favorite TV program is the light-hearted, popular 1960s situation comedy *The Dick Van Dyke Show*. Rather than Angela Davis, Mary Tyler Moore, who starred in the show as Dick Van Dyke's wife, Laura Petrie, clearly had the most significant influence on the fashionable flip hairdo that Michelle Obama often wore during the campaign—a style that was especially popular for both black and white women in the 1960s.[36]

Barack Obama never wears a turban today, nor does he dress in middle-eastern costume, although Blitt's illustration suggests that away from the public spotlight he just might. Just look at family photographs of a young "Barry" Obama sporting an Afro during his pot-smoking days while exploring the counter-culture of the 1970s.[37] But then groovy jazz musicians, poets, and intellectuals often adopted Muslim skullcaps and African dashikis in the 1960s and 1970s. Some did convert to Islam, and others joined radical or militant organizations, such as the Nation of Islam or Black Panther Party, likely reinforcing the link between exotic African American fashions and subversive or revolutionary politics.

The Obamas are too young to have been affiliated with the militant Black Panthers, and Barack Obama's strong belief in peace, a position that links him, of course, to Martin Luther King, Jr., sets him apart from the more violent aspects of the black liberation movement. However, despite what appeared to be initial promises of peace, a position that President Obama continues to advocate, and in which he personally believes, his administration has been widely criticized for its continuation of the wars in Iraq and Afghanistan, as well as its controversial use of drones—unmanned aircraft programmed to carry out attacks in enemy territory. Among members of the international community, the United States, as a result, is today perceived as no more associated with peace than it was during George W. Bush's previous administration.

Obama is, however, more often associated with the great black leaders, intellectuals, and orators of the past, such as Dr. King, writers James Baldwin and Ralph Ellison, and activists and educators W. E. B. Dubois and Frederick Douglass, the latter a close advisor to Abraham Lincoln. Nevertheless, he appears to channel the *style* of mid-century black leaders, especially Malcolm X, who with his natty suits, close-cropped hair, graceful physique, and intellectual glasses has been described as a "1960s' mod."[38] In fact, Obama did claim in his 1995 memoir, *Dreams From My Father*, to have been influenced as a young man above all by *The Autobiography of Malcolm X*, not necessarily for his political views (Malcolm X advocated at one time an armed black rebellion), but rather for his admirable self-transformation and creative construction of his own identity as a black man in America.

A portrait of Obama on the July 2008 cover of *Rolling Stone* magazine in a dark suit with cool blue tie and flag pin appears to show him laughing heartily at this inside joke of black-man-as-presidential-candidate, obligingly marked by the absurdly arbitrary signifier of patriotism, the American flag as jewelry. The portrait is a more irreverent version of that which appeared on the January 5, 2009 cover of *Time*, when Barack Obama was voted the magazine's Person of the Year. For that issue, Fairey designed a special version of his famous campaign poster, depicting Obama as cool pop art celebrity, against a wallpaper-like background pattern that evokes Warhol's parodic compositions, in which can be discerned the mighty dollar sign, the U.S. Capitol building, a wind turbine, and a partial map of the world showing Saudi Arabia and Iraq, implying that Obama is not just leader of America, but perhaps also of the world.

To some Americans, Obama's election was a tragedy. In 2010, a new group of political candidates emerged, identifying themselves with the so-called Tea Party. Their name was an anachronistic reference to the anti-taxation policy of the Boston Tea Party of 1773, and fueled by a passionate fear of liberal progress. Many liberal progressives regarded their ideology as lacking compassion for the nation's poor, and symbolic of xenophobia, isolationism, racism, entrenched militarism, greed, intolerance, and a hatred of women.[39] For these individuals, the specter of a second-term Obama presidency was apocalyptic, the initial battle of a new Civil War. The event that has enraged Obama's detractors, more than any other, is, inexplicably, his effort to provide affordable health care for all Americans. This outlandish idea has provoked Republican Representatives to vote more than fifty times to limit or to repeal entirely "Obamacare," otherwise known as the Affordable Care Act, and more recently to bring a lawsuit against the President for carrying out its provisions.[40] The bitter tears over this piece of legislation would be comical if they were not so disturbing.

America is currently the only developed nation in the world that does not provide universal health care for its citizens. And we are left to wonder why. Who among us deserves health care, and who does not? Who deserves shelter? Employment? Education? Food? Water? Protection by the law? Where do we draw the line?

One image in particular, which circulated at Tea Party rallies, depicts Obama as African savage, naked, except for his primitive decorations of shells, teeth, feathers, and bones, including a tusk that pierces his nose. A caption reads rather menacingly: "Obamacare. Coming soon to a clinic near you." The Obama campaign logo takes the place of the letter "O" in Obama, while the "C" in Care is a communist hammer and sickle.

Holy Dread

According to Sigmund Freud a taboo is something that is both sacred and unclean.[41] It is a cultural prohibition imbued with such power that its violation may be lethal. The taboo that most interested Freud was that of incest, sexual relations with a close relative, such as between siblings, or between parents and children, which can incite deep horror in many cultural contexts.

For Freud, the incest taboo, which was found to be extremely complicated in some primitive societies, where it extended to cousins, in-laws, and other distant relations, had a useful structuring function for organizing peaceful social community relations in Polynesia and Australia. It also had interesting parallels, he found, to his own context of contemporary Vienna, where the violation of such social structures could lead to obsessional neurosis.

The totem, he explained, drawing upon the work of anthropologists J. G. Frazer and Andrew Lang, is "as a rule an animal (whether edible and harmless or dangerous and feared) and more rarely a plant or a natural phenomenon (such as rain or water), which stands in peculiar relation to the whole clan."

The totem is the common ancestor of the clan, and its guardian spirit, or helper, which sends forth oracles and also protects its children.[42] The primary purpose of the totem is to insure against the incest taboo. Though today we understand the genetic reasons to avoid inbreeding, which can give rise to many congenital problems, anthropologists at the turn of the twentieth century were attempting to understand these reasons in social terms alone.

Incest is still one of the most potent taboos in many cultural contexts, but there are others, too. Many are interwoven into the American political discourse today, and include a xenophobic fear of the Other; a deep suspicion of, or anxiety toward women's reproductive capacity and their control over it; and a rejection of cultural institutions that threaten a white, patriarchal order, such as homosexuality, interracial or same sex marriage, and threatened rights to property. Let us also add to our list cultural prohibitions against unequal treatment under the law; threats to individual rights to privacy and freedom; and institutional structures that give rise to poverty, suffering, violence, death, and harm to children. These taboos, or cultural prohibitions, are kept at bay with a number of different totems, which include references to the origins of the United States (the "Founding Fathers," the Constitution, the Declaration of Independence), as well as references to important patriarchs and leaders, such as Lincoln and King. We should also consider the image of the Native American, as we have seen in Chapter 4, as an important totem in the American imagination, most visibly present in the logos of sports teams, but also at one time on the face of the five-cent nickel coin.

Totemic symbols of clan identity in the United States, such as the nation's flag, the Constitution, or the bald eagle, do not serve to prohibit incest, but rather to maintain a sense of national identity so strong as to prohibit treason, the dangerous and unclean crossing of boundaries into enemy territory. The Red State, Blue State map, however, is a totem that prevents the mixture of groups of people with ideologically opposed views. But as we round the turnstile once again, we discover that the mixing of reds and blues prohibited by the map signifies another more submerged taboo, the prohibition against miscegenation, or the mixing of different racial groups through marriage, sexual relation, or procreation. The horror that was unleashed by the election of President Obama may arguably have been, in part, the horror of racial mixing, which he and others celebrated in the story of his own mixed-race identity. America has traditionally been obsessed by the holy dread of miscegenation, which outweighs even that of incest. Indeed the Red State, Blue State map implicitly encourages unhealthy, incestuous relationships by disavowing the possibility of purple.

In his 1936 novel, *Absalom, Absalom!*, American writer William Faulkner describes the horror felt by the southern plantation owner Confederate Army Colonel Charles Sutpen, when the protagonist discovered that his son, Charles Bon, from the Colonel's previous marriage to a black woman in the West Indies, has fallen in love with Colonel Sutpen's white daughter, Charles Bon's half-sister, Judith. Colonel Sutpen has another white son, Judith's brother, Henry, upon whom falls the tragic responsibility of ending the relationship between the half-siblings. As Henry confronts his brother, Charles Bon remarks: "So, it's the miscegenation, not the incest, which you can't bear."[43]

Ob/sama

Freudian slips run amuck on the campaign trail.

In 2008, many television announcers tripped over their own tongues pronouncing "Obama" instead as "Osama." Barack Obama is a rather unusual name in the United States, although not necessarily throughout the world. Indeed President Obama seems to operate in two different, totally separate universes. In one, he speaks to the international community as a world leader. He is a respected and highly regarded diplomat who presented in 2009 important speeches, for example, on nuclear disarmament in Prague, and on the future of Islam in Cairo; he has also been awarded the Nobel Peace Prize.[44] And yet, at home, throughout his presidency, he has been ridiculed and attacked at every turn, stymied in any attempts to push forward policy or to enact federal regulations that will protect consumers and ordinary Americans.

"Barack" is a name of Semitic origin, found in both Arabic and Hebrew, that means "blessed." Similarly, "Obama," a Swahili name, denotes the Luo tribal affiliation from East Africa. It also sounds a lot like the name of the late Osama bin Laden, mastermind of the terrorist attacks on the World Trade Center in New York on September 11, 2001, who was America's enemy Number One until he was killed by U.S. special military forces in 2011.

Barack Obama's Arabic middle name, "Hussein," which means "the handsome one," is also the name of one of America's most feared and hated historical foes, the late President of Iraq, Saddam Hussein, sentenced to death in 2006. In that year, amidst rumors that the young senator might run for President, comedian Jon Stewart noted on his late night "fake news" program, *The Daily Show with Jon Stewart*, that only in America could the paradox of Barack Obama emerge.

"His first name rhymes with Iraq, his last name rhymes with Osama, and his middle name rhymes with—no—actually *is*—Hussein!"[45]

The discourse of red states and blue states may not be one that will last historically, but it is even more potent today than it was when it entered the American political vocabulary in 2004.

What will be its legacy?

Notes

1 Dr. Seuss, *One Fish Two Fish Red Fish Blue Fish* (New York: Random House, 1960). See also Tom Zeller, "Ideas and Trends: One State, Two State, Red State, Blue State," *New York Times* (February 8, 2004), available online: http://www.nytimes.com/2004/02/08/weekinreview/ideas-trends-one-state-two-state-red-state-blue-state.html (accessed August 31, 2014).

2   David Brooks in 2001 described the difference between red states and blue states in his article, "One Nation, Slightly Divisible," *The Atlantic Monthly* (December 2001): 53–65. See also Edward L. Glaeser and Bryce A. Ward, "Myths and Realities of American Political Geography," *The Journal of Economic Perspectives* 20/2 (Spring 2006): 119–44.

3   This story had been recounted earlier in his memoir, Barack Obama, *Dreams From My Father: A Story of Race and Inheritance* (New York: Times Books, 1995).

4   Barack Obama, Keynote address delivered to the Democratic National Convention, July 27, 2004, *The Washington Post*, available online: http://www.washingtonpost.com/wp-dyn/articles/A19751–2004Jul27.html (accessed June 3, 2014). See also Barack Obama, "The Audacity of Hope: DNC Keynote Address July 27, 2004," in *Words That Changed a Nation: the Most Celebrated and Influential Speeches of Barack Obama* (Seattle: Beacon Hills, 2009), 1–8.

5   Alan I. Abramowitz and Walter J. Stone, "The Bush Effect: Polarization, Turnout, and Activism in the 2004 Presidential Election," *Presidential Studies Quarterly* 36/2 (June 2006): 141–54.

6   Johanna Drucker and Emily McVarish, *Graphic Design History: A Critical Guide* (Upper Saddle River, NJ: Pearson, 2009), 82–105.

7   See, for example, William Playfair, *Commercial and Political Atlas* (London: Corry, 1786).

8   Both shows were set in fictitious towns meant to represent any place in America. Matt Groening, writer of history's longest-running television series, *The Simpsons*, writes that growing up he believed that *Father Knows Best* took place in Springfield, Oregon—his own home town. Later he realized that the television Springfield was imaginary. Groening chose "Springfield" as the name of the Simpson's home because it was the most popular, and therefore most generic, city name in the U.S. Claudia De La Roca, "Matt Groening Reveals the Location of the Real Springfield," *Smithsonian* online (May 2012), available online: http://www.smithsonianmag.com/arts-culture/matt-groening-reveals-the-location-of-the-real-springfield–60583379/?no-ist (accessed August 7, 2014).

9   By the time of the 2008 U.S. presidential election, red and blue states were analyzed regularly according to various criteria. See, for example, Andrew Gelman, David Park, Boris Shor, Joseph Bafumi, and Jeronimo Cortina, *Red State, Blue State, Rich State, Poor State* (Princeton: Princeton University Press, 2008); Hanes Walton, Jr., Josephine A.V. Allen, Sherman C. Puckett, and Donald R. Deskins, Jr., "The Red and Blue State Divide in Black and White: The Historic Election of President Barack Obama," *The Black Scholar* 38/4 (Winter 2008): 19–30; Michael Hechter, "On the 2004 Presidential Election," *Daedalus* 134/2 (Spring 2005): 131–3.

10 Thomas Frank, *What's the Matter With Kansas: How Conservatives Won the Hearts of America* (New York: Metropolitan Books, 2004).

11 Barack Obama, while on the campaign trail in Iowa, in an attempt to sympathize with the plight of the farmers, asked about the price of arugula at Whole Foods (a grocery store that sells expensive, organic foods), revealing

himself to be out of touch with the experience of everyday Americans, most of whom likely do not frequently eat the lettuce-like green, also called rocket, nor shop at Whole Foods. Jeff Zeleny, "Obama's Down on the Farm," *New York Times* (July 27, 2007), available online: http://thecaucus.blogs.nytimes.com/2007/07/27/obamas-down-on-the-farm/?_php=true&_type=blogs&_r=0 (accessed August 6, 2014).

12 See what happened to lifelong friends from red and blue states, for example, in "Red State Blue State," *This American Life*, Episode 478, transcribed on This American Life Radio Archive, Copyright Chicago Public Media and Ira Glass, available online: http://www.thisamericanlife.org/radio-archives/episode/478/transcript (accessed June 14, 2015).

13 For further explanation of the redrawn map, also known as a cartogram, see Michael Kleber, "Cartographiana," *The Mathematical Intelligencer* 22/2 (Spring 2005): 35–40.

14 Eileen J. Canavan and Jason Bucelato (eds), *Federal Elections 2004. Election Results of the U.S. President, the U.S. Senate and the U.S. House of Representatives* (Washington, DC: Federal Election Commission, 2005), available online: http://www.fec.gov/pubrec/fe2004/federalelections2004.pdf (accessed August 6, 2014).

15 Mark Twain, *Tom Sawyer Abroad* (New York: Charles L. Webster and Company, 1894), 42–3.

16 Mark Monmonier, "Lying with Maps," *Statistical Science* 20/3 (August 2005): 215–22; Mark Monmonier, *How to Lie with Maps* (2nd edn, Chicago: University of Chicago Press, 1996); Nathan Gale and William C. Halperin, "A Case for Better Graphics: The Unclassed Choropleth Map," *The American Statistician* 36/4 (November 1982): 330–6; Howard Wainer and David Thissen, "Graphical Data Analysis," *Annual Review of Psychology* 32 (1981): 191–241.

17 Michael Friendly, "The Golden Age of Statistical Graphics," *Statistical Science* 23/4 (November 2008): 502–35; Michael Friendly, "Visions and Re-Visions of Charles Joseph Minard," *Journal of Educational and Behavioral Sciences* 27/1 (Spring 2002): 31–51. See also C. J. Minard, *Des tableaux graphiques et des cartes figuratives* (Paris: E. Thuno et Cie, 1862), and C. J. Minard, *La Statistique* (Paris: Cusset, 1869); Edward Tufte, *The Visual Display of Quantitative Information* (Cheshire, CT: Graphics Press, 1983); S. E. Fienberg, "Graphical Methods in Statistics," *The American Statistician* 33 (1979): 165–78; James R. Beniger and Dorothy L. Robyn, "Quantitative Graphics in Statistics: A Brief History," *The American Statistician* 32/1 (February 1978): 1–11.

18 Leland Wilkinson, Daniel J. Rope, Daniel B. Carr, and Matthew A. Rubin, "The Language of Graphics," *Journal of Computational and Graphical Statistics* 9/3 (September 2000): 530–43; Richard Dunn, "A Dynamic Approach to Two-Variable Color Mapping," *The American Statistician* 43/4 (November 1989): 245–52.

19 Zeller, "Ideas and Trends"; Adena Schutzberg, "A Brief History of Red and Blue on U.S. Election Maps, *Directions Magazine* (October 4, 2012), available

online: http://www.directionsmag.com/articles/a-brief-history-of-red-and-blue-on-u.s.-elections-maps/281323 (accessed August 31, 2014). *Time* magazine and the *Washington Post* both published maps of the 1996 electoral results in which Bill Clinton's Democratic states were Red, while Bob Dole's Republican states were blue. This is the color scheme used by the United States National Atlas, available online: http://www.nationalatlas.gov/printable/images/pdf/elections/08_elect13.pdf (accessed August 31, 2014).

20 Reproduced in Philip B. Meggs and Alston W. Purvis, *Meggs' History of Graphic Design* (4th edn, Hoboken, NJ: John Wiley and Sons, 2006), 290.

21 Allegra Stratton, "Labour: Now it's kind of blue" [making reference to American jazz trumpeter Miles Davis's 1959 Blue Note album, *Kind of Blue*], *Guardian* Politics Blog (April 24, 2009), available online: http://www.theguardian.com/politics/blog/2009/apr/24/blue-labour-conservative-socialism (accessed August 7, 2014).

22 Andrew Hacker, "Obama: The Price of Being Black" [review of recent publications on the legacy of the Civil Rights Movement], *The New York Review of Books* 55/14 (September 25, 2008): 12–16.

23 Frere-Jones designed Gotham in 2000 for *GQ* magazine, which wanted a typeface that was "masculine, new, and fresh." The geometric, sans-serif form was inspired not only by the influential 1920s German typeface, Futura, but also by American vernacular signage in Manhattan from the 1930s to the 1950s. The name "Gotham" also evokes Manhattan as a 1930s Gotham City, and, perhaps, Obama as superhero. For the influence of the 1930s Social Realism in Shepard Fairey's HOPE poster, see also Steven Heller, "Beyond Red, White and Blue," *New York Times* (February 15, 2008), available online: http://campaignstops.blogs.nytimes.com/tag/shepard-fairey/ (accessed August 7, 2014).

24 Shepard Fairey and Jennifer Gross, *Art for Obama: Designing Manifest Hope and the Campaign for Change* (New York: Harry N. Abrams, 2009).

25 "Artist, AP Disagree Over Photo Credit, Payment," *NPR* [National Public Radio] (February 5, 2008), available online: http://campaignstops.blogs.nytimes.com/tag/shepard-fairey/ (accessed August 7, 2014).

26 The patriotic hymn, "America," with music by Samuel A. Ward and lyrics by Katharine Lee Bates, was first published in 1895. Its most familiar version dates back to 1913: "O beautiful for spacious skies, For amber waves of grain, For purple mountains majesties Above the fruited plain! America! America! God shed his grace on thee And crown thy good with brotherhood From sea to shining sea!"

27 On the campaign trail Obama was accused of being unpatriotic because he had decided not to wear a small pin in the shape of the American flag on his jacket lapel—something that some other politicians had made a habit of doing. His explanation that such a gesture was "false patriotism" did not go down well with the conservative pundits. See "Breaking News: Obama Caves! Flag Pin Returns to His Coat Lapel," *Los Angeles Times* (April 10, 2008), available online: http://latimesblogs.latimes.com/washington/2008/04/obamaflagpinlap.html (accessed August 7, 2014).

28 Susan Sontag, "Posters, Advertisement, Art, Political Artifact, Commodity," in Michael Bierut, Jessica Helfand, Steven Heller, and Rick Poynor (eds), *Looking Closer 3: Classic Writings on Graphic Design* (New York: Allworth Press, 1999), 196–218, originally published in Dugald Stermer (ed.), *The Art of Revolution: 96 Posters From Cuba* (New York: McGraw-Hill, 1970).

29 Despite their slick signage the Obama rallies, with their eclectic, rag-tag crowds of supporters, were closer in spirit to Woodstock 1969, the pivotal music festival in Woodstock, NY, than to fascist spectacles of the 1930s. See Mark Danner, "Obama, and Sweet Potato Pie," *New York Review of Books* 55 (November 20, 2008): 12–20.

30 Ibid.

31 Barack Obama, "Obama's Speech on Race," *New York Times* [video and transcript] (March 18, 2008), available online: http://www.nytimes.com/interactive/2008/03/18/us/politics/20080318_OBAMA_GRAPHIC.html?_r=0 (accessed August 31, 2014). See also Barack Obama, "A More Perfect Union: Race Speech March 18, 2008," in *Words That Changed a Nation*, 37–54.

32 David Remnick, "The Joshua Generation: Race and the Campaign of Barack Obama," *The New Yorker* (November 17, 2008): 68–83. See also David Remnick, *The Bridge: The Life and Rise of Barack Obama* (New York: Alfred A. Knopf, 2010). For further on Obama and Race, see also Colm Tóibín, "James Baldwin and Barack Obama," *The New York Review of Books* 55/16 (October 23, 2008): 18–22.

33 Russel Baker, David Bromwich, Mark Danner, Joan Didion, et al., "A Fateful Election," *The New York Review of Books* 55/17 (November 6, 2008): 4–16.

34 One of the most moving images of election night 2008 was that of civil rights leader Jesse Jackson, of the Moses generation, tears running down his cheeks. Earlier that year Jackson was caught on camera expressing frustration with the young Obama, whom he said was "talking down to Black people." He whispered under his breath, "I want to cut his nuts off." Suzanne Goldenberg, "US election 2008: 'I want to cut his nuts out'—Jackson gaffe turns focus on Obama's move to the right," *Guardian* (July 10, 2008), available online: http://www.theguardian.com/world/2008/jul/11/barackobama.uselections2008 (accessed August 7, 2014).

35 "Obama. Our Next President," *Chicago Tribune* 162/310 (November 5, 2008), section 1, pp. 1–31; "Obama. Racial Barrier Falls in Decisive Victory," *New York Times* 168/54, 585 (November 5, 2008), A1–A32, P1–P16.

36 Mary Tyler Moore, just as well known for her later role in *The Mary Tyler Moore Show*, is an interesting choice of role model, signifying both, as Laura Petrie, the conservative gender roles of 1960s domesticity, and as Mary Tyler Moore's television character, a single, working woman of the 1970s' feminist generation, living in New York City.

37 Alex Spillius, "Barack Obama as You've Never Seen Him Before," *The Telegraph* (December 17, 2008), available online: http://www.telegraph.co.uk/news/worldnews/barackobama/3815226/Barack-Obama-as-youve-never-seen-him-before.html (accessed August 31, 2014).

38 Kobena Mercer, "Black Hair/Style Politics," in Russell Ferguson, Martha Gever, Trinh T. Minh-ha, and Cornel West (eds), *Out There: Marginalization and Contemporary Culture* (New York: The New Museum of Contemporary Art, 1990): 247–64.

39 The Boston Tea Party of December 16, 1773 was a key event, resulting in the United States Declaration of Independence of 1776, and instrumental to the American Civil War. In protest to the taxation policies of the British Empire, American Colonists boarded British ships in Boston Harbor, and threw shiploads of taxed precious tea into the water. Illustrator Nathan Currier portrayed the event, which would become iconic in the American imagination, with an image of American protestors dressed as Indians while tossing tea into the harbor. Comedians and satirists ridiculed the Tea Party of 2008–12 for its use of bags of tea in various rallies and gatherings. The group's self-identification with tea and the "tea bag," furthermore, evoked a vulgar colloquial expression with which they seemed to be largely unaware. Despite the humorous and embarrassing reference, the Tea Party persisted.

40 Deirdre Walsh, "GOP-led House Authorizes Lawsuit Against Obama," CNN Politics [website] (July 31, 2014), available online: http://www.cnn.com/2014/07/30/politics/gop-obama-lawsuit/ (accessed August 31, 2014).

41 "Our collocation 'holy dread' would often coincide in meaning with 'taboo'." Sigmund Freud, "Totem and Taboo" (1913), in *The Standard Edition of the Complete Psychological Works of Sigmund Freud*, trans. James Strachey, 24 vols (London: Hogarth Press, 1953–74, 1995), vol. 13, vii–162, quote on 18.

42 Freud, "Totem and Taboo," 2.

43 William Faulkner, *Absalom, Absalom!* (1936, reprint; New York: Random House, 1964, 2002), 356.

44 Barack Obama, "Barack Obama's Full Prague Speech" [video and transcript], BBC News [website] (5 April 2009), available online: http://news.bbc.co.uk/2/hi/7984353.stm (accessed August 31, 2014); Barack Obama, "Text: Obama's Speech in Cairo," *New York Times* (4 June 2009), available online: http://www.nytimes.com/2009/06/04/us/politics/04obama.text.html?pagewanted=all (accessed August 31, 2014). See also Barack Obama, "A New Beginning" (2009), in *Barack Obama's Speeches/Los discursos de Barack Obama* (Berkeley, CA: Ulysses Press, 2010), 148–79.

45 Comedy Central, *The Daily Show With Jon Stewart*, episode 11156 (December 12, 2006).

CHAPTER SEVEN

DS

Touch Screen Goddess

For his eighth birthday, my son received a Nintendo DS. For months he had pined for this mysterious object, sleeplessly and breathlessly counting the days before that moment when the magical symbol of fantasy and social status might materialize. I fiercely resisted his wish—to no avail—being no match for the power and persuasion of technology and consumption that swept through my household. I stood by helplessly with a vision of children mindlessly, obsessively staring at a screen that flashed with seductive, violent images, and eagerly clamoring for each new improvement, addition, or replacement for the tantalizing, soon-to-be-obsolete device, and of the bloody results of such seduction, of the Columbine school shooting and other atrocities.

When he opened the box, however, I could not help but admire the sleek minimalism and elegance of the smooth red device (see Fig. 7.1).

Was this a child's toy, this small, compact rectangle with a satisfying weight in the hands? In 1954, theorist Roland Barthes described the sensuous new Citroën sports car, which was embodied in its model name "DS," pronounced in French "*déesse*" meaning "goddess."

> The DS has the beginnings of a new phenomenology of assembly, as if we were leaving a world of welded elements for a world of juxtaposed elements held together by the sole virtue of their marvelous shape ... As for the material itself, there is no question that it promotes a taste for lightness in a magical sense. ... Such spiritualization can be discerned in the importance of the quality, and the actual substance of the glazed surfaces. The Déesse is visibly an exaltation of glass ...[1]

Although we cannot make the same clever linguistic association with the English-language pronunciation of the Nintendo DS, this chapter argues that the small device, a similar technological goddess of industry, speed,

Fig. 7.1 Nintendo DS™ Lite, 2009. Author's collection. Photo by author.

and style, has a seductive power of its own which, like that of handheld mobile devices more generally, may surpass that of the 1950s automobile in the imagination of its twenty-first-century players.

According to the anonymous responses to the Frequently Asked Questions section on Nintendo's corporate website, "DS ... stands for 'Developers' System,' since we believe it gives game creators brand new tools which will lead to more innovative games for the world's players. It can also stand for 'Dual Screen'."[2]

The Nintendo DS, a handheld console for playing video games, was first released in the United States to great fanfare in November 2004, just in time for the Christmas shopping season. The success of the product—it quickly became the world's most popular gaming device—re-energized Nintendo, a Japanese company which had specialized in the design of video games and game platforms since the 1970s.

In fact, Nintendo Co., Ltd. dates to 1889, when its founder, Fusajiro Yamauchi, opened Nintendo Koppai, producer and purveyor of *hanafuda*, hand-crafted playing cards, featuring elegant illustrations of flowers painted on paper made from the bark of mulberry trees.[3] European playing cards had first been introduced to Japan by Portuguese explorers more than three hundred years before, and came to be associated with gambling. They were subsequently banned in 1633, when the country ceased trade with the West. However, decks of cards decorated with flowers and other symbols instead of numbers could more easily evade the gambling restrictions and, thus, became popular in the nineteenth century. The name *Nin-ten-do*, composed of three kanji characters, is translated roughly as "luck–heaven–hall," or "leave luck to heaven," and evokes the origin of the company in producing playing cards for games of chance.

Yamauchi's great-grandson, Hiroshi Yamauchi, who took over the company in 1949, explored a variety of business ventures beyond the production of playing cards, including the manufacture of electronic games and toys in the early 1970s.[4]

After developing a number of popular shooting games, played with light guns in old, unused bowling alleys, Nintendo produced its first consoles for playing video games in the home.[5] The company began a long collaboration with the artist Shigeru Miyamoto, who over the years has designed many of Nintendo's signature products. In the late 1970s, Miyamoto helped Nintendo to design a console game called *Space Fever*, similar to the popular game *Space Invaders* by Japanese company Taito. *Space Fever* never reached the same level of popularity as its predecessor.

Arguably more popular than *Space Invaders*, however, was Miyamoto's 1982 hit game *Donkey Kong*, which could also be played on Nintendo's handheld device Game and Watch. The device was imagined by Nintendo's game designer Gunpei Yokoi, whose inspiration purportedly came while traveling on a bullet train in Japan and seeing a passenger occupying himself with a handheld calculator.[6] In 1983, Nintendo released its Famicon, a family computer home video game console, which was called the Nintendo Entertainment System (NES) in the U.S. The NES came bundled with Miyamoto's *Super Mario Bros.*, but could also play different games using interchangeable cartridges. In 1988, Yokoi went on to develop the forerunner to the DS, the Nintendo Game Boy, which came bundled with the popular 1984 Soviet puzzle game *Tetris*.[7] By the early 1990s, Nintendo's rivals Sega and Sony were each marketing competing games and platforms. These big three companies were joined by Microsoft, which launched the XBox in 2001. Five years later, Nintendo ushered in a new generation of interactive gaming platforms with the Wii, in which the player controls the video game through the physical gesture of his or her body. Sony (PlayStation Move) and Microsoft (Kinect) followed suit, developing motion sensing games of their own.

Though some of the early video games, like *Pac-Man*, developed by the Japanese company Namco, were derived from puzzles and labyrinths, with others developing increasingly complex narratives, role-playing, and multi-tiered worlds of adventure, such as Nintendo's *The Adventures of Zelda*, the majority of popular games played in arcades and on home consoles in the late 1970s and early 1980s, like the Japanese game *Space Invaders* and Atari's *Asteroids*, involved shooting.[8] It was fun to vanquish alien beings with projectiles and explosive missiles, often in a cosmic landscape, set to dizzying, repetitive electronic soundtracks, with rhythmic pulsations and mesmerizing, flashing, vibrating screen graphics. The development of such games followed the space race of the 1960s and coincided with the arms race of the 1970s and 1980s, with its increasingly sophisticated development of military weaponry and proliferation of nuclear arms. The mythical narratives of the *Star Wars* trilogy and other space epics in late twentieth-century film, literature, and popular culture also dovetailed with the craze for video shooting games.

It is difficult to know what exactly to make of these late twentieth-century space battle video games without a lengthier investigation of military policy and weapons manufacture during the Cold War, which began after the end of the Second World War, and of the relationship of these activities to toys, games, and popular culture more generally. It is worth remembering, however, that Barthes also took note of the popular fascination with flying saucers in the mid-1950s. In a footnote to his essay "Martians," Barthes wrote that in the fall of 1954 more than 100 sightings of UFOs (unidentified flying objects) were reported in France. Following official investigations that failed to determine their origin, it was widely suspected that they had come from the Soviet Union. Not long after, however, the flying saucers were presumed to be extra-terrestrial, or Martian. Barthes explains:

> if the saucer of Soviet contrivance so readily became a Martian one, it was because in fact Western mythology attributes to the Communist world the very alterity of a planet: the USSR is a world intermediate between Earth and Mars.

In the course of the evolution of this interpretation of UFOs, he continues, the myth shifted from one of combat to one of judgment.

> Mars seeks to observe, to understand. The great USSR–USA contestation is therefore perceived from now on as a guilty state, because here the danger bears no relation to reason; hence the mythic resort to a celestial consideration, sufficiently powerful to intimidate both parties.[9]

By the later twentieth century, we might add, the potential apocalypse of mutual nuclear annihilation in an imagined showdown between the USA and USSR was projected into space.[10]

Nintendo's games, especially those designed by Miyamoto, engage the world of childhood with amusing characters and zany music. They could be seen as the electronic parallel to *Pee-wee's Playhouse*, a television program which aired in 1986 for children, written by, and starring, actor Paul Reubens. The charming and absurdist show, which acquired a cult following of adults, too, took place entirely in a make-believe land inhabited by a talking chair, a baby dinosaur, a carnival genie in a glass box, and other funny characters.

The imaginative worlds of the *Super Mario* brothers, *Donkey Kong*, and *Zelda* are rooted in Miyamoto's own low-tech childhood of outdoor adventures, in which he claims to have discovered caves, explored the bamboo forest behind a Shinto temple, carved wooden toys, and fished with his bare hands. When interviewed about his own children and their use of video games, Miyamoto replied, cheerfully, that on sunny days, of course, his son and daughter were always obliged to go outside and play. It is easy to see why Miyamoto is sometimes compared to Walt Disney. In fact, Nintendo and Disney may be linked in more ways than one. When he became president of Nintendo in 1949, Hiroshi Yamauchi licensed from Disney the rights to publish images of its cartoon characters on Nintendo's playing cards.[11] The Nintendo game stories revolving around quests to save princesses in mythical lands of enchanted creatures were likely inspired as much by Disney's beloved animated characters as by Miyamoto's own outdoor play.

Pokémon, a Nintendo franchise of games, toys, manga, animated series, and trading cards, originated as a set of role-playing video games designed in 1996 by Satoshi Tajiri. They featured the adorable Pikachu. "Pokémon," a term shortened from the name of the Japanese brand "Pocket Monsters," were all the rage among children through the turn of the twenty-first century, a phenomenon that likely resulted from Nintendo's Disney-like saturation of all children's media with the cute creatures that recall the characters in Dr. Seuss's 1974 children's book, *There's a Wocket in my Pocket!* Other useful comparisons might be drawn between Nintendo's aesthetic and the jewel-like animated films of Hayao Miyazaki (also sometimes compared to Disney), with their whimsical characters, like the memorable Totoro of the 1988 *My Neighbor Totoro*, as well as to the elaborate world of manga, Japanese comics, which Miyamoto has also said that he admires.

Fetish

When the new Nintendo DS was launched in 2004, the Chicago-based ad agency Leo Burnett was hired to design a sexy campaign, which became "touching is good," to draw in older players, especially young men, thus moving the company away from its conservative image as a purveyor of children's games. In print advertisements that ran in the somewhat risqué men's lifestyle magazine *Maxim*, Nintendo teased:

> Touching is ... thrilling, exciting, fun, weird, interesting. Sometimes a bit taboo. It's how we connect—with each other, the stuff around us, and now, our games. Here, we celebrate the most under appreciated of your five senses. We make contact. We get in touch with touching. Because with the Nintendo DS, touching is good.[12]

In late-night television spots two blue rectangles floated on a static-dotted screen, while a suggestive woman's voice, masked by electronic feedback, whispered: "Touch the bottom rectangle. Please. Go ahead, touch it. You might like it." In two additional trailers for the DS, the woman's voice and the crackling blue rectangles reappear: "See the bottom rectangle? Draw or write something in it. Don't worry; this isn't a test or anything. It's just good practice." She further urges: "Touch the screen. Someone, somewhere, wants to play with you."[13]

The ads drew attention to the DS's novel feature, two screens: the lower one for input; the upper one for display. The lower touch screen was designed to be sensitive to the touch of a finger, a sensation and activity implied in the advertisements, but which was more effectively manipulated by use of a plastic stylus that came included with the device. David Parisi describes the implication that the DS will put its user back in touch with the physical act of touching, and being touched thus:

> The screen in these ads ceases to be visual. It becomes the promise of tactile contact, no longer a window for the eye but for the hand as well. The DS is the promise of manipulating a remote body, but also the promise of being remotely manipulated by another body, becoming the touching object and the touched object. The screen is sexualized, not as a scopophilic interface that allows pleasure through remote viewing, but rather as an interface that allows for pleasurable mutual manipulation.[14]

But these are false promises. Though the user may touch the screen, he or she does not receive a reciprocal physical sensation from the device, and though the penetration of the screen with the finger is suggested, the glass surface remains impervious to touch (though the liquid crystals of the screen wriggle a little bit beneath the glass). In fact, Parisi notes, the handling of the DS, which relies upon our interface with the hard, smooth glass, is much less tactile than the more traditional joystick or textured buttons on video game controls.

The ads imply that touch is the more fundamental, more human, more primitive of our senses, something slightly dirty, or naughty, "a bit taboo."

The idea appeals to our pleasure in the forbidden. Children are often told, "Don't touch!," but with the DS they (and we) feel free to indulge the physical sensation. Barthes noted that touch was also key to the fascination with the new Citroën DS. Its admirers liked to run their fingers along its smooth and seamless surfaces and to feel the wide rubber grooves around the windows:

> this is the great tactile phase of discovery, the moment when the visual marvelous will submit to the reasoned assault of touching (for touch is the most demystifying of all the senses, unlike sight, which is the most magical).[15]

For Barthes the celebration of touch in the case of the Citroën DS signified a denigration of the visual, and brought the desired object under our control, domesticating that which had been transcendent and spiritual.[16] The same argument might be made about the Nintendo DS, which is not merely enjoyed, but rather controlled through touch.

The Nintendo DS is a fetish in both the Freudian and Marxian senses of the term. It is a ritual object that mediates the realm of social interaction. Children desire it because to possess one will give them standing among their peers. They know that it is expensive and therefore valuable. In one television ad, we can see the DS being used by teenage boys and girls for whom it signifies social status, connection to a group, and potential romance. The playfulness of an innocent game, such as *Nintendogs*, is equated with the erotic playfulness of flirtation. In another, we see a young man walk through an empty, icy, vaguely Eastern European landscape. Perhaps he is lonely, or maybe he just feels the romantic melancholy of youth. He uses his finger to write "hello" on a frosted windowpane. The windowpane writes back! By using the wireless network feature of the DS, its players can interact with one another virtually as well, potentially bridging vast distances of time and space, and bringing the world of social interaction to one's very lap. "Someone, somewhere, wants to play with you."

In addition to demonstrating Marx's concept of the commodity fetish, the strange and magical quality of an object that results from its exchange value as it becomes equated with capital, rather than labor, the DS also exemplifies Freud's notion of the fetish as substitute for sexual gratification. In his 1927 essay "Fetishism," Freud set out to explain the not uncommon practice by some men to attach feelings of desire to special objects, such as shoes, fur, velvet, or ladies' undergarments, from which they derive sexual pleasure. With his usual flair for the dramatic he wrote:

> When I now announce that the fetish is a substitute for the penis, I shall certainly create disappointment; so I hasten to add that it is not a substitute for any chance penis, but for a particular and quite special

penis that had been extremely important in early childhood but had later been lost ... To put it more plainly: the fetish is a substitute for the woman's (the mother's) penis that the little boy once believed in and ... does not want to give it up.[17]

According to Freud, the young boy, upon accidently seeing that his mother has no penis (for example, from looking up her skirt), is traumatized, and begins to fear the loss of his own. The reason that fur, velvet, shoes, and undergarments are so often fetishized is because these may remind a boy of that last moment before he gazed upward from shoes to undergarments, and glimpsed his mother's furry, velvety pubic hair. Though most boys, he writes, move beyond this experience to develop more conventional sexual relations with women, some do not, and find that they must rely for satisfaction upon these alternate, earlier developed routes.

Though many of Freud's theories of gender have been long rejected, the concept of sexual fetishism still resonates.[18] If we take Freud's idea a bit less literally, and think of the young boy's discovery as the disconcerting realization that parental (maternal) power is not all that it appears to be, it is possible to apply the experience to girls as well. But for Freud, the sexual dynamic of the mother–son relationship was particular, and the patients he treated for fetishism were exclusively male. We can easily consider the DS, particularly as advertised with erotic overtones, as representing a source of erotic gratification, though one that is actually still submerged and pre-pubescent. According to our broader interpretation, the electronic device is also a ritual object of power that enables a child to form his or her own individual identity, in relation to his peers and distinct from his parents. Just think of the tired, yet still apt, cliché of the television (or video game) as babysitter or substitute parent.

The use of the term "joystick" to refer to the control lever for video games lends further credence to game playing as sexual.[19] In his 2010 profile of Shigeru Miyamoto, writer Nick Paumgarten suggests of video games: "The best analogue for their combined disreputability and ubiquity may be masturbation."[20] Nowhere is the fetishistic character of the DS and other electronic gadgets more evident, however, than in the peculiar genre of "unboxing" videos on the Internet, in which one voyeuristically watches someone else slowly dramatize the opening of the package that contains a new electronic device, undressing it, so to speak.[21]

Pandora's Box

My highly exaggerated fear of eight-year-olds playing a game of *Mario Kart*, or a group of tweens dancing to the Wii in the living room, may seem irrational. Indeed Nintendo president Satoru Iwata has explained that the Wii was designed because the company wanted to make a game "that moms would like." (Wii Fit, Wii Sports, and Wii Dance were touted for their health benefits, since their players are arguably more physically active.) But that's not really what I fear. In my mind it is difficult to separate the goofy escapades of Mario and Luigi from those of the gangsters in *Grand Theft Auto*, from the glorification of war in *Call of Duty*, or the gratuitous violence of *Doom*—a distinction that it is often difficult for non-gamers to perceive. I know, I know.

There are all sorts of arguments for and against video games, with some claiming their power to induce psychosis, others arguing that they sharpen mental skills and improve coordination, and yet others who see them as works of art. In these quarrels video games are responsible for both mass murders, and innovative expressions of creativity. They are useful tools for childhood development and education, as well as instigators of antisocial behavior, violent racism and sexism, and even suicide.[22] But what kind of pandemonium is locked inside this box?

In 1983, Nintendo, together with several other manufacturers, including Sega, Electronic Arts, and Atari, lobbied the U.S. Congress to institute and enforce a video games rating system to help them protect and control the content of games played on their consoles. The morality of video game content had been debated since the new medium entered the public realm in the mid-1970s, and Nintendo, like its competitors, wanted to control the content of the games played on its own devices.[23] In 1982, the U.S. National Institute of Mental Health had published a report concluding that children are adversely affected by watching violent television programs. They may be less sensitive to the pain and suffering of others, more fearful of the world around them, and more likely to behave in aggressive and harmful ways toward others.[24] Video games introduced new concerns because the player is an active participant in, rather than a passive viewer of, violent content. Congress did debate the issue, though ultimately the game companies developed their own self-regulating organization, the Entertainment Software Ratings Board (ESRB), which in 1994 replaced many of the individual console-specific ratings systems. The ESRB, similar to the Motion Picture Ratings System, devised a range of classifications, from E (everyone) to AO (adults only), to categorize the games for the consumers in the United States. (Rating systems vary by nation.) A few companies, including Apple and Google, continued to use in-house rating systems, however, to rate their own computer games and apps (applications). Since the popularization of personal computing in the 1980s, and its descendant plethora of electronic devices introduced in the 1990s, video games can now be played on a variety of media and platforms. In 2010, among the top-selling games were *Call of Duty: Black Ops*; *Halo: Reach*; *Red Dead Redemption*; *Call of Duty: Modern Warfare 2*; and *Assassin's Creed: Brotherhood*, each rated M (mature).[25]

One of the first games to initiate intense public controversy was *Death Race*, introduced in 1976 by the company, Exidy (short for "Excellence in

Dynamics"). The game was modeled on the 1975 film, *Death Race 2000*, starring David Carradine and Sylvester Stallone, which achieved something of a cult following due to its sensational, violent subject matter. Ostensibly conceived as a social satire, the plot of the film involved driving racecars to run over pedestrians on purpose. The graphics of the game version were extremely rudimentary, with the pedestrians represented only by horizontal bars, and the cars by simple boxes with wheels. Nevertheless, the game provoked a "moral panic," and, it has been argued, set in place an association of video games with violence that only increased in following decades.[26]

The popular *Grand Theft Auto* franchise, marketed by the New York-based multinational company Rockstar Games, was created in 1997 by the British video game developer, DMA Design. Its origins can be traced to the 1976 *Death Race* game, with which it shares the theme of violent, and, some would argue, satirical, car crime. *Grand Theft Auto*, a fascinating world of lush images and choose-your-own-adventure style narrative, has been highly acclaimed for its aesthetic innovations in animation and gaming, in which the player inhabits a complex, immersive environment, which is represented by hyperrealistic, three-dimensional graphics. The game's visual features surely account for its success as much as does its overt violence and questionable subject matter, which includes player-initiated drunk driving, drug dealing, torture, and sex, as well as degrading portrayals of women and ethnic minorities.[27]

The representation of violence in the visual arts has a long history that dates to the prehistoric representations of the hunt in the caves at Lascaux. Violent images and subject matter are often more readily accepted when they are understood as "art," or when they are perceived to have a deeper ideological basis, such as certain forms of satire and criticism, or when they are viewed as historical artifact. The richly detailed, cinematic world of Ubisoft's game, *Assassin's Creed*, first introduced in 2007, enables the player to step back in time, and to inhabit the meticulously created cityscapes of Damascus, Constantinople, and Paris. The player's experience of violence in the imagined historical world is at once more visceral and more aestheticized. The contrast between the lavish, gilt surfaces of the Palace of Versailles, and the tattered clothing of the French peasantry in *Assassin's Creed: Unity*, for example, generates an unsettling tension, and the player is caught off guard as the camera slowly pans away from a twitching face, with naturalistically wrinkled skin, strands of hair, and blinking eyes, to reveal that we are looking at the bloody head of a decapitated noblewoman, paraded before us on a spike.

More troubling are the alleged links between game playing and real criminal behavior. Investigations of the 1999 mass shooting at Columbine High School in Littleton, Colorado, revealed that the perpetrators, two students, regularly spent time playing violent video games on their computers, the favorite among them being the science-fiction-horror-adventure game

Doom.[28] When it was introduced, in 1993, *Doom,* produced by id Software, quickly popularized the new FPS (First Person Shooter) genre in which the player perceives the game environment from the point of view of the shooter, or more specifically, from the shooter's firearm.[29] In this case, the protagonist is a "space marine" who defends himself against an array of demons. One of the Columbine shooters was a particularly avid player of *Doom* and had devised a number of mods, customized environments, and narratives, which he discussed with the gaming community in an online blog. For a time it was rumored that one of his mods was modeled on the architecture of Columbine High School and populated with its students, though this suspicion was never confirmed.

Doom was also controversial for its graphic violence. In the earliest versions of the game, set to a pulsating electronic soundtrack, the shooter blasts away at figures that groan and moan as they explode into bloody, red, pixelated pulp, while he wanders around a dark, right-angled, maze of grey cinderblock cells. In later versions of the game, introduced after Columbine, *Doom*'s CGIs (Computer Generated Images) have a smoother and more realistic look, and the fiery dungeons are slightly more visually interesting, further obscuring the boundary between fantasy and reality.[30]

The First Person Shooter genre introduced by *Doom* offers a new way to navigate virtual space. As Lev Manovich explains, the player must move through space in order to advance the game's narrative. In FPS games such as *Doom,* the player moves forward by shooting.[31] The weapon is an extension of the eye (or eye, feet, and hand combined).[32] It is a vehicle of vision and mobility that functions through destruction. Many avid gamers consider *Halo,* a military themed science-fiction game first introduced in 1999 by Bungie, and now owned by Microsoft, to be among the best designed FPS games. Considered the "killer app" for Microsoft's Xbox, *Halo* features a more complex narrative and cinematic graphics, which are set to a moody soundtrack of spiritualized chanting. Its painterly environment with bright flashes of gunfire and glowing, iridescent blue monster blood, is ostensibly more artistic and tasteful than its predecessors. Like all other fashions and trends, video games may be divided into social distinctions as well: players of *Halo* perhaps are more stylish and affluent (the game was designed to be played on a Macintosh computer) than their working class, *Doom*-playing counterparts (Walmart vs. Target?).

By contrast, Manovich writes, the navigable space of Cyan's game, *Myst,* introduced like *Doom* in 1993, is non-linear. The player wanders around a world, discovering its features along the way, rather than following pre-determined pathways and corridors. Rather than shooting things to advance the game's narrative, *Myst* enables the player to encounter a wider variety of discoveries and challenges. More broadly, he claims, virtual reality as navigable space is a new mode of thinking about the world that precedes the development of video games, FPS or otherwise. The concept of cyber-space is often attributed to William Gibson's 1984 novel, *Neuromancer,* in which the protagonist, a "space cowboy," makes his way about the virtual environment. Actually, the term "cyberspace," Manovich points out, is derived from the term "cybernetics," an idea introduced by mathematician Norbert Wiener in 1947, as he developed control systems for guided gunfire and missiles during the Second World War. Wiener defined cybernetics (based on the Greek word *kybernetikos*, "good at steering"), as "the science of control and communications in the animal and the machine."[33]

For Sherry Turkle, one of the most significant aspects of virtual reality is its capacity for simulation. "The computer offers us both new models of the mind and a new medium on which to project our ideas and fantasies. Most recently, the computer has become even more than tool and mirror: we are able to step through the looking glass."[34] *Myst*, she writes, with its branching narratives, gave way to a new type of video game based on simulation. *SimCity*, designed by Will Wright for Maxis (today a division of Electronic Arts), was first introduced in 1989. It enabled the player not only to inhabit and explore a virtual world, but also to design it, setting into motion the development of ecosystems.[35] These games, in which the player models the mind of the computer, originated in the MUD (Multiple-User Domain) games that were popular among programmers in the 1970s. In these games the player/user constructed and performed a different identity that interacted with, indeed lived, an alternate, parallel life online.

The uncanny hybrid of human–computer player, or online avatar, might be considered a version of the cyborg, a being with superhuman capabilities resulting from its combination of biological and technological parts. Though versions of the cyborg may be traced to the nineteenth century, the concept became common in science fiction literature and entertainment beginning in the 1960s.[36] The new world of virtual reality was forecasted in much poststructuralist and postmodern theoretical writing of the 1970s and 1980s, above all, that of Jean Baudrillard, who, in his influential 1981 text, *Simulacra and Simulation*, described simulation as the ultimate form of late twentieth-century capitalism. "Today what we are experiencing is the absorption of all virtual modes of expression into that of advertising. All original cultural forms, all determined languages are absorbed in advertising because it has no depth, it is instantaneous and instantaneously forgotten."[37]

In 2000, in the wake of Columbine, the American Psychiatric Association, the American Psychological Association, the American Academy of Pediatrics, the American Academy of Child and Adolescent Psychiatry, and the Parent Teacher Association together stated: "We are convinced that repeated exposure to entertainment violence in all its forms has significant public health implications." But in 2007, based on his analysis of materials belonging to the Columbine shooters, including their computer games, blogs, and diaries, psychologist Jerald Block argued that it was not the violent content of the games per se that had affected the shooters, as much as their excessive playing of them. When their computer privileges were withheld, he claimed, the shooters experienced gaming withdrawal, and began to act out their virtual fantasies in real life. In a class writing assignment for school, one of the student shooters described just such a blurring of fantasy and reality:

> Doom is so burned into my head my thoughts usually have something to do with the game. Whether it be a level or environment or whatever. In fact a dream I had yesterday was about a "Deathmatch" level that I have never even been to. It was so vivid and detailed I will probably try to recreate it using a map editor ... What I cant do in real life, I try to do in doom ... The thing is, I love that game and if others tell me "hey, its just a game." I say, "ok, I dont care." [sic][38]

The "Deathmatch" described above refers to a mode of the game in which two players connected via a computer network compete for the greatest number of kills. Games like *Doom*, Block explains, have been described as "murder simulators," which desensitize the player to violence, training him in effect, to shoot and kill.

Block's findings seem to suggest, however, that the excessive playing even of Nintendo's games, which open up many imaginary worlds to children, who sometimes play them for hours in a near catatonic state, could lead to a dangerous condition of media withdrawal. His interpretations recall Marshall McLuhan's theories of the effects of electronic media, the content of which is independent from the mechanism of the media and its effect upon our bodies and our psyches. In one of his best-known examples, McLuhan writes of the electric light bulb, a new medium introduced toward the end of the nineteenth century:

> Whether the light is being used for brain surgery or night baseball is a matter of indifference. It could be argued that these activities are in some way the "content" of the electric light, since they could not exist without the electric light. This fact merely underlines the point that "the medium is the message" because it is the medium that shapes and controls the scale and form of human association and action.[39]

In the same manner, therefore, it is not the violent content of the television program upon children that is problematic so much as the destabilizing effect of the medium itself. Though McLuhan's theories were developed before the popularization of video games and personal computing, his perceptions of the effects of television, which he described as a "cool," low-definition technology, requiring its viewers to experience it imaginatively in totality, like stepping into a bathtub, seem particularly applicable to an understanding of virtual reality at the turn of the twenty-first century.

Of course many claims have also been made linking the content of specific games to sociopathic tendencies. Among the most chilling examples is that of the 2011 mass shooting in Norway of sixty-nine teenagers at a summer camp retreat outside Oslo, and the simultaneous killing of eight additional people in a bomb explosion that the shooter set as a diversion. In that case, the killer claims, he had practised for the event by playing the popular military-themed game, *Call of Duty*, first introduced in 2003. Like *Doom* and *Halo*, *Call of Duty* is a First Person Shooter game, in which the player sees through the eyes of his avatar on screen, signified by the barrel of a gun that he directs through the game environment. The shooter can play alone in single-player mode, or together with his fellow soldiers to carry out various missions in cooperative (co-op) mode. The first version *Call of Duty* game was set during the Second World War and featured historically authentic weaponry; sequels of the game, including the popular *Call of Duty: Black Ops* version, are set during the Cold War, and take place in Vietnam, Korea, and other locations. The games are not merely recreations of battle, but rather historical fantasy fiction that combine war drama with monster fighting. The 2014 *Call of Duty: Advanced Warfare* game expanded the genre by moving the stories into the future.

Call of Duty was also cited as a possible instigating factor in the 2012 mass shooting of twenty first-graders at Sandyhook Elementary School in Newtown, Connecticut. Investigators found evidence that the shooter had spent many hours playing *Call of Duty* in the basement of his home, where he may have also practiced target shooting, using a large stockpile of firearms and ammunition. It is unclear, however, if the game had any direct influence on the Sandyhook Elementary School shooting, or if it was just one of many environmental factors and pieces of evidence that revealed the perpetrator's preoccupation with mass shootings. In addition to the guns, ammunition, and video games were found a number of newspaper articles and photographs documenting the grizzly results of similar school shootings, including the one that took place at my own institution, Northern Illinois University, on February 14, 2008.[40]

In her analysis of *Death Race*, Carly Kocurek argues that the reason the game caused such controversy in its time is that its violence operated outside the confines of "state sanctioned" violence in military-themed games, or of long established genres of romanticized violence, such as westerns or law enforcement dramas. While many of the earliest video games, especially those played in arcades, were the legacy of shooting gallery entertainment at fairs and carnivals, today such games are used to train United States military forces. Much controversy has arisen, for example, from the fact of unmanned drones flown by the United States to carry out attacks in Pakistan, and other suspected terrorist lairs, in a secretive and largely unreg- ulated war. These drones, as it turns out, often controlled from a remote location, such as a military base in Colorado, are effectively operated by gamer-soldiers, whose skills are honed on simulators.[41] Shooting games are not exclusively designed for men, but they play upon the machismo of the cowboy, the sheriff, the pioneer, and the gangster, while also evoking childhood playground games—cowboys and Indians, cops and robbers, dodge ball, freeze tag. Such motifs are repeated in the imaginative wars of fantasy superheroes and space battles as well. Games that fall outside this familiar and normative structure are suspect. But I think what troubles us so is perhaps something different; we are ambivalent about childhood. We want to protect children from harm, while also indoctrinating them into approved narratives of violence. We allow, indeed encourage them to read comic books, to play shooting games, and to play with guns. It is likely for this reason that the Newtown shooter's matricide was so distressing. Before opening fire on the children at Sandyhook Elementary School, he blasted away his mother beyond recognition by shooting her in the face, with her own weapons, while she slept.[42]

Propaganda produced during wartime always encourages and fuels a hatred of the enemy, particularly when that "enemy Other" can be visually described in terms of ethnic difference. Though we could study this phenomenon from the point of view of every historical war, today the Arab or Muslim represents the "enemy Other" in many war games.[43] Iraqi conceptual artist Wafaa Bilal commented provocatively on new media's ability to let players psychologically distance themselves from the "enemy Other" in his 2007 performance/installation, *Domestic Tension*. While living in a Chicago gallery for thirty days, Bilal invited viewers via webcam to virtually "shoot an Iraqi" with yellow paintballs rigged to a web-operated gun. While raising questions about post-traumatic stress, racism, violence, and the alienation of new media, Bilal was shot 60,000 times during the course of the experiment.[44]

Forbidden Fruit

The new Citroën manifestly falls from heaven insofar as it presents itself first of all as a superlative *object*. It must not be forgotten that the object is the supernatural's best messenger: in this object there is easily a perfection and an absence of origin, a completion and a brilliance, a transformation of life into matter (matter being much more magical than life), and all in all a *silence* which belongs to the order of the marvelous.[45]

In comparison to Apple's many computing and mobile devices, upon which video games are often played today, the DS touch screen seems rather primitive. If Nintendo's launch of the childishly innocent, yet erotically charged, DS let loose a wave of covetous desire among its consumers, the release of Apple's iPhone, dubbed the "Jesus phone" in 2007, was nothing short of a supernatural event (see Fig. 7.2).[46]

In accordance with the plan that had been set in place by the computing company's CEO, Steve Jobs, before he passed away in 2011, Apple, Inc. envisioned a family of products that appeal to young, hip customers with

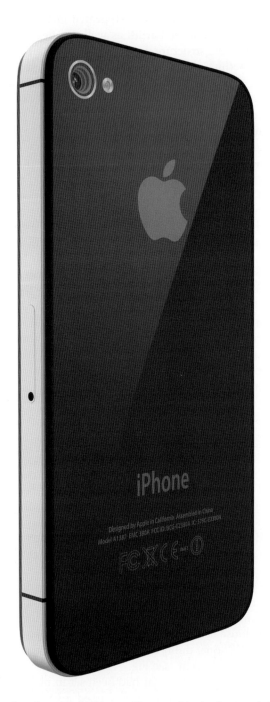

Fig. 7.2 A 3D render of an Apple iPhone 4S on a white background, February 28, 2012: (Image by Simon Edwards / Future Publishing via Getty Images).

disposable income. The iPhone was followed in 2010 by the iPad, a touch screen tablet, and then by the iPod Touch, which was introduced in 2013 as the most recent and most sophisticated in a line of devices that first appeared in 2001 for playing music and storing audio files. The objects are visually appealing in a modernist way, with their smooth "optical glass" screens and sleek casings of aluminum or polycarbonate plastics and colorless palette of silver, black, and white. When the device is turned off or in its stand-by mode, one can see one's own reflection in the deep black glass surface, as well as in the silvery chrome apple-shaped logo on its back. A new generation of iPod, iPhone, or iPad is designed at least once a year in conjunction with operating system upgrades. The constant improvements to and novel features for each new device, as well as its limited battery life, assure its obsolescence and fuel the consumer's desire for the new. This makes good sense, not only because it generates tremendous revenue for Apple and its powerful telecommunications partners, but because such small, fragile, and expensive items, constantly fondled and caressed, are often lost, stolen, or broken in that short period of time.

Far more than simply a means of staying in touch, the iPhone is a telephone with the capability to connect to the Internet with cellular phone service, or through a wireless computing network. The "smartphone" is, thus, a small computer equipped with camera, speakers, and global positioning system (GPS), and it can be used with a limitless array of apps that allow one to read, watch television and movies, play games, keep a calendar of events and appointments, make photo albums, monitor fitness, follow investments and social media, shop, check the weather, look up a recipe, pay bills, find a map and directions, use a flashlight, or tell the time. It combines the utility of a Swiss Army knife with the chic elegance of a cosmetics compact that fits neatly into one's purse. It is the apple of your eye and the Wocket in your pocket.

Steve Jobs and Steve Wozniac, bright college students with backgrounds in computing and engineering, founded the California-based Apple Computer Co. in 1976. The counter-culture ethos of their first experimental computers is expressed in the company's original trademark, designed by Ronald Wayne, an eighteenth-century style illustration of Sir Isaac Newton seated beneath an apple tree. The glowing orb of the apple dangles above his head as he contemplates. The moment depicted is just before the apple falls, hits Newton on the head, and leads him to formulate his theory of gravity. The antiquated look of the original logo was in keeping with the handcrafted appearance of the original wooden circuit board computer, Apple I, which was sold without monitor, case, or keyboard. It had the homemade, DIY (do-it-yourself) character of the *Whole Earth Catalogue*, and was designed in part to help facilitate the at-home production of flyers, mailings, and databases. It looked quite different from the magical, fetishized objects that fell from Apple's tree in the twenty-first century.

The iMac, the great-grandchild of the Apple II, Macintosh, Power Mac, and PowerBook laptop computers, was launched in 1998, when Jobs returned to lead the company after being ousted from it and spending a decade away.[47] Its soft translucent blue and white orb with a single electrical cord and no messy cables let its users connect directly to the Internet, and was introduced with an appealing advertisement campaign highlighting the clean, minimal look of the object and the creativity and innovation that it signified with the catchy slogan: "Think different." While first introducing the iMac in 1998, Jobs explained the use of the letter i in the new product name, which stood for "Internet, individual, instruct, inform, and inspire," highlighting Apple's intended educational market.[48]

In 1999, Apple introduced the iBook laptop computer in a similar rounded shape, which could be purchased in a tangerine or blueberry color. Shown together with the subsequent models in graphite, indigo, and Key lime, the candy-colored iBook laptops evoked the colorful rainbow of the company's apple logo, designed by Rob Janoff, which had been used for over twenty years. When it was closed and carried like a briefcase, the new iBook laptop, with its built-in amber colored handle, looked very much like a stylish handbag. These new products were thrilling, and made their users feel both smart and fashionable.

Jobs touted the first iMac, just as critics had hailed television a half century earlier, as looking like something from another planet, but in this case, "a good planet ... with better designers!"[49] In addition to their intriguing translucence and sensuous, self-contained shape, the new computers featured Apple's signature display graphics and typefaces, the first of which were designed in-house by Susan Kare with great attention to their aesthetic features.[50] The familiar-yet-futuristic space age form of the iMac was a marked visual contrast, Jobs claimed, to the "ugly" PCs then in use. The many creative programs for arranging photos, organizing music, and making movies in Apple's iLife suite of software likewise contributed to the symbiotic relationship between consumer and product. Apple's new advertising strategy, which included the elimination of the rainbow stripes from its second logo (the colors were absorbed into the products themselves), and a series of witty television spots, played upon the contrast between the hip Mac and the square PC.[51]

The antipathy which today remains between Apple and its competitors, results from an ideological split that occurred the 1970s. While computing had been a modernist culture of calculation, Turkle explains, by the 1980s those who worked with personal computers were increasingly comfortable with working on the surface, and had no knowledge of or interest in the coded inner workings of the machine. Apple contributed to this visual and psychological ease of use by producing a postmodern system in which one could work seamlessly with a set of interactive screen icons, "getting to know the computer by interacting with it, as one might get to know a person or explore a town," a model that was emulated as well in Microsoft's Windows operating system in 1985.[52] In subsequent revisions in 2001 and

2007, which coincided with the introduction of its new iproducts, Apple's logo became ever more ethereal. Though the shape of the apple remained, it turned from a colorless, flat black or white, to a kind of quicksilver with the character of liquid mercury, which reflects the matte silver sheen of the new iMac and MacBook Pro, housed in seamless aluminum casings. The backlit apple icon in the casing glows whenever the computer is active, which ensures its constant product-placement advertising in coffee shops, classrooms, television shows, films, and anywhere else it is used.

The apple is an interesting and evocative trademark, much like Golden's CBS eye, because it is simultaneously an abstract icon, perceived in Gestalt, and a naturalistic representation of something in the world. The flattened, conventionalized shape of the apple, which has already been bitten, is richly layered with cultural and historical associations. If Isaac Newton's apple-induced revelation is one association, linking the company to notions of brilliance, science, intelligence, creativity, innovation, and enlightenment, the forbidden fruit of the tree of knowledge of good and evil is another.

In the biblical creation story, described in Genesis, we learn that as he created the world:

> [T]he Lord God planted a garden eastward in Eden; and there he put the man whom he had formed. And out of the ground made the Lord God to grow every tree that is pleasant to the sight, and good for food; the tree of life also in the midst of the garden, and the tree of the knowledge of good and evil.[53]

God put Adam in charge of the garden's care, and warned: "Of every tree of the garden thou mayest freely eat; But of the tree of the knowledge of good and evil, thou shalt not eat of it: for in the day that thou eatest thereof thou shalt surely die."[54] God then made for Adam a companion, Eve, who was shortly thereafter charmed in the garden by a serpent who persuaded her to go ahead and eat the fruit from the tree, which would be sure to bring enlightenment: "your eyes shall be opened, and ye shall be as gods, knowing good and evil."[55]

Desiring wisdom, Eve tasted the fruit and shared it with Adam, too. Before eating the fruit, the two had been naked together in the garden, as God had created them, and they were not ashamed. Once they tasted the fruit, however, "the eyes of them both were opened, and they knew that they were naked," and sewed fig leaves together to cover themselves.[56]

The result of Eve's seduction (of her beguilement by the serpent, followed by her own tempting of Adam) is the awareness of sin, signified by the first humans' recognition of their own nude bodies as shamefully naked, and of their exile from the garden, banishment from Paradise, and curse of eternal misery of hard, physical labor and pain of childbirth. Because of their disobedience and rejection of authority Adam and Eve *do* gain knowledge, but they suffer for it. The story might have been written today specifically for Apple Inc., signified by the image of a bitten apple, the fruit of the tree of knowledge of good and evil that has already been tasted. Its seductive products, "pleasing to the eye," and with a promise of tasting good (or good taste), tempt consumers to indulge rebelliously in the sensual and intellectual pleasures of the Apple, as well as its resulting sins of pride and envy.

One noticeable side effect of the smartphone today is the tendency of its users to stare obsessively at its screen, in public or in private, at work or at home, on the train, in a restaurant, on a date, while walking down the street, ordering coffee, attending a parent–teacher conference, concert, or a business meeting, in the doctor's office, or even while driving a car. Texting while driving is a dangerous, potentially deadly activity that is now illegal in some form in all U.S. states and territories. This obsessive staring at "smartphones" ironically makes their users appear far from smart, perhaps even mentally impaired, as anyone knows who has had an uncanny encounter with a person speaking loudly to an invisible conversation partner while walking down the street. The pandemonium of violent video games with their often alleged, but rarely substantiated, links to homicidal and sociopathic behavior is one sort. The pandemonium unleashed by our dependence on electronic devices with their clearly substantiated links to destructive activities, from our excessive consumption of energy to our lethal texting-while-driving, is quite another. It is possible that new voice recognition software will help to alleviate the dangers and cumbersome inconvenience of texting. After Eve was banished from the garden of Eden she changed her name to Siri, and now spends her time tempting those who have a taste for apples with the infinite pleasures of information.

A Game that Moms Will Like

For children the real message of the DS with its promise of social acceptance and admiration by one's peers is not that having one will make them "cool," but more painfully that *not* to have one will make them unpopular. The jealous desire they feel for electronic devices is not a metaphor. It is real, and results in real tears, real frustration, real rage, and sometimes in real pleasure. Once in hand the object's supernatural aura is quickly domesticated and just as rapidly abandoned for the next glittering promise of something new. Is the Nintendo DS or Wii, as Satoru Iwata had hoped, "a game that moms like"? Parents are told that they ought to limit a child's screen time, and many believe that excessive television or video games may somehow damage her tender psyche, or at the very least prevent her from getting her homework done.

In 2011, legal scholar and Yale professor Amy Chua published a bestselling, controversial memoir, *Battle Hymn of the Tiger Mother*, an account of her own adventures as the American daughter of Chinese immigrants, raising her two young girls.[57] She insisted in her book that playing video games (like sleepovers, visits to water parks, and even after school theater club) was a tremendous waste of time, when a child could and should be groomed to play music and perform highly on her academic work by practising her instrument and studying for hours every day. Her hilarious, tongue-in-cheek, self-deprecating indictment of the obsessive parent, incited rage among some readers, however. Many felt attacked for their kinder, gentler, more relaxed style of parenting. Such progressive parenting methods, with sources in the kindergarten experiments of the early nineteenth century, had become popular in the 1960s and 1970s, when it was fashionable to nurse, nurture, and attend to one's baby around the clock.[58] More disciplinarian methods went out of favor in the 1950s.

So readers were not quite sure how to respond to Chua's politically incorrect identification of herself as a stereotypical "Chinese mother" with high academic demands for her children, which uneasily called to question America's slipping world status academically, as well as economically, in the face of a rising China. But I think Chua's characterization of the Asian or Asian American immigrant experience might have been a red herring. I think parents (moms especially) were angry because they felt secretly guilty and jealous. It's awfully easy to set a child down in front of an electronic device. It's much harder to resist the serpent's temptation of the tasty apple, and to make a child do anything difficult, whether practise piano scales or write out math problems. Where on earth did this glamorous law professor find the time to take her daughters to music lessons and to practise their instruments with them for several hours every day, all while pursuing a demanding academic career?

Chua's out of hand rejection of video games in favor of more traditional intellectual and artistic pursuits for children seemed old-fashioned and reactionary in 2011, recalling the 1980s and Tipper Gore's war on video games, taken up by mothers concerned about violence and profanity in popular media.[59] The amusingly cynical title of Chua's book evokes stereotypes of American patriotism mixed with those of Protestant religious fervor and Asian ferocity.

"The Battle Hymn of the Republic," with lyrics by Julia Ward Howe, was first published in *The Atlantic* in 1862. With its apocalyptic verses and rousing chorus, "Glory, glory, hallelujah!," it became a popular rallying song during the American Civil War.[60] What are we to do about our children as we forge ahead inevitably into the future? As Turkle states, when it comes to new technology: "It is our children who are leading the way, and adults who are anxiously trailing behind."[61]

It's been a long day and I'd like to soothe away its tensions by gazing numbly into the screen of the "family" tablet. Chances are, however, that I won't be able to find it, and if I do, it will not be charged. (Chargers in our household usually go missing after having been yanked violently from the electrical outlets in the wall.)

Aha! There it is.

The cover is tattered and torn and the screen is cracked because children like to store things between sofa cushions and in the middle of the floor. I can't figure out how to escape from this frozen video game, and I can't quite see through the blurry smear of greasy fingerprints and snack seasoning on its touch screen.

Yuck.

Notes

1   Roland Barthes, "The New Citroën," in *Mythologies*, trans. Richard Howard and Annette Lavers (New York: Hill and Wang, 2012), 169–71.

2   "What does DS stand for?" Nintendo Support [website], available online: http://en-americas-support.nintendo.com/app/answers/detail/a_id/3904/p/606 (accessed August 4, 2014).

3   Chris Kohler, "Sept. 23, 1889: Success is in the Cards for Nintendo," *Wired* (23 September 2010), available online: http://www.wired.com/2010/09/0923nintendo-founded/ (accessed August 4, 2014).

4   David Sheff, *Game Over: How Nintendo Conquered the World* (Wilton, CT: Cyberactive Publishing, 1999), 12–21.

5   The light gun, which could be considered a predecessor to the gaming mouse or joystick, is shaped like a pistol or rifle and emits a beam of light. Players shoot at images projected on a screen, which registers whether or not targets have been hit. In 1971 Gunpei Yokoi designed Nintendo's first light gun, the Opto-Electronic Gun SP (the forerunner to Nintendo's Beam Gun) for use in the abandoned bowling alleys. Florent Gorges and Isao Yamazaki, *The History of Nintendo, Volume 1, 1889–1980, From Playing Cards to Game and Watch* (London: Pix'n Love, 2010), 182.

6   Lara Crigger, "Searching for Gunpei Yokoi," *The Escapist* (6 March 2007), available online: http://www.escapistmagazine.com/articles/view/video-games/issues/issue_87/490-Searching-for-Gunpei-Yokoi (accessed August 4, 2014).

7   Kate Carmody, "Less is More: Technology and Toys," in Juliet Kinchin and Aidan O'Connor (eds), *Century of the Child: Growing By Design 1900–2000* (exh. cat., New York: Museum of Modern Art, 2012), 208–9.

8   Atari is a Japanese expression meaning "to hit the target."

9   Roland Barthes, "Martians," in *Mythologies*, 38–40.

10 The Cold War military strategy of Mutually Assured Destruction (MAD) reached its height in the United States under the presidency of Ronald Reagan in the 1980s. It was dramatized in the 1983 film *WarGames*, written by Lawrence Lasker and Walter E. Parkes. The film coincided with the introduction of the United States' Strategic Defense

Initiative (SDI), nicknamed the "Star Wars" program after the 1977 film by George Lucas.

11 Seth Schiesel, "Resistance is Futile," *New York Times* (May 25, 2008), available online: http://www.nytimes.com/2008/05/25/arts/television/25schi. html?pagewanted=all&_r=0 (accessed August 4, 2014).

12 "Touching is …" Touchingisgood [website], available online: http://www. touchingisgood.com/ (accessed August 4, 2014).

13 David Parisi, "Fingerbombing, or 'Touching is Good': The Cultural Construction of Technologized Touch," *Senses and Society* 3/3 (2008): 307–27; Advertisements for Nintendo DS, YouTube, available online: https:// www.youtube.com/watch?v=a8iclKPzrEc (accessed August 4, 2014).

14 Parisi, "Fingerbombing," 313.

15 Barthes, "The New Citroën," 171.

16 For further see Martin Jay, *Downcast Eyes: The Denigration of Vision in Twentieth-Century French Thought* (Berkeley: University of California Press, 1993).

17 Sigmund Freud, "Fetishism" (1927), in *The Standard Edition of the Complete Psychological Works of Sigmund Freud*, trans. James Strachey, 24 vols (London: Hogarth Press, 1953–74, 1995), vol. 21, 149–57.

18 Laura Mulvey, "Some Thoughts on Theories of Fetishism in the Context of Contemporary Culture," *October* 65 (Summer 1993): 3–20. See also Emily Apter, *Feminizing the Fetish: Psychoanalysis and Narrative Obsession in Turn-of-the-Century France* (Ithaca: Cornell University Press, 1991); William Pietz, "Fetish," in Robert S. Nelson and Richard Shiff (eds), *Critical Terms for Art History* (Chicago: University of Chicago Press, 1992), 197–207.

19 "joy-stick, *n*.," *Oxford English Dictionary Online* (June 2014), available online: http://www.ulib.niu.edu:2846/view/Entry/101795?redirectedFrom=joys tick#eid40463102 (accessed August 4, 2014).

20 Nick Paumgarten, "Master of Play: The Many Worlds of a Video-Game Artist," *The New Yorker*, 86/41 (December 20, 2010): 86–99.

21 Mike Rugnetta, "What's the Deal With Unboxing Videos?" PBS Idea Channel [website] (February 12, 2014), available online: https://www.youtube.com/ watch?v=xSUuO84BTSA&feature=youtu.be&t=1m18s (accessed September 1, 2014).

22 Among the most outspoken critics of video game violence and its detrimental effects on children is Craig A. Anderson, Professor of Psychology at Iowa State University. See Craig A. Anderson, Douglas A. Gentile, and Katherine E. Buckley, *Violent Video Game Effects on Children and Adolescents: Theory, Research, and Public Policy* (Oxford: Oxford University Press, 2007); C. A. Anderson, Ihori Nobuko, B. J. Bushman, et al., "Violent Video Game Effects on Aggression, Empathy, and Prosocial Behavior in Eastern and Western Countries: A Meta-Analytic Review," *Psychological Bulletin* 126/2 (2010): 151–73. By contrast, Christopher J. Ferguson, Professor of Psychology at Stetson University in DeLand, Florida, finds that such research does not reveal a link between video games and violence. See Christopher J. Ferguson, "Video Games Don't

Make Kids Violent," *Time* (December 7, 2011), available online: http://ideas.
time.com/2011/12/07/video-games-dont-make-kids-violent/ (accessed August
4, 2014); Christopher J. Ferguson, "Blazing Angels or Resident Evil? Can
Violent Video Games Be a Force for Good?" *Review of General Psychology*
14/2 (2010): 68–81. On the relationship of video games to education see Ben
Matthews, Marcella Stienstra, and Tom Djajadiningrat, "Emergent Interaction:
Creating Spaces for Play," *Design Issues* 24/3 (Summer 2008): 58–71.

23   Carly Kocurek, "The Agony and the Exidy: A History of Video Game
Violence and the Legacy of Death Race," *Game Studies: The International
Journal of Computer Game Research*, 12/1 (September 2012), available
online: http://gamestudies.org/1201/articles/carly_kocurek (accessed August 4,
2014).

24   David Pearl, Lorraine Bouthilet, and Joyce B. Lazar, *Television and Behavior:
Ten Years of Scientific Progress and Implications for the Eighties*, 2 vols
(Rockville, MD: U.S. Dept. of Health and Human Services, Public Health
Service, Alcohol, Drug Abuse, and Mental Health Administration, National
Institute of Mental Health, 1982), vol. 1.

25   "Top 10 Video Games of December and Full Year 2010," *Los Angeles
Times* (January 13, 2011), available online: http://latimesblogs.latimes.
com/entertainmentnewsbuzz/2011/01/top–0-games-of-december-2010-and-
full-year-2010.html (accessed August 4, 2014).

26   Kocurek, "The Agony and the Exidy."

27   Nate Garrelts (ed.), *The Meaning and Culture of Grand Theft Auto: Critical
Essays* (Jefferson, NC: McFarland and Company, 2006).

28   Dirk Johnson and James Brooke, "Terror in Littleton: The Suspects; Portraits
of Outcasts Seeking to Stand Out," *New York Times* (April 22, 1999),
available online: http://www.nytimes.com/1999/04/22/us/terror-in-littleton-
the-suspects-portrait-of-outcasts-seeking-to-stand-out.html (accessed August 4,
2014).

29   David Kushner, *Masters of Doom: How Two Guys Created an Empire and
Transformed Pop Culture* (New York: Random House, 2004).

30   Fethi Kaba, "Hyper-Realistic Characters and the Existence of the Uncanny
Valley in Animation Films," *International Review of Social Sciences and
Humanities* 4/2 (2013): 188–95.

31   Lev Manovich, *The Language of New Media* (Cambridge, MA: MIT Press,
2001), 151.

32   For Marshall McLuhan, "the rifle is an extension of the eye and teeth."
Marshall McLuhan, *Understanding Media: The Extensions of Man* (New
York: McGraw-Hill, 1964), 341.

33   Manovich, *The Language of New Media*, 250–1.

34   Sherry Turkle, *Life on the Screen: Identity in the Age of the Internet* (New
York: Touchstone, 1995), 9.

35   Turkle, *Life on the Screen*, 69; Manovich, *The Language of New Media*, 223.
See also Michael Heim, "The Design of Virtual Reality," *Body and Society*
1/3-4 (1995): 65–77; Ken Hillis, *Digital Sensations: Space, Identity, and*

Embodiment in Virtual Reality (Minneapolis: University of Minnesota Press, 1999).

36 Donna Haraway, "A Manifesto for Cyborgs: Science, Technology, and Socialist Feminism in the 1980s," in *The Haraway Reader* (London: Routledge, 2004), 7–46.

37 Jean Baudrillard, *Simulacra and Simulation*, trans. Sheila Faria Glaser (Ann Arbor: University of Michigan Press, 1994), 87.

38 Jerald J. Block, "Lessons From Columbine: Virtual and Real Rage," *American Journal of Forensic Psychiatry* 28/2 (2007): 5–33. Quotation on p. 15.

39 McLuhan, *Understanding Media*, 8–9.

40 N. R. Kleinfeld, Ray Rivera, and Serge F. Kovaleski, "Newtown Killer's Obsessions, Chilling Detail," *New York Times* (March 28, 2013), available online: http://www.nytimes.com/2013/03/29/nyregion/search-warrants-reveal-items-seized-at-adam-lanzas-home.html?pagewanted=all (accessed August 5, 2015). "6 Dead in NIU Shooting: Gunman Opens Fire in Lecture Hall, Then Kills Self; 16 Others Injured in 3 p.m. Attack; Shooter a Former Graduate Student," *Chicago Tribune* (February 15, 2008), section 1, 1.

41 Carrie Elizabeth Anderson, "Game of Drones: The Uneasy Future of the Soldier-Hero in *Call of Duty: Black Ops II*," *Surveillance and Society* 12/3 (2014): 360–76.

42 Matt Flegenheimer and Ravi Somaiya, "A Mother, A Gun Enthusiast and the First Victim," *New York Times* (December 15, 2012), available online: http://www.nytimes.com/2012/12/16/nyregion/friends-of-gunmans-mother-his-first-victim-recall-her-as-generous.html?_r=0 (accessed August 5, 2015).

43 Vit Sisler, "Digital Arabs: Representation in Video Games," *European Journal of Cultural Studies* 11/2 (2008): 203–20.

44 Wafaa Bilal, *Shoot an Iraqi: Art, Life and Resistance Under the Gun* (San Francisco: City Lights, 2008).

45 Barthes, "The New Citroën," p. 169.

46 "Apple's 'magical' iPhone unveiled," *BBC News* (9 January 2007), available online: http://news.bbc.co.uk/2/hi/technology/6246063.stm (accessed August 5, 2015); John Heilmann, "Steve Jobs in a Box," *New York Magazine* (June 17, 2007), available online: http://nymag.com/news/features/33524/ (accessed August 5, 2015).

47 Walter Isaacson, *Steve Jobs* (New York: Simon and Schuster, 2011).

48 "Original iMac Introduction – Apple Special Event (1998)," May 6, 1998, Flint Center, Cupertino, California, Every Steve Jobs Video [website], available online: http://everystevejobsvideo.com/original-imac-introduction-apple-special-event-1998/ (accessed May 27, 2015).

49 Ibid.

50 Johanna Drucker and Emily McVarish, *Graphic Design History: A Critical Guide* (2nd edn, Upper Saddle River, NJ: Pearson, 2013), 314–15.

51 Seth Stevenson, "Mac Attack: Apple's Mean-Spirited New Ad Campaign," *Slate* (June 19, 2006), available online: http://www.slate.com/articles/business/ad_report_card/2006/06/mac_attack.html (accessed August 4, 2014).

52 Turkle, *Life on the Screen*, 23.

53 Genesis 2:8-9 (King James Version).

54 Ibid.

55 Genesis 3:5 (King James Version).

56 Genesis 3:7 (King James Version).

57 Amy Chua, *Battle Hymn of the Tiger Mother* (New York: Penguin, 2011).

58 William and Martha Sears promoted the attachment method of parenting in their popular manual, *The Baby Book: Everything You Need to Know About Your Baby From Birth to Age Two* (Boston: Little, Brown and Company, 1993).

59 Mary Elizabeth Gore, *Raising PG Kids in an X-Rated Society* (Nashville, TN: Abingdon Press, 1987).

60 The lyrics to "Battle Hymn of the Republic," written by Julia Ward Howe, American abolitionist and social activist, were published in *The Atlantic* (February 1872). See John Stauffer and Benjamin Soskis, *The Battle Hymn of the Republic: A Biography of the Song That Marches On* (Oxford: Oxford University Press, 2013).

61 Turkle, *Life on the Screen*, 10.

CHAPTER EIGHT

Just Do It

Mythologies of the Athletic Shoe

Sporting activities, together with the sportswear that accompanies them, are often at the center of our emotional life. Sports represent physical discipline, as well as leisure and consumption, and they inform our aesthetic of the human body. They are key to shaping feelings of patriotism and, by extension, nationalism, while also serving as ambassadors of international communication. In Chapter 4, we noticed the ways in which sports team mascots become tied to feelings of allegiance and identity, which are especially nurtured in childhood and youth. Sports are also important tools for parents and educators who instill in children ideas of what it means to be a good citizen, to be responsible, to share, to be a team player, and to have respect for authority. At the same time sports teach us about individual achievement and competition. As ubiquitous as shooting metaphors in the English language are expressions that derive from sports: *What's your game plan? Is he up to par? She's stepping up to the plate.* Similarly, sportswear is a means of communication, through a complex language of shapes and colors, materials and styles, as well as through the visual signifiers of brands. It can be both uniform and fashion statement. This chapter examines our relationship to sports and sportswear, and to the athletic shoe in particular, by focusing on one brand—Nike—whose name, products, and corporate identity are especially rich in meaning.

Winged Victory

Nike, the winged goddess of victory, was companion to Athena, patron goddess of wisdom, art, and war in ancient Greece (See Fig. 8.1).

Nike's namesake, Nike, Inc., the global athletic shoe and apparel company, features as its trademark an iconic swooping, aerodynamic "swoosh," a graphic mark that suggests speed, like one of Constantin Brancusi's elegant,

Fig. 8.1 Victory of Samothrace (Nike). Hellenistic, 2nd century BCE. Marble, h: 328 cm (129 in). MA2369. Photo: Thierry Olivier. Musée du Louvre, Paris, France. ART495152. © Musée du Louvre. Dist. RMN—Grand Palais/Thierry Olivier/Art Resource, NY.

abstract sculptures of a bird in flight. Nike, in both its name and its products, suggests several orders of myth, from the Greek goddess Nike herself to Mercury, god of travelers, known for his swift flights, who was often depicted wearing winged shoes. Mercury, due to his mercurial nature, was also the patron god of commerce, financial gain, luck, divination, eloquence, and poets, but also trickery and thieves, and he served as a guide for souls as they moved after death from this world to the underworld.

Nike's mercurial slippers are made of a blend of materials, including cotton, nylon, rubber, polyester, polyurethane, ethylene-vinyl acetate, and other polymers. Roland Barthes described plastic in the 1950s as "a magical" and "alchemical" substance with "Greek shepherds' names (Polystyrene, Phenoplast, Polyvinyl, Plyethylene)," writing:

> Thus, more than a substance, plastic is the very ideal of its infinite transformation ... it is ubiquity made visible; moreover, this is the reason why it is a miraculous substance: a miracle is always a sudden conversion of nature. Plastic remains completely impregnated by this astonishment: it is less an object than the trace of a movement.[1]

But plastic, for Barthes, like Mercury's dual nature, was also a "disgraced material, lost between the effusion of rubber and the flat hardness of metal." With its "quick-change talent," he writes, "it can form pails as well as jewels."[2]

The Nike shoe company, like Apple, has its origin in the countercultural atmosphere of the west coast. It was founded officially in 1971, though got its start in the 1960s, when owner Phil Knight, a track-and-field coach at the University of Oregon, made an unusual pair of shoes for his college runner, Otis Davis, who would later go on to win two gold medals at the 1960 summer Olympics in Rome. Knight fashioned a unique shoe for Davis, according to various accounts, by pressing its rubbery sole with a waffle iron.

Knight became partners with another runner whom he had coached in college, Bill Bowerman, when the latter returned with entrepreneurial energy after just having earned a Master of Business degree at Stanford University. Bowerman thought that Knight ought to market Japanese Tiger brand running shoes in the United States, and for a few years the coach sold them to his players out of the trunk of his car. In 1971, however, Knight and the Japanese Onitsuka Co. (today, the maker of Asics brand shoes) parted ways. Knight and Bowerman began to design their own shoes, and hired staff to market them. Runner Jeff Johnson, who was brought in to help facilitate the original start-up company, Blue Ribbon Sports, is credited with thinking of the name "Nike," while Carolyn Davidson, then a graphic design student at Portland State University, invented the swoosh logo. Olympic runner and Oregon native Steve Prefontaine was hired as the first athlete–spokesperson for the company, setting a trend that would continue to the present.[3] Prefontaine, with his long hair and mustache, lent the company an unconventional (today we might call it "hipster") style. Over the years, Nike has often identified with similarly offbeat characters, like the blue-collar San Francisco marathon runner, Walt Stack (1908–95), who was later featured in the company's first "Just do it" ad, running across the Golden Gate bridge.

Nike did not invent the running shoe, but it mythologized it. This happened in part because of the popularity of its product, but more so as a result of the company's savvy use of clever advertising. Its success derives foremost from the onomatopoetic "swoosh," which evokes the sound of air rushing past a speeding object. The elongated, slightly curving graphic mark suggests a feeling of swiftness in its aerodynamism, reminiscent of a bird's wing in flight, as well as the graceful stride of a runner. The swoosh is both an underline and a checkmark, both emphasis and task completed, a checked-off item on a list that signifies accomplishment and victory. By its association with ancient Greece, Nike also alludes to the ideals of classical antiquity, to the origins of the Olympic games, and to the aesthetic perfection of the beautiful athletic body. Before we delve more deeply into these myths, however, let us step back and consider the wider social and historical context of sports today.

Physical Education

Physical education is a big business today. The physical training of the body historically has often related to the training of military warriors, for example, in ancient Greece and China.[4] Physical training for additional pedagogical, medical, and aesthetic reasons is more closely linked in the West, however, with the introduction of gymnastics in the nineteenth century. In the United States, the theories of eighteenth- and nineteenth-century German educators Johann Friedrich GutsMuths and Friedrich Ludwig Jahn, and of Swedish physician Pehr Henrik Ling, were particularly popular.[5]

In 1918, the National Education Association endorsed physical education in America as a means to develop the body: "To build and preserve any nation, it is necessary to inculcate ideals of physical prowess, national courage, sportsmanship, fair play, and self-preservation of man. To this end it is the first duty to perfect the body."[6] Although throughout the 1920s, the National Education Association expressed anxiety about the possibility of children having too much leisure time, by the 1930s the organization advocated more physical recreational activity.[7]

Both the Swedish and German systems were incorporated into the U.S. education system, from the primary through the collegiate levels, where they were also important to early feminist reformers, who saw physical education as a means to women's emancipation.[8] The German system, which advocated a more formal training, with large apparatus activities, such as vaulting, had developed rather ominously, by the 1930s, into the intensely nationalistic and militaristic Hitler youth program, part of the National Socialist political agenda.

The less formal movement of the body cultivated in the Swedish system, by contrast, was absorbed into progressive methods of early childhood education initiated by Friedrich Froebel and Maria Montessori, for whom the movement was an important element of both self-discovery and problem solving. Such ideas, along with those of Hungarian dance theorist Rudolf von Laban, were the foundation of Movement education, a new discipline that was popularized in both the United States and England in the 1950s, and that included elements of dance, theater, and music, as well as sport. Today, physical education remains a key component of many school systems around the world, particularly at the primary and secondary levels, where physical activity is considered a counterpoint to the intellectual work that takes place while sitting in the classroom, and playing outside is seen as a reprieve from the tyranny of the video game. In addition to encouraging cooperation, discipline, and respect for authority, keeping children busy after school, sports also are believed to discourage or prevent delinquency.

But sports, especially competitive sports, which begin during the early school years, and continue for some as they enter college, are also a source of contention. On the one hand, excelling at sports can be a ticket to higher education, and perhaps for a few lucky, talented individuals it can be a ticket to a career—maybe even to fame and fortune. On the other, universities have increasingly come under scrutiny for unethical practices related to sports programs, including their exploitation of athletes, exorbitant coaches' salaries, and sometimes even criminal activity.[9]

To be fair, this problem mostly has to do with men's college basketball and football programs in the United States, which have vast media markets and are powerful industries often only tangentially linked to a school's educational mission. Such programs do generate school spirit, and, more importantly, they can attract financial donors to universities at a time when imperiled higher education can use all the help it can get.[10] There is no question that college sports are a big money affair in America. Even so, the NCAA (the National Collegiate Athletic Association) likes to promote its interests as belonging to the spirit of competition and the improvement of students' academic lives.[11] It is notable, however, that players have recently taken the initiative to unionize, arguing that they serve their universities as employees rather than as students, especially in their contributions to the financial well-being of those institutions—a move that signals that something perhaps is not quite right; or at least, not quite what it appears.[12]

Professional sports magnify the problems that percolate at the college level. Though surely less gruesome than their antecedents in ancient Roman and Mesoamerican games, the public spectacle of competitive sports today serves a symbolic political purpose, which can make one a bit uneasy.[13] Sports at all levels encourage gambling. Today, men's football and basketball join the older professional sport of baseball as the most popular American games upon which to wager. But in the early twentieth century, the arguably more dangerous and violent sports of horse racing and boxing played a grander role in the popular imagination.

Cricket has an even larger following around the world than the big American sports do, although international football ("soccer" in the United States) is by far the most popular mass media sport. Crowned every four years by the World Cup, (international) football for both men and women, like the annual spectacle of the World Series and Super Bowl in the United States, generates its share of celebrity, marketing, violence, scandal, and controversy.[14]

The non-professional pageantry of the Olympic games, which are held every other year, alternating summer and winter sports, celebrates national and international competition in a slightly different way. Though the tradition of Olympic athletic competition derives from ancient Greece, the first modern Olympics were held in 1896. In form and purpose the modern Olympic games had much in common with the great international exhibitions of the late nineteenth and early twentieth centuries.[15] From the Berlin games of 1936, to the Beijing games of 2008, the Olympics has celebrated peace and the brotherhood of nations, while also propagating the image of national power. In the poster for the 1912 Olympic games, held in Stockholm, athletes twirl a fluttering array of banners representing different nations. Most prominent in the foreground is the blue and yellow Swedish flag carried by a heroic figure, illustrated by painter Olle Hjortzberg in the characteristic Scandinavian National Romantic style of the early twentieth century (see Fig. 8.2).[16]

In such images the strong body of the athlete, like the strength of the product advertised, stands in for the political, economic, and military strength of the nation. The nationalistic displays of 1936 and 2008 were visual tours de force. German filmmaker Leni Reifenstahl's 1936 propaganda documentary *Olympia* is as mesmerizing in its slow motion footage of the beautiful bodies of divers sailing into the air, as was the dramatic orchestration of Beijing's 2008 opening ceremony, with its thousands of synchronized drummers, flying acrobats, and fireworks.[17]

The peculiar national–international tension of the Olympic games was most apparent, however, in the Cold War boycott by the United States of the 1980 Olympics in Moscow, and of the USSR's retaliatory boycott of the 1984 Olympics in Los Angeles. The Olympic village of international athletes who live together for the duration of the games signifies a global village of good will that transcends national borders. But the real global village today is that of Coca-Cola, McDonald's, GE, Panasonic, Visa, and Samsung.[18]

Fig. 8.2 Olle Hjortzberg, Poster for the 1912 Olympic games in Stockholm, Sweden. Photo Courtesy of Swedish National Archives. Reprinted with permission of The Swedish Central Association for the Advancement of Athletics.

An Ideal Body

The original Olympic games were performed in the nude. The word "gymnastics" derives from the Greek *gymnos* (naked), and more specifically *gymnazo* (to train naked). When we watch the Olympic games today, part of their appeal is in the visual pleasure we take in looking at the athletes' bodies. Among the most popular Olympic sports to watch are women's gymnastics and ice-skating, neither of which depend upon running shoes, but both of which celebrate the body, sheathed only slightly beneath the elastic fabrics that cling to the athletes' physical contours. This is true also of swimming and diving, and increasingly over the years, with the innovation of high-tech materials, of track and field, long-distance running, speed skating, and many other sports.

But it is not only the erotic and voyeuristic element, the desire of watching nearly naked bodies on screen (for most spectators see them mediated in this way), that appeals to fans of the Olympic games. The viewer is also amazed by the athletes' physical feats, and admires in a Platonic sense the perfect form and grace of their bodies, which is enhanced by their nudity. The perfection of athletic bodies like those of Olympians Greg Luganis, Michael Phelps, Nadia Comaneci, and Usain Bolt is reinforced by their perfection in performance, and signified by their winning of gold medals.

For the 1972 Olympic games in Munich, graphic designer Otl Aicher devised a comprehensive program of visual communication that centered on a set of pictographic images of the athletic body, each signifying a different sport.[19] These pictograms were not the first that had been designed for the Olympics, but they quickly became the most iconic, and have inspired many recreations and reinterpretations over the years. Aicher's rational and scientific representation of the athlete as a modular figure composed within a quadratic grid ensured the uniformity of his idealized athletic bodies, and lent the figures a harmonious look, like a modern canon of Polykleitos, the classical treatise in which the ancient Greek sculptor described the human body according to ideal mathematical proportions. Aicher's identical representation of Olympic swimmers, gymnasts, and pole-vaulters at the Munich games differed from the pictographic representations of sports at both the 1968 Mexico City and 1964 Tokyo Olympics, which preceded them. The team of designers organized by Katsumi Masaru in 1964, like Vance Wyman in 1968, had invented similarly abstracted and modular symbols, but theirs were slightly more idiosyncratic, modeled on individualized bodies and equipment for each different sport. For the 2008 Olympic games in Beijing the Chinese character "jing," meaning city, and the second part of the word "Beijing," was chosen as the event's iconic trademark. The 2008 logo also resembles the figure of an athlete, though its style is more expressive and painterly than that of the 1960s and 1970s pictograms. Its calligraphic form recalls the traditional handwritten Chinese character, made into a seal, and stamped with red ink.[20]

When Nike went public in 1980, its marketing shifted away from the image of a countercultural producer of shoes for running, a relatively low-key and democratic sport, associated less with big money, corporate sponsorship, gambling, and crime, than with camaraderie, health, recreation, friendly competition, and personal achievement. Rather, it turned to the sport of basketball, choosing as its new spokesperson Michael Jordan, star of Chicago's winning professional team, the Bulls. Jordan, widely considered to be one of the most talented basketball players of all time, had a god-like presence of his own, and was known especially for his superhuman leaps on the court, which seemed more like flight. Nike began to produce a special basketball shoe, the Air Jordan, alluding to the player's ability to jump high into the air, and later turned the abstracted silhouette of Jordan's leaping body into a secondary icon for related Nike products (see Fig. 8.3).

While many famous athletes have represented Nike over the years, only Jordan's body was developed into a trademark. When Nike Town, billed as a "retail-as-theater" space, opened in Chicago in 1991 it featured a temple-like Air Jordan Pavilion. One visitor remembers:

> When you walked in from the street through the revolving doors, you found yourself in a vaulted vestibule in which a giant alabaster statue of Jordan was suspended in his trademark "air" post, flying with basketball in hand to an invisible hoop. So, you looked up at Jordan, on whom spotlights were fixed, before walking into the store to buy Nike items. It was pretty intense.[21]

How much should we read into the image of Michael Jordan's body as icon and trademark? America has a long and violent history of using the body of the black man as currency, from its early days in which slaves were a source of labor for white plantations, to its dependence upon laborers for the railroad and for industrial production in the late nineteenth and early twentieth centuries, to its abundance of prisoners today that fuel the incarceration industry. African Americans have also played an important role in popular culture historically as musicians and entertainers, and above all as athletes, generating billions of dollars in revenue for their teams' owners. Today's black basketball player, thus, emerges from a complex and fraught history of racism, which combines performance with physical labor and capital. Michael Jordan's body is transcendent and rarefied in its iconic form, yet carries within its image a troubled history that is smoothed away by the logo, suggesting a new society, in which the black man is not property, but rather hero, champion, Olympian god, and story of success.

Black sports heroes in the United States are often upheld as symbols of triumph over racism, and certain figures have been particularly resonant. Jessie Owens's wins in track and field at the 1936 Berlin Olympics signified the triumph of the black man over the racist Nazi ideology of white Aryan

Fig. 8.3 Tom Lane/Ginger Monkey Design, Package design for Nike Air Jordan Year of the Dragon shoes, 2012. Reproduced with permission of the artist. The Air Jordan brand is owned by Nike, Inc.

supremacy. Muhammad Ali's extraordinary talents and social engagement symbolized the triumph of black man as a creatively, politically, and physically empowered force in the midst of the 1960s' Civil Rights Movement. Jackie Robinson, the first baseball player to break the "color barrier" in American professional sports, in 1947, is perhaps most often upheld as a heroic symbol of change. Michael Jordan adds to these meanings as well. The image of a tall, dark, and handsome Jordan, with powerful, athletic body, draws upon stereotypes of the black man as both menacing and virile, recalling Barbara Kruger's satirical 1986 artwork, *What big muscles you have!* Nike, though arguably unconventional in its choice of spokespeople and approach to marketing, was not immune to such stereotypes of blackness as intrinsically strong, rhythmic, musical, and entertaining, producing in 2001 a television advertisement featuring famous players dribbling the basketball in a virtuosic hip-hop dance.[22]

Talented professional athletes are often paid extraordinary sums of money. Is this actually what makes them victorious? Is this their true accomplishment? Some have questioned the potential effect that wealthy sports celebrities like Jordan have on young people, especially young African-American men, who may be seduced by the advertising image of role models into striving for athletic victory, while overlooking other aspects of their lives and careers that might offer great potential for achievement as well.[23]

The myth of Michael Jordan has led many young black men to pursue basketball with the dream of playing the game professionally and making millions. In this dream basketball is a way to rise above poverty, segregation, and discrimination, fulfilling the prophecy of Martin Luther King, Jr. There are many, many young black men who wear (and buy) Nike's Air Jordan shoes; the truth, however, is that actual athletes of Jordan's caliber are very few and far between, and the possibility of achieving his success is scant.

Sneaker Wars

In the 1980s, athletic shoes were hot property, especially in impoverished and largely African-American communities where some would do nearly anything, including commit murder, to acquire them.[24] Once known as "sneakers" because of the quiet rubber soles, which enabled one to move around silently, this type of footwear is also frequently called a "tennis shoe," a label that suggests an aspect of upper-middle class leisure.[25]

When Nike entered the scene, jogging was a popular activity. To be able to jog, especially for women runners, implies that one's neighborhood is safe. It is more common to encounter runners and joggers in affluent white communities than in poor black neighborhoods, where pick-up basketball games on derelict, concrete urban courts, are more of a cliché. The racial dynamics of the sneaker are complex, and complexly woven into the structure of Nike, Inc., which also owns Converse brand shoes.

Converse All Star canvas plimsoll shoes were first introduced in 1917, and endorsed by white basketball player Chuck Taylor, whose name they also acquired. Particularly popular among punk rockers in the 1970s, Converse All Star shoes have acquired a variety of meanings over the years, associated especially with white youth subculture.

By the 1980s, with the introduction of its Air Jordan shoe, Nike became more popularly associated with black youth culture, and with the big-money sport of basketball. When Jordan first wore his custom-made red and black

Nike shoes on the court, the NBA (National Basketball Association) fined him for violating its uniform dress code. Thus, from their very inception the shoes have been linked to the idea of breaking rules.

The phrase "sneaker wars" refers on the one hand to the violent competition for such commodities among youth. On the other it evokes the intense market competition between athletic shoe brands in the 1980s. Nike was not the only brand of choice among young black men, as seen memorably in the hip-hop group Run-D.M.C.'s 1986 song and music video "My Adidas." The song was homage to the shoe as fashion statement and symbol of wealth and power, bound together with the image of cultural and economic success for black men in both basketball and the recorded music industry.

By the end of the twentieth century, athletic shoes were—as they are today—ubiquitous throughout popular culture—worn by all, whether white, black, young, old, mainstream, alternative, or otherwise. It became trendy, for example, for women to wear comfortable running shoes during commutes to work that involved much walking. Once at the office they could be exchanged for less ergonomically designed high-heeled shoes. Athletic shoes were thus a conduit between work and leisure, worn for the physical necessity of moving the body comfortably, and with strength. Like blue jeans, t-shirts, and baseball hats, athletic shoes are part of the vernacular sartorial landscape (see Fig. 8.4).

But sportswear also often speaks a more specific language, simultaneously conveying industriousness and relaxation. To be stylishly dressed in athletic wear may imply that one has either just come from, or is on the way to, a workout. But wearing workout clothes out of context, especially if they are more slovenly than stylish, can convey laziness as much as physical fitness.

Many children wear athletic shoes to school, not only for gym class, but all the time. My favorite new school shoes, when I was in elementary school, were white leather sneakers with a white suede Nike swoosh. Recently I was obliged to make a pilgrimage to Niketown, as it is called today, with my own school-age children. The multi-storied wonderland of commerce is a fascinating place. Once you pick out the shoes you want to buy, an employee will call them up on a transparent elevator, like mining diamonds from deep within the earth. The reason it was so important for us to visit this paradise of athletic wear was to buy a pair of trendy and outrageously priced basketball socks, ostensibly designed with sophisticated technology to wick away the sweat of twelve-year-olds as they run around the school gym. These mid-length socks, knit of Dri-FIT fabric, in bright colors, are shaped to the contours of the foot and feature interesting geometric patterns that run vertically down the back of the leg, like the seam of a fishnet stocking.[26] They are designed visually to complement the look of the shoes themselves, which are made of bright red, neon yellow, or shocking electric blue synthetic leather-like fabrics with an appealing

Fig. 8.4 Nike and Converse brand shoes, 2014. Author's collection. Photo by author.

sheen. Combined with their brightly colored, shiny nylon jerseys, rainbow-hued shoes, vibrantly patterned socks, awkward sweaty bodies, mouth guards, and enormous sports goggles, these young players on the basketball court look like a cross between giant space aliens and tiny jockeys in horseracing silks.

Nike-brand footwear began in the form of deconstructed Japanese sneakers pressed with waffle irons, sold to a few groovy college athletes out of the back of a car. As the company grew over the years, however, its shoes were produced in mass quantities using the cheap labor force of garment workers in Indonesia. This practice was for many years the target of criticism by journalists, filmmakers, and labor leaders, who demonstrated Nike's complicity with the dark side of global capitalism. Wage protests began as early as the late 1980s at Nike's Asian factories, and, in 1991, critical reports began to appear in the press. In 1998, filmmaker Michael Moore interviewed Phil Knight for Moore's documentary about Nike, *The Big One*; he challenged Knight to visit one of the company's Indonesian factories with him. In 1999, college-soccer-coach-turned-labor-activist Jim Keady traveled to Indonesia, where he lived in its workers' squalid housing in order to produce his own documentary film, *Behind the Swoosh*, while journalist Naomi Klein attacked the company's sweatshop practice in her widely read book, *No Logo*.[27]

Fall From Grace

We hold our athletes to very high standards when it comes to taking care of their bodies. In addition to undergoing the rigorous discipline of physical training to hone their cardiovascular, muscular, and nervous systems in order to achieve strength, flexibility, endurance, and quick reflexes, they must stay perfectly hydrated, get precisely the correct amount of sleep, eat exactly the right balance of nutrients—carbohydrates, proteins, vitamins, minerals. They may rarely drink alcohol—at least not while performing—and must never smoke cigarettes or use illegal drugs. Prescription medications are closely regulated as well.

The high-performing body of an athlete is a scientific achievement. But there is a catch; this body must be "natural." In fact, we are more than willing—obliged—to banish our favorite athletes for transgressing these strict moral boundaries, even while implicitly encouraging them to do so. The fall from grace of athletes discovered to have performed while under the influence of banned substances, which have plagued the Olympic games and other sports over the years, is disappointing, not just for their fans who will no longer be able to watch their favorite athletes, but also because it disrupts the fairy tale aura of rags-to-riches success that many athletes represent. Success in the face of difficulty, such as the overcoming of class, race, gender, or other barriers, it might be argued, is the most important myth of American identity.

By far the most upsetting such case in recent history was that of bicycling champion Lance Armstrong. The mythically named Armstrong survived cancer and went on to win the Tour de France an astonishing seven times in a row from 1999 to 2005. Even as a youth Armstrong was a successful athlete who competed in triathlon races, and by the early 1990s he was racing professionally. At the time of his diagnosis in 1996, Armstrong's stage three testicular cancer had spread to his abdomen, brain, and lungs; he was not expected to survive. But thanks to modern medicine, with its potent chemical cocktails, he was able to beat the disease. He returned to racing in 1998, fully recovered, and joined the U.S. Postal Service bicycling team, where he became an effective spokesperson for the institution, which, before the completion of the transcontinental railroad, sent mail to be delivered by the swift and dangerous relay riders of the Pony Express.

All throughout his career Armstrong had faced nasty allegations of "doping," the illegal use of performance enhancing drugs, such as cortisone, HGH (human growth hormone), and testosterone, accusations which he regularly denied. The allegations were controversial and uncomfortable. What kind of insensitive critic would want to challenge the cancer survivor whose seemingly superhuman strength and endurance had taken him to victory, enabling him to establish an important foundation for cancer research? But following a 2012 investigation by the United States Anti-Doping Agency (USADA), Armstrong admitted that in fact he had been using illegal substances all along, including during each of his Tour de France victories. Not only had he cheated, but he had also lied—to the sporting community, to his fans, and to his sponsors. Nike announced at the time that "with great sadness" it would terminate its decade-long contract with Armstrong because it could not condone the use of illegal drugs, though the company would continue to support Armstrong's foundation.[28]

It is always disheartening when idols are discovered to be merely human, flawed and sinful, like the rest of us. In 2009, for example, one of Nike's most beloved spokespeople, the even more mythically named golf star Tiger Woods, was discovered to have cheated on his wife, when she found a number of embarrassing, sexually explicit text exchanges between Woods and his mistress on his phone. Sexual indiscretions are always frowned upon in public, common though they may be. And cheating, whether in sports or marriage, is considered ethically incorrect. But Nike did not terminate its contract with Woods; rather, the company rallied around its hero, releasing, in 2010, a startling television ad in which the athlete did not speak, but appeared rather to listen in shame to the disappointed words of his late father.[29]

Although Tiger Woods's infelicities may have let down his fans, Lance Armstrong's more costly criminal indiscretions, when they finally were proven to be true, and which had much wider implications for his sport and for the nature of cheating itself, could not be tolerated. The public (and Nike) decided that Woods was like a bad puppy that needed scolding, whereas Armstrong was a cheat and liar, and, when it came right down to it, not a very nice person. If we consider Armstrong's actions within a larger context, however, the ethics seem murkier and more problematic. Where do we draw the line between the pharmaceuticals used to cure Armstrong of cancer and the banned substances that gave him an ideal body and the physical edge to win?

Just Do It

Signifying achievement, function, and pragmatism, the graceful and emphatic swoosh embodies an ethics of discipline and perfection, the discipline that leads an athlete to win Olympic gold, or a corporation to win financial gold. Secondary to the swoosh, but nearly as rich in meaning, is Nike's famous tagline, "Just Do It." The author of that phrase, Dan

Wieden, of Nike's advertising firm Wieden + Kennedy, was under the gun, so to speak. In the last-minute pressure to turn out a result by the deadline, Wieden recalls, his mind wandered to writer Norman Mailer, to his story of convicted murderer Gary Gilmore, and Gilmore's last words before the firing squad that executed him in 1976, "Let's Do It."[30] Wieden tweaked the phrase slightly. By substituting "Just" for "Let's," he rendered it ever so slightly more imperative.

Who was Gary Gilmore, and why did Wieden think of Mailer's retelling of his story at that particular moment, while he was under pressure to meet a deadline? Gilmore was sentenced to death for murder, after having spent much of his adolescence involved in petty crime. According to lore, Gary's older half-brother was the illegitimate child of traveling magician Harry Houdini. The tragic story of Gilmore's life and death, thus, interweaves themes of tragedy, evil, violence, glamor, magic, and celebrity in a way that is both mythical and surreal. Though most consumers surely do not think about Gilmore's story when they purchase Nike products, I wonder if its strangeness and power might still resonate in the slogan: "Just do it." According to journalist Brent Hunsberger: "People reportedly wrote letters to Nike saying 'Just Do It' has inspired them to leave abusive husbands or achieve heroic rescues from burning buildings."[31]

In 1995, Nike ran an advertisement that featured very young girls at play, who range in age from about five to ten years old. "If you let me play sports," they say one after another, "I will have more self confidence ... I will be sixty percent less likely to develop breast cancer ... I will suffer less depression ... I will be more likely to leave a man who beats me."[32] The moving montage was not just a ploy to recruit more women customers, but also a response to the new Title IX legislation in the United States, which guaranteed equal funding for women's college sports.[33] Nike's products are marketed to both men and women, but its representation of women tends more to the showcasing of sexy tennis stars than modern day Nikes and Athenas, goddesses of victory and war.[34]

Wieden + Kennedy has developed numerous remarkable television advertisements promoting individual achievement over the years. Unconventional, surprising, often edgy, and sometimes weird, Nike's ads combine the romantic worship of sports heroes with alternative, cutting-edge music, and off-the-beaten-path personalities, like Spike Lee and Dennis Hopper, to encourage an anarchic mood, as in the 1995 television spot featuring tennis players Andre Agassi and Pete Sampras playing "guerrilla tennis" in the middle of a busy New York city intersection.

Similarly enjoyable is a 1999 advertisement featuring Tiger Woods playing a game of Hacky Sack with his golf club and golf ball, bouncing it between his legs and around his body until he finally tosses it into the air and hits it across the course. Golf is not just a boring game for rich white people, we learn, but something that could appeal to a cool college kid or maybe even a pot-smoking slacker, like kicking around a footbag, skateboarding, or playing Ultimate Frisbee. The image of golf as a white club sport is delightfully problematized by Woods himself, a youthful, somewhat androgynous plurality of ethnicities, the child of an African-American father with mixed Native American, white, and Chinese ancestry, and a Thai–American mother of partially Dutch and Chinese heritage. Woods, like Obama, embodies an intriguing mixture of meanings, both exotic and ordinary, and is presented optimistically as a harbinger of a future, more democratic, post-racial society. These associations were under-lined in Nike's 1996 advertisement featuring young children of all different races, both boys and girls, playing golf, each of whom states: "I am Tiger Woods."

In the grand Nike narrative the ordinary (a chubby boy, little girl, or a tenacious old man) is blended with the extraordinary (the amazing feats of Jordan or Woods). The shoes are magical, fetish objects. They are Dorothy's ruby slippers. In a 2005 spot Brazilian soccer star Ronaldinho takes a pair of Nike shoes out of a small gold case that looks like something we might expect to see in a James Bond film. We watch as he discards his old Nike shoes and slips on the new pair. They are white with a golden swoosh. He tests them out by dribbling the ball down the field and kicking it against the crossbar of the goal, retrieving the ball by bouncing it on his head. He repeats this four times before dribbling back to the golden case without ever letting the ball touch the ground. Yes, the shoes work. Like Dorothy's ruby slippers, Ronaldinho's shoes are enchanted. Thus, it seems odd to think about them in the context of Gilmore's death by firing squad, but we cannot escape the intriguing web of associations. The term "deadline" used as a noun to describe a time limit, "especially a time by which material has to be ready for inclusion in a particular issue of a publication," may have originated in 1929, when it was announced as the date of submission for a contest hosted by *Poetry* magazine. In the nineteenth century, however, "deadline" more commonly referred to the "line drawn around a military prison, beyond which a prisoner is liable to be shot down."[35] The urgency of the publishing deadline can indeed feel like a life or death situation, in which the writer races to the time limit like a sprinter toward a finish line. Wieden needed the deadline to overcome his writer's block.

Today, Nike is a global brand recognized and desired around the world. It is not only the American athletes at the Olympic games who are marked by the swoosh on their shoes, jerseys, and jackets, but all athletes, from Jamaica to Ukraine, that are so labeled. Some of Nike's athletes win Olympic gold, of course, but Nike, Inc. has achieved an even greater economic victory.

In 2013, Nike became the first sporting good company to join the powerful oil, food, and communications industries on the Dow Jones Industrial Average, one of the oldest and most relied upon stock market indices used to gauge the performance of the industrial sector.[36] While the international exhibitions of the nineteenth century may have prepared the way for global capitalism in the late twentieth, the modern Olympic games, with their visual display of trademarks and brands, are a product of it.

Is the cathartic experience of going to battle in the sports arena a peaceful substitute for battle in war? Or does it only fuel violent, competitive instinct, and reinforce tribal feelings or national identity? As we look beneath the surface of the Nike swoosh, just as with the Golden Arches, the bull's-eye target, and the color green, we discover many associations living in the collective unconscious, which are signified by the graphic mark. While imagining Mercury, with wings on the soles of his feet, our minds may wander to the homophone sole/soul. Nike taps into a deep desire for self-empowerment, which is more cosmic than economic. We desire the shoes not only because they are stylish, and will give us entry into a social community, but also because we believe they will enable us to achieve our dreams, and will make us stronger, better people, prepared to overcome adversity and to accomplish any task. Given this ethos, it's not frivolous to imagine that Nike, Inc. might return to its countercultural roots, reinventing itself as a new model of sustainable design, the ethical treatment of laborers, and the self-empowerment of consumers. And to be fair the corporation has made some changes in this direction in recent years. But Nike, Inc. is just one example among many global producers of sportswear, fashion, and clothing with similar problems. It has attracted more attention from critics than others because of its striking success.

Would you stop buying its shoes even if it didn't change a thing about itself?

Notes

1 Roland Barthes, "Plastic," in *Mythologies*, trans. Richard Howard and Annette Lavers (New York, Hill and Wang, 2012), 193–5.

2 Barthes, "Plastic," 194.

3 "History and Heritage," Nike, Inc. [corporate website], available online: http://nikeinc.com/pages/history-heritage (accessed August 27, 2014).

4 Paik Wooyeal and Daniel Bell, "Citizenship and State-Sponsored Physical Education: Ancient Greece and Ancient China," *The Review of Politics* 11/1 (Winter 2004): 7–34.

5 Anders Ottoson, "The first historical movements of kinesiology: scientification in the borderline between physical culture and medicine around 1850," *International Journal of the History of Sport* 27/11 (2010): 1892–919.

6 Proceedings of the National Education Association, 1918, quoted in Jesse Fiering Williams, "Health and Physical Education," *The Journal of Higher Education* 10/9 (December 1939): 491–6.

7 Williams, "Health and Physical Education," 494.

8 June A. Kennard, "The History of Physical Education," *Signs* 2/4 (Summer 1977): 835–42.

9   Scandals involving college sports have involved corruption, gambling, the selling of illegal drugs and firearms, and domestic violence. Robert D. Benford, "The College Sports Reform Movement: Reframing the 'Edutainment' Industry," *The Sociological Quarterly* 48/1 (Winter 2007): 1–28.

10 Obama, Barack, "Remarks by the President on College Affordability, Buffalo, NY," *The White House, Office of the Press Secretary* (August 22, 2013), available online: http://www.whitehouse.gov/the-press-office/2013/08/22/remarks-president-college-affordability-buffalo-ny (accessed August 27, 2014); Janice Nahra Friedel, Zoë Mercedes Thornton, Mark M. D'Amico, and Stephen G. Katsinas, "Performance-Based Funding: The National Landscape," Policy Brief published by The University of Alabama Education Policy Center (September 2013), available online: http://uaedpolicy.ua.edu/uploads/2/1/3/2/21326282/pbf_9–7_web.pdf (accessed August 27, 2014).

11 "Student-athletes," NCAA [website], available online: http://www.ncaa.org/student-athletes (accessed August 31, 2014).

12 Ben Strauss and Steve Eder, "College Players Granted Right to Form Union," *New York Times* (March 26, 2014), available online: http://www.nytimes.com/2014/03/27/sports/ncaafootball/national-labor-relations-board-rules-northwestern-players-are-employees-and-can-unionize.html?_r=0 (accessed August 28, 2014).

13 Linda Schele and Mary Ellen Miller, *The Blood of Kings: Dynasty and Ritual in Maya Art* (exh. cat., Fort Worth, TX: Kimbell Art Museum, 1986). Today, the game of American football, though not involving human sacrifice in quite the same way, has been increasingly questioned for the frequency with which some players suffer serious head injuries with long-term complications. Mark Fainaru-Wada and Steve Fainaru, *League of Denial: The NFL, Concussions and the Battle for Truth* (New York: Crown Archetype, 2013).

14 There are many accounts of hoodlum behavior by football fans and players over the years. One of the stranger manifestations of game-related violence in football was 2014 World Cup player Luis Suárez's bad habit of biting his opponents. Owen Gibson, "Luis Suárez banned for four months for biting in World Cup game," *Guardian* (June 26, 2014), available online: http://www.theguardian.com/football/2014/jun/26/world-cup-luis-suarez-ban-biting-uruguay (accessed August 27, 2014).

15 Maurice Roche, *Mega-Events and Modernity. Olympics and Expos in the Growth of Global Culture* (London: Routledge, 2000).

16 Jilly Traganou, "Foreword: Design Histories of the Olympic Games," *Journal of Design History* 25/3 (2012): 245–51; Alan Tomlinson and Christopher Young (eds), *National Identity and Global Sports Events: Culture, Politics, and Spectacle in the Olympics and the Football World Cup* (Albany: State University of New York Press, 2005).

17 Megan Evans, "'Brand China' on the World Stage: Jingju, the Olympics, and Globalization," *TDR: The Drama Review* 56/2 (Summer 2012): 113–30.

18 These brands, together with Dow, Acer, Atos, Omega, and P & G, were the top sponsors of the London 2012 Olympic games. "Marketing: Media Guide,

London 2012," IOC (International Olympic Commission) [website], available online: http://www.olympic.org/Documents/IOC_Marketing/London_2012/IOC_Marketing_Media_Guide_2012.pdf (accessed August 26, 2014).

19 Christopher Young and Kay Schiller, *The 1972 Olympics and the Making of Modern Germany* (Berkeley: University of California Press, 2010); Markus Rathgreb, *Otl Aicher* (London: Phaidon, 2006).

20 Jilly Traganou, "Olympic Design and National History: The Cases of Tokyo 1964 and Beijing 2008," *Hitotsubashi Journal of Arts and Sciences* 50/1 (2009): 65–79; Luis Castañeda, "Choreographing the Metropolis: Networks of Circulation and Power in Olympic Mexico," *Journal of Design History* 25/3 (2012): 285–303.

21 Peter O'Leary [recollections of Chicago's Nike Town opening, 1991], personal communication, August 31, 2014.

22 Most of the television spots discussed in this article are available online. See Aaron Taube, "25 Nike Ads that Shaped the Brand's History," *Business Insider* (September 1, 2013), available online: http://www.businessinsider.com/25-nike-ads-that-shaped-the-brands-history–2013-8?op=1 (accessed August 28, 2014).

23 The powerful lure of sports success was expressed in Steve James's award-winning 1994 documentary film, *Hoop Dreams*, a story of two African-American high school students from Chicago who hope to play professional basketball.

24 Rick Telander, "SENSELESS: In America's cities, kids are killing kids over sneakers and other sports apparel favored by drug dealers. Who's to blame?" *Sports Illustrated* (May 14, 1990), available online: http://www.si.com/vault/1990/05/14/121992/senseless-in-americas-cities-kids-are-killing-kids-over-sneakers-and-other-sports-apparel-favored-by-drug-dealers-whos-to-blame (accessed August 28, 2014). Although these kinds of killings first began in the late 1980s they have also happened in more recent years. Jay Scott Smith, "Air Jordans are more than a sneaker to some blacks," *The Grio* (December 28, 2011), available online: http://thegrio.com/2011/12/28/air-jordans-are-more-than-a-sneaker-to-black-community/ (accessed August 28, 2014); Paul Duggan, "Sneakers apparently led to killing," *The Washington Post* (January 9, 2012), available online: http://www.washingtonpost.com/local/sneakers-apparently-led-to-killing/2012/01/09/gIQAN1rVmP_story.html (accessed August 28, 2014).

25 The Oxford English Dictionary defines "tennis shoe" as "a light canvas soft-soled shoe suitable for tennis or general casual wear," tracing its first usage to author Rudyard Kipling in 1887. "tennis shoe n.," *Oxford English Dictionary Online* (June 2014), available online: http://www.ulib.niu.edu:2846/view/Entry/199141?redirectedFrom=tennis+shoe#eid18915405 (accessed August 28, 2014).

26 Dri-FIT (Functional Innovative Technology) is Nike's proprietary blend of nylon, polyester, cotton, and spandex yarn, used for various products to repel rain and wick away sweat.

27 Naomi Klein, *No Logo* (New York: Picador, 2000), 365–79. These high-profile critiques of Nike were not merely opportunistic, but rather, loud responses to a seriously troubling structure of manufacture that permeates global capitalism

today. Human rights concerns about exploitation of workers, who are paid low wages, and who work in unsafe conditions, sometimes under the threat of violent retaliation, are ever more urgent today. In 2013, worker safety reached a point of crisis when more than 1,000 garment workers were killed in the collapse of a factory in Dhaka, Bangladesh, which produced many major European and American brands of clothing. Julfikar Ali Manik, Seven Greenhouse, and Jim Yardley, "Western Firms Feel Pressure as Toll Rises in Bangladesh," *The New York Times* (April 25, 2013), available online: http://www.nytimes.com/2013/04/26/world/asia/bangladeshi-collapse-kills-many-garment-workers.html?pagewanted=all&_r=0 (accessed August 28, 2014); "Bangladesh Factory Collapse Toll Passes 1,000," BBC News [website] (May 10, 2013), available online: http://www.bbc.com/news/world-asia–22476774 (accessed August 28, 2014). For more on the crisis of sweatshop practices in the clothing industry see Elizabeth L. Cline, *Overdressed: The Shockingly High Cost of Cheap Fashion* (New York: Portfolio/Penguin, 2012).

28 Matt William, "Nike drops deal with Lance Armstrong after he 'misled us for a decade'," *Guardian* (October 17, 2012), available online: http://www.theguardian.com/sport/2012/oct/17/nike-lance-armstrong-misled-decade (accessed August 28, 2014).

29 See Barbara Lipford of *Adweek* magazine speaking on CBS television's *The Early Show*, April 8, 2010, available online: http://www.cbsnews.com/videos/tigers-emotional-new-commercial/ (accessed August 28, 2014).

30 Norman Mailer, *The Executioner's Song* (Boston: Little, Brown, 1979). See also Jeremy W. Peters, "The Birth of 'Just Do It' and Other Magic Words," *New York Times* (August 19, 2009), available online: http://www.nytimes.com/2009/08/20/business/media/20adco.html?_r=3&ref=business (accessed August 28, 2014).

31 Brent Hunsberger, "Nike celebrates 'Just Do It' 20th anniversary with new ads," *The Oregonian* (July 17, 2008), available online: http://blog.oregonlive.com/playbooksandprofits/2008/07/nike_celebrates_just_do_it_20t.html (accessed August 28, 2014).

32 Taube, "25 Nike Ads that Shaped the Brand's History."

33 United States Public Law No. 92–318, 86 Stat. 235 (June 23, 1972).

34 Of the top twelve highest paid Nike endorsements, only one was by a woman, Russian tennis sensation Maria Sharapova. Simon Cambers, "Maria Sharapova Signs £43m deal with Nike," *Guardian* (January 12, 2010), available online: http://www.theguardian.com/sport/2010/jan/12/maria-sharapova-nike-deal (accessed August 28, 2014).

35 "dead-line, n.," *Oxford English Dictionary Online* (June 2012), available online: http://www.oed.com/view/Entry/47657 (accessed 25 August 2012).

36 Jia Lynn Yang, "Dow Jones Industrial Average Drops HP, Bank of America; Nike, Visa Added," *The Washington Post* (September 10, 2013), available online: http://www.washingtonpost.com/business/economy/dow-jones-industrial-average-swaps-in-goldman-sachs-nike-and-visa/2013/09/10/54e37468-1a1e-11e3-8685–5021e0c41964_story.html (accessed August 28, 2014).

CHAPTER NINE

The Grid

Design in Play

We've now arrived at our final chapter. And I, for one, feel pretty pessimistic about these meditations on design and culture, and their rootedness in the psychology of global capitalism and the military–industrial complex. What about the positive aspects of design? What about its potential to change the world for the better, and its meaning for our children—the ones who will inherit and transform this realm of signs and symbols? Among the most popular toys for children throughout the industrial period have been building games, from wooden blocks for very young infants, to virtual worlds, in which older kids construct and inhabit imaginative spaces.[1] These kinds of activities help children to design themselves and to negotiate their relationship to the world around them. Many such creative and constructive toys enable children more specifically to envision the home as the archetypal built environment. Is there an iconography or a mythology of home? If so, what does it look like? In the 1939 film version of *The Wizard of Oz*, Dorothy is finally able to fulfill her wish to go home by clicking together the heels of her magical ruby slippers and chanting "There's No Place Like Home," a spell that transports her through time and space from the dream world of Oz back to her native Kansas.[2] This chapter investigates the symbolic forms of building one's own identity, of nation building, and the relationship of these structuring activities to the home. At the center of this relationship is a tension between order and fantasy, which is made visible in the grid.[3]

Magic, Technology, War

Three of the most popular children's toys in the United States were designed and introduced during the First World War: Erector Set (1913), Tinkertoy

(1914), and Lincoln Logs (1916). Though stylistically different, these three building toys tell us much about the growth and identity of a new nation on the brink of war.

Alfred Carleton Gilbert, an American inventor, athlete, and magician, who founded the Mysto Manufacturing Company in New Haven, Connecticut, designed the Erector Set. Originally from Salem, Oregon, Gilbert received a college degree in sports medicine from Yale University after winning a gold medal for the United States in pole-vaulting at the 1908 London summer Olympics.

Devoted to toy manufacture and progressive business practice, Gilbert was one of the first American employers to provide benefits to his employees, and successfully lobbied Congress to prevent a ban on toy production during the First World War. As a result he became known as "the man who saved Christmas." His Erector Set, a system of mechanical metal building parts, including pulleys, wheels, gears, and motors, was inspired by his fascination with the new electrification of the rail line between New Haven and New York.[4]

The railroad's 1907 bridge in New Haven was an innovative feat of engineering. Its exposed metal structure recalls the daring iron filigree of the Eiffel Tower, which had been built as a symbol of new technology for the 1889 Paris Exposition universelle. But the New Haven railroad bridge was less a civic monument than a utilitarian system of transportation for the future. It was practical, yet thrilling none the less, with electrical wires harnessing invisible energy to carry passengers with unprecedented speed—magical, indeed! Gilbert's Erector Set enabled children to imaginatively recreate the modern structures in their own homes.

Tinkertoy was devised in 1914 by Charles H. Pajeau and Robert Pettit in Evanston, Illinois, a suburb to the north of Chicago. The idea for the toy came to Pajeau, a stonemason, after he noticed children playing with sticks and wooden spools of thread. The wooden Tinkertoy pieces combine circular disks in smooth, unstained wood, drilled through the center and around the outer edge every 45 degrees, so that wooden rods of various lengths can be inserted into them to create triangular structures, according to the geometric laws of the Pythagorean theorem.

Visually, Tinkertoy constructions are more abstract than those produced with Erector Set. They resemble scientific models of molecular structures more than roads, bridges, and buildings. But the toys were first promoted to the public with models that recreated the strange and fascinating structure of the Ferris wheel, built for the 1893 Chicago World's Columbian Exposition (see Fig. 9.1).[5]

The Ferris wheel itself was envisioned as an American Eiffel Tower, a spectacular tribute to modern engineering, and a symbol of national identity for the fair. Like Erector Set, Tinkertoy combines the physical and mathematical principles of building with children's imaginative play. In the 1980s, a group of students at the Massachusetts Institute of Technology

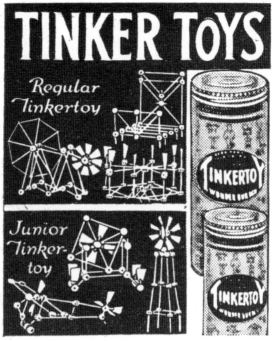

Fig. 9.1 Advertisement for "Tinker Toys", *The Golden Jubilee Sears, Roebuck and Co. Catalogue* (Chicago: Sears, Roebuck and Co., 1936), 804. TINKERTOY® is part of the K'NEX family. Image courtesy University of Michigan Libraries.

(MIT) built a giant computer out of Tinkertoy pieces, which could play a game of tic-tac-toe.[6]

Unlike its contemporaneous rivals, Lincoln Logs recreate the romance of cowboys and Indians, the wild frontier, and the self-sufficient craft of the homesteading American pioneer. Invented in Chicago, in 1916, by John Lloyd Wright, son of the famous architect Frank Lloyd Wright, the first set of Lincoln Logs, interlocking wooden parts for building houses, was sold with instructions for recreating both "The Lincoln Cabin" and "Uncle Tom's Cabin," two of the most multivalent mythical structures in American history. While Erector Set engaged ideas of science and technology in a present and future America, and Tinkertoy combined the tactile play of wooden blocks with ideas of modern engineering, Lincoln Logs engaged the past, marked by racial conflict, struggles for democracy, and war.

Despite its explicit references to American history in Abraham Lincoln's formative log cabin and the fictional slave residence of "Uncle Tom," from Harriet Beecher Stowe's influential anti-slavery novel, *Uncle Tom's Cabin; or, Life Among the Lowly* (1852), Lincoln Logs was purportedly inspired by the early designs for Frank Lloyd Wright's innovative Imperial Hotel in Tokyo, which was constructed with a unique system of interlocking parts to help the building to sustain earthquakes. Of these three wartime toys, which combine magic with technology, it is the old-fashioned seeming Lincoln Logs that most clearly reveal their mythic structure, signifying the survival of the pioneer, the industrious spirit of construction (sometimes interpreted as the democratic pursuit of happiness), and the fraught, violent encounter with the land.

Today, it is common to speak of living "on the grid," meaning that one is connected to the vast infrastructure of electrification that was put into place over the course of the twentieth century. To be "off the grid" in this discourse signifies that one is disconnected from such infrastructure, sometimes by choice. Often associated with far left- or far right-leaning political views suspicious of a heavy-handed federal government, those who choose to live off the grid, like their early homesteading pioneer ancestors, find alternative sources of energy and water by building solar panels, digging wells, using compostable toilets, and creating cooling systems that do not rely upon electric refrigerators. Erector Set, Tinkertoy, and Lincoln Logs each hover around the grid. While Erector Set most closely evokes the grid, through its dependence on electricity, Lincoln Logs most profoundly rejects it, like a remote cabin in the woods. Both toys, however, rely upon building parts that must fit together through a system of mathematical principle and precision. Tinkertoy, on the other hand, could surely be considered the most mathematical, and the most reminiscent of the creative process of engineering, and yet it is also fullest of countercultural, futuristic reference, evoking the forms of Buckminster Fuller's Dymaxion House and geodesic domes.

LEGO as Symbolic Form

I recently saw a sectional drawing of an architectural column, like those that were used to build temples in ancient Greece. It reminded me of a

LEGO brick, and led me to wonder what is signified—physically, spatially, or metaphorically—by the building block as symbolic form.[7] The LEGO "brick" is a small, rectangular plastic piece. Protruding from its upper surface is a raised grid of circular bumps, which interlock with indentations of the same proportion on the underside of another block. It is highly versatile, lending itself to the construction of simple or complex objects. Specialty parts, such as human figures, vehicle elements, weaponry, costume, and other accessories, are combined into a lively array of toys that can be used creatively for hours to construct miniature worlds (see Fig. 9.2).

The bricks are sold in several forms. They can be purchased in bins of basic building blocks, in various color palettes, including bright primary hues, sci-fi shades of black and grey, or princess pinks. They are also produced as themed kits, from which one can make models inspired by popular movies or by the fantasy characters in the LEGO universe.

Inevitably, the pieces of such kits, expensive and seductively marketed to children, find their way into larger, disorganized bins, once they have been constructed, played with, destroyed, discarded, and forgotten by their variously skilled makers. There they are mixed indistinguishably into a

Fig. 9.2 Structure built of LEGO® bricks created by Lucian O'Leary, 2014. Untitled painting by Jeff Marlin, 2009, oil on canvas, 76.2 × 81.28cm (30 × 32 in). Courtesy of the artist's estate. LEGO® is a trademark of the LEGO® Group of companies which does not sponsor, authorize, or endorse this example.

sea of parts that nevertheless can continue to fuel the imagination. LEGO projects require space to build, and an open area to set them out and place them into action.

In some ways, LEGO is the latter-day manifestation of the glued and painted model airplanes and cars, or electric model trains, sold popularly in hobby stores to children (especially boys) in the first half of the twentieth century. But the pleasure of LEGO is slightly different in that its creative play results not so much from the illusionism of those structures, composed of metal, wood, and paint, but rather from the recycling and physical clicking of the building components together and apart again, as well as from the imaginative structures that they signify in their abstract, geometric form.

The name "Lego" derives from the Danish words *leg godt* ("play well," or "good play"). First made in wooden form in the 1930s, in the workshop of carpenter Ole Kirk Christiansen, it has been popular since the Danish company began producing the colorful, modular, interlocking plastic version in 1958, under the leadership of Christiansen's son, Godtfred Kirk Christiansen.[8]

The origins of the toy coincide with the emergence in the early twentieth century of Scandinavian modernism, which itself had strong roots in the nineteenth-century Arts and Crafts movement. Much of what we identify as Scandinavian design today dates to the mid-twentieth century, such as Finnish–American designer Eero Saarinen's Womb and Tulip Chairs (1947–8 and 1955–6, respectively), Danish designer Arne Jacobsen's Egg chair (1958), and the curvy Swedish Saab automobiles of that decade— organic, ergonomic, and sensual.

Finnish designer Alvar Aalto's molded plywood chairs and amoeba-shaped glass vases in the 1930s may be seen as a transition from the more Romantic nineteenth-century craft revival, and its mythological associations with the Scandinavian forest, to the later, surrealistic, biomorphic forms of mid-twentieth-century Scandinavian design. In his serene Villa Mairea in Noormarkku, Finland (1938–41), with its interior columns made of bundled sticks, and sod-roofed sauna, Aalto channeled the spirit of Akseli Gallen-Kallela's mythic murals of the Kalevala, painted on the ceiling of Eliel Saarinen's Finnish National Museum in Helskinki, where giant stone sculptures of bears stand guard.

But Scandinavian modernism was also based, ideologically and stylistically, in the modular, industrial architecture that emerged between the First and Second World Wars (1919–39). At the 1930 Stockholm Exhibition of Swedish Arts and Crafts and Home Industries, art historian Gregor Paulsson, head of the Swedish Arts and Crafts Society, promoted the idea of "good design" that drew upon a native craft tradition, while also embracing new technologies of production. He believed that, much like the products of the Deutscher Werkbund, Swedish design could flourish with progressive partnerships between art and industry.

Paulsson was especially influenced by Swedish social reformer Ellen Key, who promoted in her 1899 essay, "Beauty for All," and 1900 book, *Century of the Child*, the importance of cultivating a world of beauty— especially for children—as a means to change society.[9] In his own 1919 book, *Better Things for Everyday Life*, Paulsson further developed Key's theories, echoing the ideas of artists Carl and Karin Larsen, whose designs for children's rooms were published in Carl Larsen's 1899 book, *At Home*.[10] At the 1930 Stockholm Exhibition products designed for the Orrefors glass and Gustavsberg porcelain manufactories that built on these traditions were hailed as embodying a new "Swedish grace."

Paulsson and his colleague, Swedish architect Gunnar Asplund, however, were inspired not by bears in the forest so much as by the modular buildings they saw at the 1927 Weissenhofsiedlung exhibition in Stuttgart, Germany. The model houses, which showcased the theories of Mies van der Rohe, Walter Gropius, and Le Corbusier, among others, previewed the type of architecture that would be selected by Henry-Russell Hitchcock and Philip Johnson of the New York Museum of Modern Art in 1932 as representing the International Style for their influential exhibition of modern architecture.[11]

Hermann Muthesius, co-founder of the Werkbund, was "appalled" by the formalism of the 1927 Stuttgart exhibition, describing it as a mere study in concrete and glass.[12] Muthesius advocated standardization, but only as a way to achieve the healthy, domestic ideal of the cozy English house, with its life-sustaining hearth. For Muthesius and other modernist architects inspired by the British Arts and Crafts ideal, including Frank Lloyd Wright, the central, warming hearth was also the social center of the home.[13]

Danish furniture designer Kaare Klint likewise followed an English model in the 1920s and 1930s, which emphasized use rather than aesthetics. He rejected popular experiments with tubular steel furniture in Denmark that had been inspired by the German Bauhaus innovations, calling them trendy "functionalism." Instead, he embraced Frederick Taylor's theories of scientific management and industrial production.[14] Although the LEGO toy company may not have had specific links to the Danish furniture industry, it emerged from a context that valued both a regional craft tradition of wood working, and rational and scientific theories of design, as exemplified by modular, geometric glass and concrete International Style buildings, which were understood to be universally comprehensible and to transcend nationalistic differences.[15]

What is the appeal of LEGO? From where does it arise?

When I asked my own ten-year-old I learned that he liked "the feel of each plastic brick or character," as well as "looking at the catalogues and collecting them."

"You can carry them around in your pocket," he said. "If a scene is your own creation you can imagine yourself in it." However, he remarked, "One negative is that the sets are too expensive, and you always want to have more. But you can understand why; they have to dig up all the oil to make the plastic."[16] Most important, it seems, is its tactility, and its ability to inspire the imagination when a child physically plays with the toys, whether he pretends to fly them around the room or carries them in his pocket. But there is also an element of consumer desire—the desire to acquire and collect, which is not unlike the fetishistic desire some children have for a Nintendo DS. Indeed, the various LEGO catalogues and magazines, to which children can subscribe, fuel this desire, as does the conversion of all popular culture images, events, or personalities into LEGO form: *LEGO® Star Wars*, *LEGO® Lord of the Rings*, *LEGO® Indiana Jones*, *LEGO® SpongeBob SquarePants*.

Everything appealing to children and their nostalgic parents, it seems, also exists in LEGO form. Children know that collectible, desirable LEGO sets, like electronic devices, are expensive and, therefore, valuable. Most curious is the lurking uneasiness about the pleasure of LEGO, which seems also to be related to its being a petroleum product. Perhaps this is just a symptom of early twenty-first-century conditioning in the problems of sustainability, but maybe it signifies something else, too.

Roland Barthes was very dismissive of plastic toys:

> Contemporary toys are made of unpromising materials, products of chemistry, not of nature. Many are now molded from elaborate compounds; the plastics out of which they are made look both crude and hygienic, they eliminate the pleasure, the gentleness, the humanity of touch.[17]

Wood, by contrast, Barthes writes, is a "poetic substance" that connects a child with the outside world of trees, as well as with wooden furniture, and the floor. A wooden toy does not break when a child bumps or drops it. It has a soft, muffled sound, and can grow older with a child, "gradually modifying relations of hand and object."[18] The individual pieces of LEGO, made today of ABS (acrylonitrile butadiene styrene), are extremely durable, but the resulting built structures can be very fragile, and the individual pieces are small and can quickly disappear under the sofa or into the vacuum cleaner.[19] Every parent knows the feeling of watching, with bated breath, as a child carries his complex creation around the house, knowing that it can so easily be dropped or bumped and break apart, resulting in frustration and tears. LEGO projects, today, are undoubtedly less messy, delicate, or toxic than the model trains and planes that children built decades ago, but even though children today "like the feel" of the smooth, plastic pieces, traces of Barthes's revulsion toward the synthetic may remain.

LEGO has also been studied in relation to theories of early childhood development.[20] German educator Friedrich Froebel (1782–1852) intro-duced the concept of Kindergarten in the early nineteenth century. His idea for a "garden of children" included singing, dancing, art projects, gardening, and free play with sets of differently shaped geometric wooden blocks, which could be arranged in various patterns (see Fig. 9.3).

He called these blocks and other related objects "gifts" (Fröbelgaben).[21] Froebel was born and raised in the Thuringian forest of Germany, an affluent region known for its curative herbs. He attributed his own educational philosophy to his religious upbringing by his Lutheran minister father, as well as to his childhood play in the region's natural environment, not unlike the later, mythical outdoor adventures of Nintendo's Shigeru Miyamoto.

As a young man, Froebel studied both mathematics and botany at the University of Jena, Germany. Upon graduation, he pursued a long teaching career in Frankfurt, Berlin, and Yverdon-les-Bains, Switzerland, under the influence of the Romantic educational reformer, Johann Heinrich Pestalozzi, who embraced Jean-Jacques Rousseau's belief in the dignity of children. Pestalozzi developed a curriculum in which learning happened "naturally," as a result of a child's curiosity and freedom to explore self-directed, hands-on object lessons, rather than through lectures, recitation, and corporal punishment.

From 1811 to 1815, Froebel worked at the University of Berlin's Mineralogical Museum with mineralogist Christian Samuel Weiss, from whom he learned about the grid-based, geometrical structures of crystals. The time that Froebel spent organizing the museum samples led him to regard the building blocks of nature as the divine handiwork of God. When Froebel later founded his first children's school in Bad Blankenberg, he introduced the block toys, which were wooden models based on the geometric crystal structures he had come to admire.[22] He also introduced, controversially, women teachers. Froebel's ideas migrated to the United States, where they were taken up in 1856 by his student Margarethe Shurz, at her German-language school for immigrants in Waterton, Wisconsin, and a few years later by Elizabeth Peabody, at her English-language kindergarten in Boston, Massachusetts.[23]

Italian physician and early childhood educator, Maria Montessori (1870–1952), like Froebel, emphasized that learning best results from free play with tactile objects, such as beads or clay, which a child manipulates with her hands. In 1909, Montessori published her theories, which were based on her work at the Casa dei Bambini, an experimental school for the children of low-income working families in Rome. Her book was translated into English in 1912 as *The Montessori Method: Scientific Pedagogy as Applied to Child Education in Children's Houses*.[24] Though criticized by some progressive educators as too restricting, Montessori's method was extremely influential on school curricula around the world throughout the twentieth century, and Montessori schools for young children remain popular today.[25] Many years later designer Victor Papanek appreciated LEGO toys for encouraging just the sort of free play that Montessori and Froebel had advocated.[26]

Fig. 9.3 Front cover with illustration of Froebel's second gift. Johanna Wierts van Coehoorn-Stout and J. H. Gunning, *De Kindertuin: handleiding bij de ontwikkeling van het kind van 3 tot 7 jaar volgens de methode van Fröbel* (The Kindergarten: Manual for the Development of Children Aged 3 to 7 Years According to the Method of Froebel), Amsterdam: H. Wierts van Coehoorn-Stout, 1904. Photo courtesy Norman Brosterman.

Much has been made of the fact that Frank Lloyd Wright was given a set of Froebel blocks as a child. Indeed, visitors can see a set in the playroom of his home and studio, in Oak Park, Illinois (and purchase contemporary versions in the museum gift shop). The blocks are an important part of the mythology of Wright's creative genius, along with the story that his mother decorated his infant nursery with images of famous cathedrals in the hopes that he would one day become an architect. Did Wright's early introduction to these educational toys help to determine his later career as one of the most admired twentieth-century designers?

Wright, like Froebel, came from a progressive religious family. Raised by his Welsh Unitarian schoolteacher aunts in Spring Green, Wisconsin, he incorporated the creative spirit of experimental education into his own work and into the curricula of the schools he established at Taliesin East and West, where students not only learned about architecture, but also played music, performed theater, and grew their own food. One can imagine that Wright's unconventional Prairie style, with its geometric emphasis and unexpected cantilevered forms, may have resulted from his imaginative play with wooden Froebel blocks as a boy, carefully balancing and stacking their smooth, geometric shapes, to create unusual, dynamic structures.[27]

The playroom of Wright's home and studio is an inspiring space, with high, barrel-vaulted ceiling, broad stained glass windows, open wooden floor for play, child-sized benches and chairs, plenty of built-in storage for toys, balcony seating for grown-ups to attend the children's theater productions, and a piano. A space for creative design in play, it is a miniature children's version of his own adjacent work studio, which he built a few years later on the same property, an open octagonal atrium with working tables and skylights, warmed with earth-toned textured stone and concrete, and infused with an enchanting colored light that filters through the stained glass ceiling. It recalls the imaginative designs for children's rooms proposed at the turn of the century by Carl and Karin Larsen, and other modern artists who were influenced by similar ideas.[28] Such rooms were also promoted in *The Craftsman* magazine, edited by Gustav Stickley, beginning in 1901, as a vehicle to promote the ideas of William Morris and the British Arts and Crafts movement in the United States.

Though quite different aesthetically, Wright's home and studio emerges from the same ideological context as German Bauhaus Director Walter Gropius's 1924 plans for the Friedrich Froebel House, a kindergarten and youth center to be built of standardized, pre-fabricated panels.[29] Stylistically, the houses that one builds with LEGO resemble the bold geometric forms and primarily colors of Gerrit Rietveld's contemporaneous Schröder House in Utrecht, a combination of rectangular volumes, like a three-dimensional version of Piet Mondrian's grid paintings of that period.

Many innovators of De Stijl, Dada, Constructivism, and Bauhaus design crossed paths in the 1920s, intersecting as well with the Scandinavian experiments of Aalto, Klint, and others. Thus, it is probably not surprising that today one finds LEGO kits for Frank Lloyd Wright's 1906 Prairie style Robie House and his later 1936 home Fallingwater, Le Corbusier's 1929 Villa Savoye, and Mies van der Rohe's iconic 1945–1951 Farnsworth House, which are likely intended more for adult collectors than for children. The geometric forms of each lend themselves well to their reproduction in rectangular plastic bricks, which mimic traditional bricks of clay, stone, concrete, and glass.[30]

Good Things

Between 1950 and 1955, the New York Museum of Modern Art (MoMA) curated five exhibitions of "good design," an idea that had motivated many architects, designers, and critics since the industrial revolution. Edgar Kaufmann, Jr., Director of MoMA's Department of Industrial Design, organized them in conjunction with Chicago's Merchandise Mart to promote a functional, modernist aesthetic for household objects and furnishings. The shows highlighted work by Charles and Ray Eames, Greta von Nessen, Russel Wright, Hans Wegner, Earl S. Tupper, Eva Zeisel, Eero Saarinen, and other designers and manufacturers from Italy, Germany, and Scandinavia. Many of the featured objects were unusual chairs and innovative kitchen tools.[31] Under the leadership of its first Director, Alfred Barr, MoMA had already curated a number of similar exhibitions throughout the 1930s and 1940s, including "Useful Objects" (1938), "Organic Design in Home Furnishings" (1940), and "Printed Textiles for the Home" (1946). Kaufmann, Jr., a prominent voice at MoMA for many years, was the son of Edgar Kaufmann, owner of Kaufmann's department store in Philadelphia, who in 1936 commissioned Frank Lloyd Wright to design the Kaufmann family's vacation home, Fallingwater, in Bear Run, Pennsylvania. Kaufmann, Jr. also studied architecture with Frank Lloyd Wright at Taliesin East in Spring Green, Wisconsin. But even before he met Wright, Kaufmann, Jr. had cultivated a taste for modern, especially European, design while studying art in Vienna and Florence in the 1920s.

In the midst of the Merchandise Mart shows, which coincided with periodic shopping seasons, MoMA also curated the 1953 exhibition, "Premium Toys Designed for Industry," featuring the work of toymakers A. F. Arnold and Joseph Zalewski. Director of MoMA's Department of Education, Victor d'Amico, wrote:

> Toys have an important place in the creative growth of the child, both in influencing his art expression and developing his taste. They are his first possessions and the objects of profound interest and affection. Through them he is introduced to the elements of design, texture, pattern, form, color and rhythms as they become tools of his activity and his imagination.[32]

MoMA's shows were thus envisioned not only as a way to train consumers to practise good taste and judgment in their purchases, but also, more explicitly, to extend this notion of good taste and appropriate design to children. The museum, thus, was in tune with Rousseau's and Pestalozzi's notion that children possess a less encumbered imaginative life, and that this life should be protected and nurtured.[33] It is an idea readily associated with nineteenth-century Romanticism, as well as with avant-garde Expressionism before the First World War. The fascination with and validation of children's rich inner lives was often featured in the art and literature of the period from Lewis Carroll's 1865 tale, *Alice's Adventures in Wonderland*, to Freud's psychoanalytic case studies of children, to Dada, an art movement that some believe drew its name from the French word for hobby horse (though the term may just as readily be regarded as baby babble).[34]

The legacy of the long investment in the creative and constructive child in Europe and North America has been revisited recently. In 2012, MoMA presented the exhibition "Century of the Child: Growing By Design 1900–2000," curated by Juliet Kinchin and Aidan O'Connor, which largely celebrated the modernist ideal of the creative child, invoking in its title the earlier ideas of Ellen Key. It focused on the work of progressive social reformers, and showcased canonical, innovative designs, like Gerrit Rietveld's delightful 1919 high chair, the iconic Rubik's Cube designed in 1974 by Hungarian architect Ernő Rubik, and LEGO.[35] Though more critical than the earlier 1950s "Good Design" shows, MoMA's "Century of the Child" exhibition brought to light again the formal clarity and appeal of objects that would likely have had a place in Key's world of "beauty for all."

Amy Ogata's contemporaneous 2013 book, *Designing the Creative Child: Playthings and Places in Midcentury America*, more rigorously challenges the concerning way in which the concept of the creative child was marketed in the United States and came to signify national identity, particularly after the Second World War.[36] MoMA's 2012 exhibition appeared to be, however, less worried about the future of children than were the participants of the 1990 International Design Conference in Aspen, Colorado, organized around the same theme, "Growing by Design."

Co-convened by Jane Clark Chermayeff and Ivan Chermayeff, the conference featured presentations by designers of toys, children's illus-trators, educators, child psychologists, and directors of innovative social programs, galvanized by the conviction that "the environment we have created for children is getting worse."[37] Barthes had already expressed the idea that the environment for children is getting worse in the 1950s, when he criticized new plastic toys. He was also wary of toys as imitative of the adult world, encouraging consumption, rather than generating creativity, as he believed that traditional wooden blocks do.[38]

Good Games

One of my children, while playing the popular video game *Minecraft*, once became so frustrated that he threw a metal water bottle through a window, shattering it. When I recounted this alarming experience to a fellow parent of three young boys, he responded without surprise: "Oh, you mean 'mindcrack'." Like many video games, this one can induce obsessive behavior that can sometimes turn violent, transforming a child into an irrational addict. But most observers of *Minecraft*, since its 2009 release by the Swedish start-up company Mojang, have noted its striking difference from other more violent games in the industry. "It isn't destruction that makes *Minecraft* unique," wrote Harry McCracken for *Time* magazine, "It's construction."[39]

Minecraft originated not as a big budget video game with flashy graphics and narrative, but rather as an indie (independent) "sandbox" game, in which players inhabit an open-ended environment. There they "mine" various materials, such as iron ore and emeralds, in standardized blocks, which they then use to "craft" their tools, and assemble into modular, grid-based worlds. The term sandbox, used to describe the genre, evokes the image of open-ended play in a limited and protected environment designed especially for children, like a real sandbox in a Montessori classroom. But in a "real" sandbox children's minds and bodies are nurtured and expanded as they fill their buckets and shovels with the soft, gritty mineral that runs through their fingers and under their toes.

Like Lincoln Logs, *Minecraft* is strangely anachronistic, set even further back in time, or so it seems, with its medieval references to mining and crafting. Its graphics are also antiquated. The low-resolution (16-bit) building blocks that players move around the screen have the aesthetic of video puzzle games from the 1980s, and seem to be imbued with nostalgia for the primitive, pixelated form (see Fig. 9.4).

Players are not so much interested in the illusionism of their virtual worlds as in the fun of building them. By working together to share the building of virtual places some players have designed vast worlds that recreate both real and fictional environments. *Minecraft*, like its spiritual and stylistic predecessor, LEGO, to which it is frequently compared, originated in Scandinavia. It is a game that has received a lot of attention, not just from children but also from educators, some of whom have employed it in the classroom as a teaching tool.[40] The ingenuity of *Minecraft*, and perhaps the reason for its strong appeal, is that it combines a modernist interest in the highly structured, mathematical, built environment on a regular grid, with a fantastical, romantic pioneer spirit in which one smelts mineral ore, fashions tools, and farms animals.

Minecraft and LEGO satisfy the same impulse to construct, and are often used by children interchangeably. Both can hold attention and inspire

Fig. 9.4 Environment constructed using MINECRAFT™ game by Gabriel O'Leary, 2015. MINECRAFT™ is a trademark of the game developer Mojang, owned by Microsoft Corporation, which does not sponsor, authorize, or endorse this example.

imagination, as well as incite desire and frustration. Both can keep a child quiet and occupied for hours. But there are important distinctions, too. What is the difference between manipulating a computer mouse or gliding one's fingers across a screen or keyboard, and pulling apart the smooth plastic LEGO bricks, or clicking them back together? What is the difference between imagining that one is wielding an axe or physically chopping wood? Do both activities get the blood pumping, muscles contracting, and respiratory system straining? Is intensive brain activity the equivalent of physical motion? Is one form of game healthier than another? Does the material matter? The color? Are the shapes of the blocks or the images on screen important? Is the medium the message?

Creative Survival

Minecraft can be played in either Creative or Survival mode. In Creative mode, the sandbox is endlessly full of building materials, whereas in Survival mode players need to quickly scramble to assemble a rudimentary shelter and to vanquish threatening foes that soon appear. In this sense, *Minecraft* recalls the mythology of the log cabin. In each of her novels, children's author Laura Ingalls Wilder described in detail the dwellings in which she lived. The first log cabin that her father built for his young family in the Big Woods of Wisconsin was a "little gray house made of logs," far from any neighbors. "The house was a comfortable house," she writes:

> Upstairs there was a large attic, pleasant to play in when the rain drummed on the roof. Downstairs was the small bedroom, and the big room. The bedroom had a window that closed with a wooden shutter. The big room had two windows with glass in the panes, and it had two doors, a front door and a back door.[41]

When the Ingalls family picked up and moved westward across the Mississippi River, Pa built the famous "little house on the prairie," a project that Wilder documented as carefully as if writing a DIY manual for the enterprising pioneer (or instructions for a *Minecraft* player). Pa felled the trees needed to build the little dream house, and physically transported the logs, hoisting them into place using the physics of leverage. He ingeniously fashioned wooden pegs and leather thongs in place of manufactured nails and hinges.[42]

Embellished with charming illustrations by Garth Williams, Wilder's books enable the reader to visualize the log structures and to associate them in his imagination with the project of westward expansion, of settlement, and of self-sufficiency (see Fig. 9.5).

The houses, which look in Williams's illustrations exactly like they are made of hand-crafted Lincoln Logs, become symbols of the family's survival of malaria, scarlet fever, locusts, prairie fires, Indians, wolves, and a long, cold, winter in which they nearly starved to death.[43]

For readers of the "Little House" books today the adventures of the Ingalls family are nearly incomprehensible. Multiple times, as their survival was threatened, the family simply abandoned their carefully crafted home, moving on to the next adventure. While waiting for Pa to build their third home, on the banks of Plum Creek, the family occupied a pre-existing underground dwelling with a sod roof, built into the side of a hill. The cave-like house had been made by another pioneer, a Norwegian immigrant who spoke no English. After a few months in the soft earth dwelling the Ingalls family moved into the new house of modern, milled lumber, which Laura describes glowingly as a "wonderful house," bright and sunny with clean, yellow pine floors, and clear panes of glass—a luxury, like a show window from which the natural elements could be watched: an approaching blizzard; a dark and glittering cloud of locusts; a parade of ants; the sparkling fresh snow after a storm. The house protects and sustains life with its shelter, warmth, shade, and mosquito netting. It is cold in the morning, when first emerging from bed, but warm by the stove. The wood is solid and clean, a wild material domesticated.[44] The suite of books revolves around Wilder's descriptions of the various spaces she inhabits, and the aesthetic pleasure she takes in them. Recurrent motifs include the few furnishings that travel from place to place with the family: a red-checked table-cloth, Pa's lovingly carved decorative wooden bracket shelf for Ma's china doll, Laura's Dove-in-the-Window quilt.

Fig. 9.5 Building the little house on the prairie. Illustration by Garth Williams, in Laura Ingalls Wilder, *Little House on the Prairie* (New York: HarperCollins, 2004). © 1953 by Garth Williams. Copyright renewed 1991. Reproduced with permission of Garth Williams estate.

Each of the houses Pa builds protects the family from the natural elements, which are beyond human control, and which threaten life itself. But these spaces are ephemeral, and used only for a short time before moving on, despite the love and labor in their construction and appointment. Much stronger for them, it seems, was the pleasure of moving, of starting anew, the pioneer spirit. Perhaps this pleasure was similar to playing with LEGO or Tinkertoy, in which structures are assembled and disassembled with pieces constantly reshuffled.

About a year after residing in the—in Laura's words—"wonderful" house at Plum Creek, the Ingalls moved on again to stake a claim on property in the Dakota Territory, by the shores of Silver Lake. Finally, Laura moved to her own homestead, where she lived with her husband, Almanzo, and their little daughter, Rose, until it accidentally burned down in a kitchen fire—an event that recalls the morning I woke to find my younger son in tears because his *Minecraft* homestead had burned down overnight, and all his sheep and pigs had perished.[45]

Most fascinating in the *Little House* books is the urge to build and the satisfaction in making something from nothing, an impulse that is similarly satisfied by Froebel blocks, LEGO, and *Minecraft*, and one that has also been noted by feminist scholars over the years.[46] Maybe the Ingalls girls were more liberated than many children today, with their many toys and electronic devices.

I do not mean to suggest that all children today live with an abundance of material goods, nor do I want to ignore the difference between the material wealth of the West and the devastating poverty in other parts of the developing world. Even in wealthy nations, of course, there are many who lack even the most basic elements of food and shelter for survival. But we do live in a global world today, much more so than we did a century ago, and this world is shaped by an image of abundance that circulates in advertising media—a condition that has been described as "affluenza."[47]

This is the legacy of design of which critics from John Ruskin to Victor Papanek have cautioned. The Ingalls girls did not play *Minecraft*, but rather occupied themselves with the real tasks of running a homestead—grazing their cows, tending their crops, making bread, preserving food for the winter, sewing clothes, and keeping their little houses tidy by sweeping clean the wooden floors and airing out their straw bedding. In their leisure time they played with homemade dolls, read books, listened to music, and did (real) craft activities like beadwork, embroidery, or quilting—the quintessential symbol of pioneer survival and art (Plate 11).

The dream house is not just a toy for children, but also a driving concept for adults. In the United States, the notion of the dream house is more explicitly related to the idea of the American dream. It signifies creative survival, free play, and fantasy, as well as aspiration. From 1908 to 1940, Sears, Roebuck & Co., sold kit homes through its mail-order catalogue. One could thus purchase a home in much the same way that one might order a pair of shoes, a stove, or a sewing machine. The kit would typically arrive by rail with pre-cut lumber and hardware; the homeowner was responsible for constructing it, and for connecting himself to the grid, much like putting together a LEGO set.

In 1908 London most of the city's population lived in rented dwellings, but a competition held in conjunction with the Olympic games that year featured hundreds of examples of single-family homes. The first Ideal Home Exhibition, organized by the *Daily Mail* newspaper, advertised an image of suburban domesticity in the U.K. that would continue to expand in the mid-twentieth century, just as it did in the United States.[48]

When we hear Dorothy's incantation, "There's no place like home," the phrase implies that there is no place as good as home, no place that we would rather be. At the same time it also suggests that "home" is a utopian ideal, literally "no place" to which we always aspire, but never quite reach.

The dream house is just that, a dream, or as Freud put it, the fulfillment of a wish. All of the children's toys we've surveyed here share a common aspiration. When building, it is understood that we will build something better, different, or new, and that we will grow, improve ourselves, or the world around us. The act of building can also evoke the divine. In contrast to imitative toys, Barthes writes: "The most elementary set of building blocks, if not too refined, implies an altogether different apprenticeship to the world ... [a child's] actions are not those of a user but those of a demiurge ... he creates life, not property."[49]

It is a truism that children will often play as happily with the cardboard box in which a toy was packaged as with the toy itself. Building toys, from Froebel blocks to *Minecraft* to LEGO, embody the human impulse to build, structure, miniaturize, collect, and combine—in short, to design. Trying to make sense of the architecture that surrounded him in the nineteenth century, and the tower of babbling visual languages in which it spoke, German architect and art historian Gottfried Semper wrote:

> Surrounded by a world full of wonder and forces whose laws we may divine, may wish to understand but will never decipher, that touch us only in a few fragmentary harmonies and suspend our souls in a continuous state of unresolved tension, we conjure up in play the perfection that is lacking. We make for ourselves a tiny world in which the cosmic law is evident within the strictest limits, yet complete in itself and perfect in this respect. In such play we satisfy our cosmogonic instincts.[50]

As we continue to play with our games and toys, let's try to think more carefully about what kind of instincts our play satisfies. Are they instincts to increase our various consumptions of goods and energy? Or are they the ones that inspire us to create a world? And if so, what kind of world do we imagine living in? And how will we live in that world once we have built it?

Notes

1 Amy F. Ogata, *Designing the Creative Child: Playthings and Places in Midcentury America* (Minneapolis: University of Michigan Press, 2013).

2 In the original version of the story, Dorothy's magical shoes are silver, rather than red, and the phrase she uses, clapping her heels together three times, is "Take me home to Aunt Em!" Frank L. Baum, *The Wonderful Wizard of Oz* (Chicago: Geo. M. Hill Co., 1900; reprint, New York: Harper Trophy, 1987), 304.

3 I'm alluding here in part to Rosalind Krauss's study of the grid as a structuring mechanism in early twentieth-century modern painting. Rosalind E. Krauss, "Grids," in *The Originality of the Avant-Garde and Other*

Modernist Myths (Cambridge, MA: MIT Press, 1985), 8–22. I'm also motivated by the notion of "Swiss" typography as grid-based. See Emil Ruder, "The Typography of Order," in Michael Bierut, Jessica Helfand, Steven Heller, and Rick Poynor (eds), *Looking Closer 3: Classic Writings on Graphic Design* (New York: Allworth Press, 1999), 135–8, originally published in *Graphis*, 85 (September–October 1959); and Anthony Froshaug, "Typography is a Grid," in Bierut et al. (eds), *Looking Closer 3*, 177–9, originally published in *Designer* 167 (January 1967).

4   A. C. Gilbert and Marshall McClintock, *The Man Who Lives in Paradise: the Autobiography of A. C. Gilbert* (New York: Rinehart, 1954); Bruce Watson, *The Man Who Changed How Boys and Toys Were Made* (New York: Viking, 2002), and *The Man Who Saved Christmas*, directed by Sturla Gunnarsson (CBS television, 2002); "The 1908 London Olympics" [original film footage], BFI (British Film Institute) [website] (July 13, 2012), available online: http://www.youtube.com/watch?v=3IqE2KEqZJI (accessed June 14, 2013).

5   Karen Hewitt and Louise Roomet, *Educational Toys in America: 1800 to the Present* (exh. cat., Burlington, VT: Robert Hull Fleming Museum, 1979), 44–5; Gary Cross, *Kids' Stuff: Toys and the Changing World of American Childhood* (Cambridge, MA: Harvard University Press, 1997), 60–1, 161, 182.

6   A. K. Dewdney, "Computer Recreations: A Tinkertoy Computer that Plays Tic-Tac-Toe," *Scientific American* 261/4 (October 1989):120–3.

7   I'm borrowing here the following uses of the term: Lev Manovich, "Database as Symbolic Form," *Convergence* 5/2 (1999): 80–99; Erwin Panofsky, *Perspective as Symbolic Form*, trans. Christopher S. Wood (New York: Zone Books, 1991), originally published as "Die Perspektive als 'symbolische Form'," in *Vorträge der Bibliothek Warburg 1924–1925*, ed. Fritz Saxl (Leipzig: B. G. Teubner, 1927), 258–330.

8   Kjetil Fallan, "LEGO," in Grace Lees-Maffei (ed.), *Iconic Designs: 50 Stories About 50 Things* (London: Bloomsbury, 2014), 177–9.

9   Barbara Miller Lane, "An Introduction to Ellen Key's 'Beauty for All'" (1900), in Lucy Creagh, Helena Kåberg, and Barbara Miller Lane (eds), *Modern Swedish Design: Three Founding Texts* (New York: Museum of Modern Art, 2008), 18–31; Ellen Key, "Beauty for All," in Creagh, Kåberg, and Lane, (eds), *Modern Swedish Design: Three Founding Texts*, 32–57. See also Juliet Kinchin, "Hide and Seek: Remapping Modern Design and Childhood," in Juliet Kinchin and Aidan O'Connor (eds), *Century of the Child: Growing By Design 1900–2000* (exh. cat., New York: Museum of Modern Art, 2012), 10–27.

10 Helena Kåberg, "An Introduction to Gregor Paulsson's *Better Things for Everyday Life*," in Creagh, Kåberg, and Lane (eds), *Modern Swedish Design: Three Founding Texts*, 58–71; Gregor Paulsson, *Better Things for Everyday Life* (1919), republished in Creagh, Kåberg, and Lane (eds), *Modern Swedish Design: Three Founding Texts*, 72–125.

11 Philip Johnson, Alfred Barr, Jr., and Henry-Russell Hitchcock (eds), *Modern Architecture: International Exhibition* (exh. cat., New York: Museum of

Modern Art, 1932); Henry-Russell Hitchcock and Philip Johnson, *The International Style: Architecture Since 1922* (New York: W. W. Norton and Co., 1932).

12 Gillian Naylor, "Swedish Grace ... or the Acceptable Face of Modernism?" in Paul Greenhalgh (ed.), *Modernism in Design* (London: Reaktion, 1990), 164–83.

13 Hermann Muthesius, *The English House*, trans. Janet Seligman (London: Crosby, Lockwood, Staples, 1979), originally published as *Das englische Haus: Entwicklung, Bedingungen, Anlage, Aufbau, Einrichtung und Innenraum*, 3 vols (Berlin: W. Wasmuth, 1904–5). See also Hermann Muthesius and Henry van de Velde, "Werkbund Theses and Antitheses" (1914), in Ulrich Conrads (ed.), *Programs and Manifestoes on 20th-Century Architecture*, trans. Michael Bullock (Cambridge, MA: MIT Press, 1971), 28–31.

14 Per H. Hansen, "Networks, Narratives, and New Markets: The Rise and Decline of Danish Modern Furniture Design, 1930–1970," *The Business History Review* 80/3 (Autumn 2006): 449–83.

15 Kevin Davies, "Twentieth-Century Danish Furniture Design and the English Vernacular Tradition," *Scandinavian Journal of Design History* 7 (1997): 41–57. For more recent investigations that tease out the complexities and nuance of design and its national histories in Denmark, Finland, Sweden, and Norway, see Kjetil Fallan (ed.), *Scandinavian Design: Alternative Histories* (Oxford: Berg, 2012).

16 Gabriel O'Leary, [thoughts on LEGO], personal communication, December 15, 2011.

17 Roland Barthes, "Toys," in *Mythologies*, trans. Richard Howard and Annette Lavers (New York: Hill and Wang, 2012), 58–61.

18 Barthes, "Toys," 60–1.

19 Jeffrey L. Meikle, *American Plastic: A Cultural History* (New Brunswick, NJ: Rutgers University Press, 1997), 188.

20 Karen Hewitt, "Blocks as a Tool for Learning: Historical and Contemporary Perspectives," *Young Children* 56/1 (January 2001): 6–13; Mitchel Resnick, "Technologies for Lifelong Kindergarten," *Educational Technology Research and Development* 46/4 (1998): 43–55.

21 Norman Brosterman, *Inventing Kindergarten* (New York: Abrams, 1997).

22 Ibid., 24–5.

23 Daniel J. Walsh, Shunah Chung, and Aysel Tufekci, "Friedrich Wilhelm Froebel," in Joy Palmer, Liora Bresler, and David E. Cooper (eds), *Fifty Major Thinkers on Education: From Confucius to Dewey* (London: Routledge, 2001), 94–9.

24 Maria Montessori, *Il Metodo della Pedagogia Scientifica applicator all'educazione infantile nelle Case dei Bambini* (Rome: M. Bretschneider, 1909); Maria Montessori, *The Montessori Method: Scientific Pedagogy as Applied to Child Education in "The Children's Houses,"* trans. Anne E. George (New York: Frederick A. Stokes, 1912); Maria Montessori, *The Discovery of the Child* (Madras, India: Kalakshetra Publications, 1948).

25 William Heard Kilpatrick, *The Montessori Method Examined* (Boston: Houghton Mifflin, 1914); Jane Roland Martin, "Maria Montessori," in Palmer, Bresler, and Cooper (eds), *Fifty Major Thinkers on Education*, 224–8. See also Rita Kramer, *Maria Montessori: A Biography* (Chicago: University of Chicago Press, 1976). Other influential thinkers on the role of play in early childhood development were psychologists Jean Piaget, *Play, Dreams, and Imitation in Childhood*, trans. C. Gattegno and F. M. Hodgson (New York: Norton, 1962), and Erik H. Erikson, *Toys and Reasons: Stages in the Ritualization of Experience* (New York: W. W. Norton, 1977).

26 Aidan O'Connor, "Design for the Real World," in Kinchin and O'Connor (eds), *Century of the Child*, 228; Victor Papanek, *Design for the Real World: Human Ecology and Social Change* (London: Granada Publishing Limited, 1974).

27 Anthony Alofsin, *Frank Lloyd Wright: The Lost Years, 1910–1922: A Study of Influence* (Chicago: University of Chicago Press, 1993), 359, n. 69. Alofsin refers the reader to Jeanne S. Rubin, "The Froebel-Wright Kindergarten Connection: A New Perspective," *Journal of the Society of Architectural Historians* 48/4 (December 1989), 24–37.

28 Juliet Kinchin, "Hungary: Shaping a National Consciousness," in Wendy Kaplan (ed.), *The Arts and Crafts Movement in Europe and America: Design for the Modern World* (exh. cat., Los Angeles County Museum of Art, 2004), 142–77; Elisabet Stavenow-Hidemark, "Scandinavia: 'Beauty for All'," in Kaplan (ed.), *The Arts and Crafts Movement in Europe and America*, 178–217.

29 Mark Dudek, *Kindergarten Architecture: Space for the Imagination* (2000; reprint, New York: Routledge, 2013), 39.

30 For more on the brick as one of several archetypal grids that have influenced modes of building through history see Hannah B. Higgins, *The Grid Book* (Cambridge, MA: MIT Press, 2009), 13–32.

31 The Good Design shows, held November 21, 1950 to January 28, 1951; November 27, 1951 to January 27, 1952; September 23 to November 30, 1952; September 22 to November 29, 1953; February 8 to March 2, 1955, are described in catalogues published by MoMA. See Edgar Kaufmann, *What is Modern Design?* (exh. cat., New York: Museum of Modern Art, 1950); *Good Design: An Exhibition of Home Furnishings Selected by the Museum of Modern Art, New York, for the Merchandise Mart, Chicago* (five catalogues, New York: Museum of Modern Art, published annually 1950–5 in conjunction with the exhibitions). See also Roberta Smith, "The Ordinary as Object of Desire" [Review of exhibition, "What Was Good Design? MoMA's Message: 1944–56"], *New York Times* (June 5, 2009), available online: http://www.nytimes.com/2009/06/05/arts/design/05desi.html?pagewanted=all&_r=0 (accessed August 15, 2014).

32 "Exhibition of Toys at Museum of Modern Art," Museum of Modern Art Press Release, MoMA exh. no. 544, October 14, 1953, archival document no. 531008-73, available online: http://www.moma.org/momaorg/shared/pdfs/docs/press_archives/1754/releases/MOMA_1953_0084_73.pdf?2010 (accessed August 15, 2014).

33 Jean-Jacques Rousseau, *Émile; or, On Education*, trans. Allan Bloom (New York: Basic Books, 1979). First published in French as *Émile; ou de l'éducation* (4 vols, Amsterdam: Jean Néaulme, 1762).

34 Tristan Tzara, "Dada Manifesto 1918," in Dawn Ades (ed.), *The Dada Reader: A Critical Anthology* (Chicago: University of Chicago Press, 2006), 36–41, originally published in *Dada* 3 (March 1918).

35 Kinchin, "Hide and Seek," 20–1; and Juliet Kinchin, "De Stijl, Children, and Constructivist Play," in Kinchin and O'Connor (eds), *Century of the Child*, 70–1.

36 Ogata, *Designing the Creative Child*, x.

37 CBS correspondent Robert Krulwich, quoted in Jane Clark Chermayeff, "Notes on Policy and Practice. Growing by Design: The 1990 International Design Conference in Aspen, A Notebook," *Children's Environments Quarterly* 8/3–4 (1991): 88–96.

38 Barthes's views were echoed by many thinkers on childhood, including American pediatrician and best-selling author Benjamin Spock, who wrote in a 1961 article for *Ladies' Home Journal*, "The less specific [the toy] is, the more it stimulates a child's imagination," describing the best such toys as wooden blocks. See Spock, quoted in Gary Cross, *Kids' Stuff: Toys and the Changing World of American Childhood* (Cambridge, MA: Harvard University Press, 1997), 161. See also Benjamin Spock, "The Creative Use of Toys," *Ladies' Home Journal* 78/12 (December 1961): 36–7; Benjamin Spock, *The Common Sense Book of Baby and Child Care* (New York: Duell, Sloan, and Pearce, 1946).

39 Harry McCracken, "The Mystery of Minecraft," *Time* 181/21 (June 3, 2013): 40ff. *Minecraft* also became quickly popular among academic scholars. See Nate Garrelts (ed.), *Understanding Minecraft: Essays on Play, Community, and Possibilities* (Jefferson, NC: McFarland and Co., 2014).

40 "Minecraft: Is it more than just a game? Gaming phenomenon being hailed as a teaching tool," *The Toronto Star* (June 1, 2013), IN1; Nick Bilton, "Minecraft, a Child's Obsession, Finds Use as an Educational Tool," *New York Times* (September 16, 2013), B8.

41 Laura Ingalls Wilder, *Little House in the Big Woods* (1932; reprint, New York: Harper Trophy, 2004), 1, 4.

42 Laura Ingalls Wilder, *Little House on the Prairie* (1935; reprint, New York: Harper Trophy, 2004), 54–9, 63–5, 99–106, 122–31.

43 Laura Ingalls Wilder, *The Long Winter* (1940; reprint, New York: Harper Trophy, 2004).

44 Laura Ingalls Wilder, *On the Banks of Plum Creek* (1937; reprint, New York: Harper Trophy, 2004), 107–17.

45 Laura Ingalls Wilder, *The First Four Years* (1971; reprint, New York: Harper Trophy, 2004), 127–30.

46 Lucy R. Lippard, "Making Something From Nothing (Toward a Definition of Women's 'Hobby Art')," in *The Pink Glass Swan: Selected Feminist Essays on Art* (New York: The New Press, 1995), 128–38.

47 Marian Wright Edelman, President of the Children's Defense Fund, quoted in Chermayeff, "Notes on Policy and Practice," 91.

48 Deborah S. Ryan, *The Ideal Home Through the Twentieth Century* (London: Hazar, 1997).

49 Barthes, "Toys," 60.

50 Gottfried Semper, *Style in the Technical and Tectonic Arts; or, Practical Aesthetics*, trans. Harry Francis Mallgrave and Michael Robinson (Los Angeles: Getty Publications, 2004), 82, originally published as *Styl in den technischen und tektonischen Künsten; oder, Praktische Aesthetitik: Ein Handbuch für Techniker, Künstler und Kunstfreunde*, 2 vols (Frankfurt am Main: Verlag für Kunst und Wissenschaft, 1860; Munich: F. Bruckmann, 1863).

SELECT BIBLIOGRAPHY

Adams, J. T., *Epic of America*. Boston: Little, Brown & Co., 1931.

Alofsin, A., *Frank Lloyd Wright: The Lost Years, 1910–1922: A Study of Influence*, Chicago: University of Chicago Press, 1993.

Anderson, C. A., D. A. Gentile, and K. E. Buckley, *Violent Video Game Effects on Children and Adolescents: Theory, Research, and Public Policy*, Oxford: Oxford University Press, 2007.

Arnheim, R., *Art and Visual Perception: A Psychology of the Creative Eye*, Berkeley: University of California Press, 1954.

Audubon, J. J., *The Birds of North America. From Drawings Made in the United States and Their Territories*, 7 vols, Philadelphia: J. B. Chavallier, 1840–4.

Badmington, N. (ed.), *Roland Barthes: Critical Evaluations in Cultural Theory*, 4 vols, London: Routledge, 2010.

Bakhtin, M., *Rabelais and His World*, translated by H. Iswolsky, Bloomington: Indiana University Press, 1984.

Bamberg, J., *British Petroleum and Global Oil, 1950–1975: The Challenge of Nationalism*, Cambridge: Cambridge University Press, 2000.

Barthes, R., *Mythologies*, translated by R. Howard and A. Lavers, New York: Hill and Wang, 2012.

Barthes, R., *The Fashion System*, translated by M. Ward and R. Howard, Berkeley: University of California Press, 1990.

Bass, J. and P. Kirkham, *Saul Bass: A Life in Film and Design*, London: Laurence King Publishing, 2011.

Baudelaire, C., *The Painter of Modern Life and Other Essays*, translated and edited by J. Mayne, London: Phaidon, 1995.

Baudrillard, J., *Simulacra and Simulation*, translated by S. F. Glaser, Ann Arbor: University of Michigan Press, 1994.

Baum, F. L., *The Wonderful Wizard of Oz*, Chicago: George M. Hill Co., 1900. Reprint, New York: Harper Trophy, 1987.

Bayer, H., "Towards a Universal Type," in M. Bierut, J. Helfand, S. Heller and R. Poynor (eds), *Looking Closer 3: Classic Writings on Graphic Design*, New York: Allworth Press, 1999, 60–2.

Benjamin, W., "The Work of Art in the Age of Mechanical Reproduction" (1936), in *Illuminations*, translated by H. Zohn, New York: Schocken Books, 1968, 217–52.

Bennett, P. and J. McDougal (eds), *Barthes' "Mythologies" Today: Readings of Contemporary Culture*, London: Routledge, 2013.

Bhabha, H. K., "The Other Question: Difference, Discrimination and the Discourse of Colonialism," in R. Ferguson, M. Gever, T. T. Minh-ha, and C. West (eds), *Out There: Marginalization and Contemporary Culture*, New York: The New Museum of Contemporary Art, 1990, 71–88.

Blaszczyk, R. L., *The Color Revolution*, Cambridge, MA: MIT Press, 2012.

Brands, H. W., *The Age of Gold: The California Gold Rush and the New American Dream*, New York: Doubleday, 2002.

Brandt, A. M., *The Cigarette Century: The Rise, Fall, and Deadly Persistence of the Product that Defined America*, New York: Basic Books, 2007.

Breton, A., *Manifestoes of Surrealism*, translated by R. Seaver and H. R. Lane, Ann Arbor: University of Michigan Press, 1972.

Brosterman, N., *Inventing Kindergarten*, New York: Abrams, 1997.

Bruegmann, R., *Sprawl: A Compact History*, Chicago: University of Chicago Press, 2005.

Carson, R., *Silent Spring*, 1962, reprint, Boston: Mariner Book, 2000.

Chermayeff, J. C., "Notes on Policy and Practice. Growing by Design: The 1990 International Design Conference in Aspen, A Notebook," *Children's Environments Quarterly* 8/3–4 (1991): 88–96.

Cheskin, L., *Color For Profit*, New York: Liveright, 1951.

Columbus, C., *Four Voyages to the New World: Letters and Selected Documents*, edited and translated by R. H. Major, New York: Corinth Books, 1961.

Cross, G., *Kids' Stuff: Toys and the Changing World of American Childhood*, Cambridge, MA: Harvard University Press, 1997.

Curtis, E., *The North American Indian; Being a Series of Volumes Picturing and Describing the Indians of the United States and Alaska*, 20 vols, Cambridge: The University Press, 1907–30.

Debord, G., *The Society of the Spectacle*, trans. D. Nicholson–Smith, New York: Zone Books, 1994.

Dickens, C., "The Noble Savage," *Household Words* 7/168 (1853): 337–9.

Doordan, D., "Design at CBS," *Design Issues*, 6/2 (1990): 4–17.

Drucker, J. and E. McVarish, *Graphic Design History: A Critical Guide*, second edition, Upper Saddle River, NJ: Pearson, 2009, 2013.

Ellingson, T., *The Myth of the Noble Savage*, Berkeley: University of California Press, 2001.

Erikson, E. H., *Toys and Reasons: Stages in the Ritualization of Experience*, New York: Norton, 1977.

Fairey, S. and Gross, J., *Art for Obama: Designing Manifest Hope and the Campaign for Change*, New York: Harry N. Abrams, 2009.

Fallan, K. (ed.), *Scandinavian Design: Alternative Histories*, Oxford: Berg, 2012.

Faulkner, W., *Absalom, Absalom!*, 1936, reprint, New York: Random House, 2002.

Fer, B., D. Batchelor, and P. Wood, *Realism, Rationalism, Surrealism: Art Between the Wars*, New Haven: Yale University Press, 1993.

Ferrier, R. W., *The History of the British Petroleum Company*, vol. 1, *The Developing Years 1901–1932*, Cambridge: Cambridge University Press, 1982.

Forty, A., *Objects of Desire: Design and Society from Wedgwood to IBM*, London: Thames and Hudson, 1986.

Frank, T., *What's the Matter With Kansas: How Conservatives Won the Hearts of America*, New York: Metropolitan Books, 2004.

Frederick, C., *Household Engineering: Scientific Management in the Home*, Chicago: American School of Home Economics, 1920.

Freud, S., *The Standard Edition of the Complete Psychological Works of Sigmund Freud*, translated by J. Strachey, 24 vols, London: Hogarth Press, 1953–74, 1995.

Friendly, M., "The Golden Age of Statistical Graphics," *Statistical Science* 23/4 (November 2008): 502–35.

Froshaug, A., "Typography is a Grid," in Bierut, M., Helfand, J., Heller, S., and Poynor, R. (eds), *Looking Closer 3: Classic Writings on Graphic Design*, New York: Allworth Press, 1999, 177–9.

Fuller, R. B., *Operating Manual for Spaceship Earth*, New York: Simon and Schuster, 1969.

Garland, K., "First Things First" (1964), in M. Bierut, J. Helfand, S. Heller, and R. Poynor (eds), *Looking Closer 3: Classic Writings on Graphic Design*, New York: Allworth Press, 1999, 154–5.

Garrelts, N. (ed.), *Understanding Minecraft: Essays on Play, Community, and Possibilities*, Jefferson, NC: McFarland and Co., 2014.

Geisel, T. S. (see Seuss, Dr.)

"The Gift to Be Simple," *Portfolio*, 1/1 (1950), edited by F. Zachary, unpaginated.

Gilman, S., *Difference and Pathology: Stereotypes of Sexuality, Race, and Madness*, Ithaca, New York: Cornell University Press, 1985.

Good Design: An Exhibition of Home Furnishings Selected by the Museum of Modern Art, New York, for the Merchandise Mart, Chicago, five catalogues, New York, Museum of Modern Art, published annually, 1950–5, in conjunction with the exhibitions.

Gorges, F. and I. Yamazaki, *The History of Nintendo, Volume 1, 1889–1980, From Playing Cards to Game and Watch*. London: Pix'n Love, 2010.

Gurney, G. and T. T. Heyman (eds), *George Catlin and His Indian Gallery*, exhibition catalogue, Washington, D.C.: Smithsonian Museum of American Art, 2002.

Hacker, A., "Obama: The Price of Being Black," *The New York Review of Books* 55/14 (September 25, 2008): 12–16.

Hall, S. and T. Jefferson (eds), *Resistance Through Rituals: Youth Sub-Cultures in Post-War Britain*, London: Hutchinson, 1976.

Hardwick, M. J., *Mall Maker: Victor Gruen, Architect of an American Dream*, Philadelphia: University of Pennsylvania Press, 2003.

Hayden, D., *Building Suburbia: Green Fields and Urban Growth, 1820–2000*, New York: Pantheon Books, 2003.

Hebdige, D., *Subculture: The Meaning of Style*, London: Methuen, 1979.

Heller, S., "Thoughts on Rand," *Print* 51/3 (May–June 1997): 106–9.

Heskett, J., *Industrial Design*, London: Thames & Hudson, 1980.

Hess, A., "The Origins of McDonald's Golden Arches," *Journal of the Society of Architectural Historians* 45/1 (1986): 60–7.

Hewitt, K. and L. Roomet, *Educational Toys in America: 1800 to the Present*, exhibition catalogue, Burlington, VT: Robert Hull Fleming Museum, 1979.

Hine, T., *Populuxe*, 1986, reprint, New York: Knopf, 1987.

Hitchcock, H. R. and P. Johnson, *The International Style: Architecture Since 1922*, New York: W. W. Norton and Co., 1932.

Hollis, R., *Swiss Graphic Design: The Origins and Growth of an International Style, 1920–1965*, New Haven: Yale University Press, 2006.

Holm, Bill, *Northwest Coast Indian Art: An Analysis of Form*, Seattle: University of Washington Press, 1965.

Horkheimer, M. and T. W. Adorno, "The Culture Industry: Enlightenment as Mass Deception" (1944), in M. Horkheimer and T. W. Adorno, *Dialectic of*

Enlightenment, translated by J. Cumming, New York: Continuum Publishing Company, 1994, 120–67.

Hounshell, D., *From the American System to Mass Production, 1800–1932: The Development of Manufacturing Technology in the United States*, Baltimore: Johns Hopkins University Press, 1984.

Howard, E., *Garden Cities of To-Morrow* (1902), edited by F. J. Osborn, new edn, Cambridge, MA: MIT Press, 1965.

Huyssen, A., *After the Great Divide: Modernism, Mass Culture, Postmodernism*, Purdue: Indiana University Press, 1987.

Jameson, F., *Postmodernism; or, the Cultural Logic of Late Capitalism*, Durham, NC: Duke University Press, 1991, 1994.

Jobling, P. and D. Crowley, *Graphic Design: Production and Presentation Since 1800*, Manchester: Manchester University Press, 1996.

Kaplan, W. (ed.), *The Arts and Crafts Movement in Europe and America: Design for the Modern World*, exhibition catalogue, Los Angeles County Museum of Art, 2004.

Kaufmann, E., *What is Modern Design?*, exhibition catalogue, New York: Museum of Modern Art, 1950.

Kepes, G., *Language of Vision*, Chicago: Paul Theobald, 1944.

Key, E., "Beauty for All," in L. Creagh, H. Kåberg, and B. M. Lane (eds), *Modern Swedish Design: Three Founding Texts*, New York: Museum of Modern Art, 2008, 32–57.

Kinchin, J. and A. O'Connor (eds), *Century of the Child: Growing By Design 1900–2000*, exhibition catalogue, New York: Museum of Modern Art, 2012.

King, M. L., Jr., "Letter from a Birmingham Jail" (16 April 1963), in M. L. King, Jr., *Why We Can't Wait*, 1964, reprint, New York: Signet Classic, 2000, 64–84.

Klein, N., *No Logo*, New York: Picador, 2000.

Krauss, R. E., *The Originality of the Avant-Garde and Other Modernist Myths*, Cambridge, MA: MIT Press, 1985.

Lacan, J., *Écrits: A Selection*, translated by Alan Sheridan, New York: Norton, 1977.

Larrick, N. and R. Martin, *First ABC. An Educational Picture Book*, New York: Platt & Munk Publishers, 1959.

Lawrence, D., *A Logo For London: The London Transport Bar and Circle*, London: Laurence King Publishing, 2013.

Le Corbusier, *The City of To-morrow and its Planning* (1929), translated by F. Etchells, New York: Dover Publications, 1987.

Leach, W., *Land of Desire: Merchants, Power, and the Rise of a New American Culture*, New York: Pantheon, 1993.

Lears, J., *Fables of Abundance: A Cultural History of Advertising in America*, New York: Basic Books, 1994.

Lees–Maffei, G. (ed.), *Iconic Designs: 50 Stories About 50 Things*, London: Bloomsbury, 2014.

Lepore, J., "Battleground America: One Nation, Under the Gun," *The New Yorker* (April 23, 2012): 38–47.

Lévi–Strauss, C., "The Structural Study of Myth" (1955), in C. Lévi–Strauss, *Structural Anthropology*, translated by C. Jacobson and B. G. Schoepf, New York: Basic Books, 1961, 207–31.

Lévi–Strauss, C., *The Way of the Masks*, translated by S. Modelski, Seattle: University of Washington Press, 1975.

Lewis, M. and W. Clark, *The Journals of Louis and Clark*, edited by J. Bakeless, 1964, reprint, New York: Signet Classics, 2011.

Lippard, L. R., "Making Something From Nothing (Toward a Definition of Women's 'Hobby Art')," in *The Pink Glass Swan: Selected Feminist Essays on Art*, New York: The New Press, 1995, 128–38.

Loewy, R., *Industrial Design*, Woodstock: Overlook Press, 1979.

Loewy, R., *Never Leave Well Enough Alone*, New York: Simon and Schuster, 1951.

Longfellow, H. W., "Song of Hiawatha" (1855), in *Poems and Other Writings*, edited by J. D. McClatchy, New York: Literary Classics of the United States, 2000, 141–279.

Loos, A., *Ornament and Crime: Selected Essays*, edited by A. Opel, translated by M. Mitchell, Riverside, CA: Ariadne Press, 1998, 167–76.

Lovelock, J. E. and L. Margulis, "Atmospheric Homeostasis by and for the Biosphere: the Gaia Hypothesis," *Tellus* 26/1–2 (1974): 2–10.

Lynch, M., *The Arab Uprising: The Unfinished Revolutions of the New Middle East*, New York: Public Affairs, 2012.

Lyotard, Jean–François, *Postmodernism Explained: Correspondence 1982–1985*, Sydney: Power Publications, 1988, 1993.

Maass, P., *Crude World: The Violent Twilight of Oil*, New York: Vintage Books, 2009.

Madge, P., "Ecological Design: A New Critique," in R. Buchanan, D. Doordan, and V. Margolin (eds), *The Designed World: Images, Objects, Environments*, Oxford: Berg, 2010, 328–38.

Mailer, N., *The Executioner's Song*, Boston: Little, Brown, 1979.

Malcolm X, *Malcolm X Speaks: Selected Speeches and Statements*, edited by G. Breitman, New York: Merit Publishers, 1965.

Manovich, L., "Database as Symbolic Form," *Convergence* 5/2 (1999): 80–99.

Manovich, L., *The Language of New Media*, Cambridge, MA: MIT Press, 2001.

McCracken, G., *Culture and Consumption: New Approaches to the Symbolic Character of Consumer Goods and Activities*, Bloomington: Indiana University Press, 1990.

McDonough, W. and M. Braungart, *The Hannover Principles: Design for Sustainability, for the City of Hannover, Germany, EXPO 2000, the World's Fair*, Charlottesville, VA: William McDonough Architects, 1992.

McKenney, T. L. and J. Hall (eds), *History of the Indian Tribes of North America*, 3 vols, Philadelphia: Edward C. Biddle, 1836–44.

McLuhan, M., *The Mechanical Bride: Folklore of Industrial Man*, 1951, reprint, Berkeley, CA: Gingko Press, 2001.

McLuhan, M., *The Medium is the Massage* [*sic*], 1967, reprint, Corte Madera, CA: Gingko Press, 2001.

McLuhan, M., *Understanding Media: The Extensions of Man*, New York: McGraw-Hill, 1964.

Meggs, P. B. and A. W. Purvis, *Meggs' History of Graphic Design*, fourth edition, Hoboken, NJ: John Wiley & Sons, Inc., 2006.

Meikle, J. L., *American Plastic: A Cultural History*, New Brunswick, NJ: Rutgers University Press, 1997.

Miller, M. B., *The Bon Marché: Bourgeois Culture and the Department Store, 1869–1920*, Princeton: Princeton University Press, 1981.

Moholy-Nagy, L., *Vision in Motion*, Chicago: Paul Theobald, 1947.

Monmonier, M., *How to Lie with Maps*, second edition, Chicago: University of Chicago Press, 1996.

Montessori, M., *The Montessori Method: Scientific Pedagogy as Applied to Child Education in "The Children's Houses,"* translated by A. E. George, New York: Frederick A. Stokes, 1912.

Morris, W., *The Collected Works of William Morris*, edited by M. Morris, 24 vols, London: Longmans, Green, and Company, 1910–15.

Mulvey, L., "Visual Pleasure and Narrative Cinema," *Screen* 16/3 (1975): 6–18.

Nader, R., *Unsafe at Any Speed: The Designed-In Dangers of the American Automobile*, New York: Grossman, 1965.

Naylor, G., "Swedish Grace ... or the Acceptable Face of Modernism?" in P. Greenhalgh (ed.), *Modernism in Design*, London: Reaktion, 1990, 164–83.

Nickerson, W. S., *Early Encounters. Native Americans and Europeans in New England. From the Papers of W. Sears Nickerson*, edited by D. B. Carpenter, East Lansing: Michigan State University Press, 1994.

Nixon, R. and N. Khrushchev, "The Kitchen Debate," in C. Gorman (ed.), *The Industrial Design Reader*, New York: Allworth Press, 2003, 172–4.

Obama, B., *Dreams From My Father: A Story of Race and Inheritance*, New York: Times Books, 1995.

Obama, B., *The Audacity of Hope: Thoughts on Reclaiming the American Dream*, New York: Crown Publishers, 2006.

Ogata, A. D., *Designing the Creative Child: Playthings and Places in Midcentury America*, Minneapolis: Minnesota University Press, 2013.

Olins, W., *The Corporate Personality*, London: Design Council, 1978.

Olmsted, F. L., *Civilizing American Cities: Writings on City Landscapes*, edited by S. B. Suton, 1971; New York: De Capo Press, 1997.

Oreskes, N. and E. M. Conway, *Merchants of Doubt: How a Handful of Scientists Obscured the Truth on Issues from Tobacco Smoke to Global Warming*, New York: Bloomsbury, 2010.

Packard, V., *The Hidden Persuaders*, New York: Simon and Schuster, 1957.

Palmer, J., L. Bresler, and D. E. Cooper (eds), *Fifty Major Thinkers on Education: From Confucius to Dewey*, London: Routledge, 2001.

Panofsky, E., *Perspective as Symbolic Form* (1927), translated by C. S. Wood, New York: Zone Books, 1991.

Papanek, V., *Design for the Real World: Human Ecology and Social Change*, London: Granada Publishing Limited, 1971.

Parisi, D., "Fingerbombing, or 'Touching is Good': The Cultural Construction of Technologized Touch," *Senses and Society* 3/3 (2008): 307–27.

Paulsson, G., *Better Things for Everyday Life* (1919), in L. Creagh, H. Kåberg, and B. M. Lane (eds), *Modern Swedish Design: Three Founding Texts*, New York: Museum of Modern Art, 2008, 72–125.

Paumgarten, N., "Master of Play: The Many Worlds of a Video-Game Artist," *The New Yorker* 86/41 (December 20, 2010): 86–99.

Petrini, C., *Terra Madre: Forging a New Global Network of Sustainable Food Communities*, White River Junction, VT: Chelsea Green, 2010.

Piaget, J., *Play, Dreams, and Imitation in Childhood*, translated by C. Gattegno and F. M. Hodgson, New York: W. W. Norton, 1962.

Pollan, M., *In Defense of Food: An Eater's Manifesto*, New York: Penguin Press, 2008.

Pollock, G., *Vision and Difference: Femininity, Feminism, and the Histories of Art*, London: Routledge, 1988.

Price, S. L., "The Indian Wars," *Sports Illustrated* (March 4, 2002): 68–72.

Rand, P., "Confusion and Chaos: The Seduction of Contemporary Graphic Design," in S. Heller and M. Finamore (eds), *Design Culture: An Anthology of Writings from the AIGA Journal of Graphic Design*, New York: Allworth, 1997, 119–24.

Rand, P., "Logos, Flags, and Escutcheons," in M. Bierut, W. Drenttel, S. Heller, and D. K. Holland (eds), *Looking Closer: Critical Writings on Graphic Design*, New York: Allworth Press, 1994, 88–90.

Rand, P., *Thoughts on Design*, New York: Wittenborn and Company, 1947.

Remnick, D., "The Joshua Generation: Race and the Campaign of Barack Obama," *The New Yorker* (November 17, 2008): 68–83.

Roche, M., *Mega-Events and Modernity. Olympics and Expos in the Growth of Global Culture*, London: Routledge, 2000.

Rousseau, J., *Émile; or, On Education* (1762), translated by A. Bloom, New York: Basic Books, 1979.

Rousseau, J., "Discourse on the Origin of Inequality" (1754), in *The First and Second Discourses Together With the Replies to Critics and Essay on the Origin of Languages*, edited and translated by V. Gourevitch, New York: Harper and Row, 1986, 117–238.

Ruder, E., "The Typography of Order," in M. Bierut, J. Helfand, S. Heller, and R. Poynor (eds), *Looking Closer 3: Classic Writings on Graphic Design*, New York: Allworth Press, 1999, 135–8.

Ruskin, J., *Unto This Last, and Other Essays on Art and the Political Economy*, London: J. M. Dent, 1907.

Said, E., *Orientalism*, New York: Vintage Books, 1979, 2003.

Schönberger, A. (ed.), *Raymond Loewy: Pioneer of American Industrial Design*, exhibition catalogue, Berlin: International Design Center; Munich: Prestel Verlag, 1990.

Schlosser, E., *Fast Food Nation: The Dark Side of the All-American Meal*, Boston: Houghton Mifflin, 2002.

Schumacher, E. F., *Small is Beautiful: Economics as if People Mattered*, New York: Harper and Row, 1973.

Semper, G., *Style in the Technical and Tectonic Arts; or, Practical Aesthetics* (1860–3), translated by H. F. Mallgrave and M. Robinson, Los Angeles: Getty Publications, 2004.

Seuss, Dr. [Theodor Seuss Geisel], *One Fish Two Fish Red Fish Blue Fish*, New York: Random House, 1960.

Sheff, D., *Game Over: How Nintendo Conquered the World*, Wilton, CT: Cyberactive Publishing, 1999.

Sinclair, U., *The Jungle*, 1906, reprint, New York, Bantam Books, 1981.

Sinclair, U., *Oil!*, 1926, reprint, New York, Penguin, 2007.

Sontag, S., "Posters, Advertisement, Art, Political Artifact, Commodity" (1970), in M. Bierut, J. Helfand, S. Heller, and R. Poynor (eds), *Looking Closer 3: Classic Writings on Graphic Design*, New York: Allworth Press, 1999, 196–218.

Spigel, L., *Welcome to the Dreamhouse: Popular Media and Postwar Suburbs*, Durham, NC: Duke University Press, 2001.

Spock, B., "The Creative Use of Toys," *Ladies' Home Journal* 78/12 (December 1961): 36–7.

Starch, D., *Principles of Advertising*, New York: McGraw Hill, 1923.

Stephanson, A., *Manifest Destiny: American Expansionism and the Empire of Right*, New York: Hill and Wang, 1995.

Stocking, G. W., Jr., *Objects and Others: Essays on Museums and Material Culture*, Madison: University of Wisconsin Press, 1985.

Tarbell, I. M., *The History of the Standard Oil Company*, 2 vols, New York: McClure, Phillips and Company, 1905.

Taylor, F. W., *The Principles of Scientific Management*, New York: Harper & Brothers, 1911.

Tomlinson, A. and C. Young (eds), *National Identity and Global Sports Events: Culture, Politics, and Spectacle in the Olympics and the Football World Cup*, Albany: State University of New York Press, 2005.

Traganou, J., "Foreword: Design Histories of the Olympic Games," *Journal of Design History* 25/3 (2012): 245–51.

Tufte, E., *The Visual Display of Quantitative Information*, Cheshire, CT: Graphics Press, 1983.

Turkle, S., *Life on the Screen: Identity in the Age of the Internet*, New York: Touchstone, 1995.

Turkle, S., *The Second Self: Computers and the Human Spirit*, New York: Simon and Schuster, 1984.

Turner, F. J., *The Frontier in American History*, New York: Henry Holt & Co, 1921.

Twain, M., *Tom Sawyer Abroad*, New York: Charles L. Webster and Company, 1894.

Umland, A. (ed.), *Magritte: The Mystery of the Ordinary, 1926–1938*, exhibition catalogue, New York: Museum of Modern Art, 2013.

Venturi, R, Scott–Brown, D., and S. Izenour, *Learning From Las Vegas: The Forgotten Symbolism of Architectural Form*, Cambridge, MA: MIT Press, 1972.

Votolata, G., "Bullets and Beyond (The Shinkansen)," in H. Clark and D. Brody (eds), *Design Studies: A Reader*, Oxford: Berg, 2009, 511–15.

Wilder, L. I., *Little House in the Big Woods*, 1932, reprint, New York: Harper Trophy, 2004.

Wilder, L. I., *Little House on the Prairie*, 1935, reprint, New York: Harper Trophy, 2004.

Williams, R. H., *Dream Worlds: Mass Consumption in Late Nineteenth-Century France*, Berkeley: University of California Press, 1982.

Wright, F. L., *The Disappearing City*, New York: W. F. Payson, 1932.

X, M. (see Malcolm X)

INDEX

The letter *f* after an entry indicates a figure.